T0287509

WILLFUL
MISCONDUCT

THE **TRAGIC STORY** OF
PAN AMERICAN FLIGHT 806

CamCat Publishing, LLC
Brentwood, Tennessee 37027
camcatpublishing.com

Hardcover ISBN 9781931540346
Paperback ISBN 9780744300833
Large-Print Paperback ISBN 9780744300840
eBook ISBN 9780744300857
Audiobook ISBN 978074430xxxx

Library of Congress Control Number: 2020936170

Cover design by Mimi Bark

5 3 1 2 4

WILLFUL
MISCONDUCT

THE TRAGIC STORY OF
PAN AMERICAN FLIGHT 806

WILLIAM NORRIS

CamCat
Perspectives

BY WILLIAM NORRIS

Fiction

A Grave Too Many

Make Mad the Guilty

The Badger Game

Nonfiction

A Talent to Deceive

Snowbird

The Man Who Fell from the Sky

Willful Misconduct

TABLE OF CONTENTS

PRELUDE

Room 64G, in the cellars beneath the United States District Court for the Central District of California, is some way off the Los Angeles tourist route. Above it, in the filing section on the ground floor of the imposing building on North Spring Street, a stern notice forbids public entry. Beyond this sign, a steep flight of stairs leads down to a catacomb of roughcast concrete and dusty pipes. Here is a tomb without bones, a mortuary of long-forgotten files and long-abandoned catalogues of legal pain. It is a place where hopes and dreams and aspirations share the upright coffins of the filing cabinets with tragedy and pain. The paper detritus of the act of dying is all around.

Room 64G contains more than its fair share of death. Behind a dull green door, its lock stiff with disuse, are the exhibits that catalogue the end of ninety-seven lives: those of the men, women, and children who took their last trip on Flight 806 of Pan American World Airways from Auckland to Pago Pago on January 30, 1974. I had gone to the courthouse in search of something; I knew not what. I only knew that the crash at Pago Pago, so small and insignificant by later standards of disaster, had spawned the longest, most complex, and most expensive legal case in aviation history. I wanted to find out why. Perhaps here, where the exhibits were left at the conclusion of the first trial in July of 1978, I would find some clue.

I was dredging for inspiration, seeking to find some foothold from which to climb the mountain of research that would undoubtedly lie ahead. I was not to know that before the day was out I would hold in my hands an unexploded bomb, a document so explosive that lawyers and judges had spent years making sure it would never reach the public. It was called the Hudson Report.

I had heard of this document, at least by repute. In December 1975, in a progress report to his clients who were suing Pan American for damages, Los Angeles attorney Daniel C. Cathcart had referred to "a detailed FAA (Federal Aviation Administration) investigation of the Pan Am operation from the point of view of aviation safety." He was full of confidence. "I feel we have reason to believe," he added, "that the Pago Pago air crash litigation will be a matter of past history by this time next year." Read in 1981, with the action still going full blast, the words had an air of sad bravado.

On March 24, 1976, in his fourth progress report, Cathcart wrote:

> In addition, we have uncovered a group of reports by
> Pan American pilots based at San Francisco, citing the
> dangerous practices engaged in by Pan American . . .
> with the information which is now in admissible form,
> contained in the FAA investigation reports, Pan Am's
> own in-house investigations of its operation, as well as

the report submitted by Pan Am pilots, I cannot believe that the management will permit this case to go to trial.

The contents of these reports are by court order not to be released to anyone. Once this case goes to trial the order will not apply, and the press will undoubtedly pick up these reports, and the international dissemination of these documents has the potential to destroy Pan American as an operating entity.

It was strong stuff. Clearly, these documents were of the utmost importance. Yet at this point the trail went cold. There were no press accounts that I could trace, nor any indication that the reports had been produced at the trial. And there was one further mystery: I had been shown the report quoted above by one of the survivors of the crash. Yet when the lawyer subsequently opened his files to me, with apparent total frankness, that letter was missing from the sequence of progress reports stretching over seven years. What was more, the later documents had been renumbered, so that there was no reason to suppose one was missing. Had I not happened to chance upon it in New Zealand and had the accidental foresight to make a copy, I would never have known of this alleged sensational evidence.

Had the FAA report ever existed? That was the question that worried me. If so, had it been the subject of an elaborate cover-up operation to protect the reputation of America's most prestigious airline? One thing seemed certain: if such a cover-up had taken place, no one would have been so careless as to leave the report lying around where inquisitive people like me could find it.

I resolved to take up the search in Washington, D.C., where I had friendly contacts in the aviation community. In the meantime, there seemed no harm in having a look at the archives of the California court where the long drama had taken place. There was no telling what might turn up.

The clerk in charge of the exhibits section of the district court was a pleasant and efficient young man named Lee Torbin Junior. Mr. Torbin received my request to look at the relics of the Pago Pago trial with polite disbelief. It was clearly beyond his experience that anyone, even a crazy British author, should want to see such things. I had the distinct impression that he had no idea where the stuff was kept, but luckily my total ignorance of its file numbers, which by regulation had to be written down before the request could be granted, saved him from having to admit the fact. Still, he was very nice about it.

The response was discouraging, but I had all day. Having traveled a long way and spent a lot of money to stand in that office, I was disinclined to give up without a struggle. I stayed on one side of the barbed-wire fence. Mr. Torbin stayed on the other, and for an hour or two we swapped polite suggestions and refusals while the more orthodox business of the records office went on about us.

At length, he seemed intrigued by my persistence. It was becoming plain that I had no intention of going away and leaving him in peace. "Hey, Charlie," he called to one of the other clerks, "didn't they put all that Pago Pago stuff in a cellar someplace?" Charlie thought they had. Someplace. All at once Lee Torbin Jr. reached a decision, probably born of desperation. "Come on," he said to me. "Let's go look." And to my great surprise he beckoned me behind the counter, past the prohibiting notice, and down the stairs. We were headed for room 64G.

For a journalist, there is a very special thrill in being where he ought not to be, seeing what authority wishes him not to see, or reading what he is not supposed to read. I felt it strongly that day.

It took some effort to shift the stubborn lock on 64G, but at last we were in. Mr. Torbin and I were alone with the legal relics of Pago Pago. It was a shock. Where I had expected neat rows of filing cabinets and boxes of exhibits in duly labeled sequence, I saw instead a mountainous jumble of paper. The cellar, perhaps thirty feet square, was filled on every side to a height of about six feet with a great amorphous hotchpotch of boxes and files. Here and there the top of a filing cabinet poked through the surface like an iceberg in an angry sea. The records of Flight 806 had not been laid to rest by a tidy mind.

Where the hell did I start? I looked at Mr. Torbin and Mr. Torbin looked at me. I cleared the front of one filing cabinet and began to open the drawers. It became rapidly apparent that there was no more order inside the cabinets than outside.

Sheaves of paper—some in folders, some not, and none with any discernible label—tumbled out as I dug deeper. The damn things must have been breeding in the dark. A quick glance seemed to show that none was of any interest, though it was difficult to tell. I had the horrid feeling that the story of the century could be lurking in this Augean cellar, and I would be none the wiser.

I abandoned the first cabinet and took off my coat, wading into the pile of boxes as though there might still be a survivor beneath them. Mr. Torbin stood uncertain, bemused by this latest evidence of literary derangement, then decided to humor me and lend a hand. It was clearly going to be the only way to get rid of me.

At length, in a far corner, a green filing cabinet emerged. It was like the rest, save for one thing: this one had numbers on the drawers. Hardly daring to hope, I pulled open the first to discover orderly file covers numbered in sequence. If someone had taken the trouble to put the contents in order while all around was chaos, it just might contain something important. I began leafing through the papers. The sharp, regular sound behind me was Lee Torbin Jr., tapping his foot.

And then I had it. Inside a plain brown envelope, unsealed, was an unmarked file cover. But the title page of the papers within made me catch my breath. It read: "Report of Pan American pilots of Council 56, and FAA Special Investigation Team at Training Building, San Francisco airport, May 6, 1974."

A swift glance through the contents showed that Cathcart had hardly been exaggerating. I hurriedly put the file back in the envelope and laid it aside, trying not to betray my excitement. Then I went back to the cabinet to resume the search. Where there was one gold nugget there might well be two. And so, it proved. The second was dated June 13, 1975. It was a report addressed to the assistant administrator, AEU-1 (whoever he might have been), from a certain Jack W. Hudson. Hudson was described as team coordinator as well as chief of the FAA's Air Carrier District Office at Fort Worth, Texas.

It was the third line that caught my eye: "SUBJECT: Special Inspection - Pan American World Airways, 1974." I had found it.

That was the limit of my success. There was no sign of the alleged in-house report by Pan American, which I later discovered was known as the Thomas Report, but it was enough. I was confident that I held in my hand evidence that had long been concealed. Would its revelation do anything to help the plight of those who were still suffering, uncompensated, more than seven years after the Pago Pago crash? I did not know, but I had to try.

Lee Torbin Jr. held out his hand. "I'll take those," he said. I reluctantly handed over the files as we left room 64G, which looked even more chaotic than when we had entered, and went back to the wire cage that served as his office. Torbin laid them on his desk and I stood there, unable to take my eyes off the brown envelopes, like a child in a candy store. My palms itched.

Torbin said, "I don't think I can let you have these." Oh shit, I thought. There they are, so close, I could just grab them and run. I had visions of being pursued from the courthouse by a screaming mob of legal bureaucrats, led by Lee Torbin Jr. But the thought came and went. Anyway, the wire cage was locked. Surely, I was not about to fail now. I knew it would be fatal to appear too anxious.

"Why not?" I asked as though it did not matter.

"I have a vague feeling," Torbin said, "that some of those exhibits were put under judicial seal by Judge Byrne. [He had tried the Pago Pago case.] I think these might be among them."

My heart did a double flip and landed in the region of my toecaps. It could well be so. That would explain why the documents had disappeared so completely, never coming up in open court and never having been pried loose under the Freedom of Information Act. A judicial prohibition would have stopped all that. It would stop me, too. There was no way that Lee Torbin Jr. was going to put his job on the line for the sake of my bright blue eyes.

"I'll have to check," he said.

The next fifteen minutes lasted a long time. First, Torbin telephoned Judge Byrne's clerk, Lori Serif. She was new to the job and did not know the answer. He rang the court reporter, who could not remember. He rang and rang, until my nerves were in shreds and there seemed to be no one left in the whole court building who had not been asked the question. But none of them knew the answer.

"Surely," I ventured, "that must mean that they are clear. If they are under seal, one of these people is bound to know."

But the ultracautious Mr. Torbin was having none of it. He had to have a positive answer before he would let me see those papers. I could not blame him. It was his neck.

Finally, he had an idea. "I know who can tell us," he said. "Judge Byrne had a clerk at the time of the trial who retired not long ago. I'll call her." He found the number and explained the problem. His next words were ominous. "Is all the Pago evidence under seal?"

Four-letter words passed silently in coarse procession through my mind. The envelopes on the desk before me seemed to blur and recede. So near, and yet . . . I stood there like a dummy while the conversation continued. I could make little sense of what was being said and by now was paying scant attention. It was just a question of gritting my teeth, thanking Mr. Torbin for his help with as much sincerity as I could muster, and writing off the whole episode to experience. Perhaps there would be another way to get hold of the Hudson Report. I doubted it.

At length Lee Torbin Jr. put down the receiver and smiled. "Do you want copies?" he asked. "They'll cost you fifty cents a page."

(I subsequently discovered that the lady in question had disliked Judge Byrne with a passion and had seized the opportunity to get her own back from the safety of retirement.)

———

Later that day, with the copies locked in my briefcase, I recounted the episode to one of the lawyers involved in the case. The reports, he told me, were definitely under judicial seal and had been for years. They would remain so at least until all the appeals had been heard—perhaps forever. He and the other lawyers in the case had copies but had been sworn not to reveal their contents to anyone.

So where did that leave me?

"Go ahead and publish," he said. "No one can stop you. Remember the First Amendment to the Constitution."

And so I will. For though the scandals they reveal are now history, history has a nasty way of repeating itself if nothing is done to prevent it. Things happened, and without public awareness, they could happen again. Somewhere, on some airline, they may be happening still. No one really knows.

The deeper I researched this story, the more unpleasantness came to light. Long-shut cupboard doors swung open to reveal a host of skeletons. For the tale of Flight 806 is more than the suppression of the Hudson Report, the training records of the flight crew, and all the rest of the evidence that the jury was never allowed to hear. It is basically the story of man's inhumanity to man: a little vanity, a little greed, and a little ruthlessness all added up to a major act of injustice.

In the view of some lawyers, the tale was not ready for telling at the time this book was first published. The last page in the saga had yet to be written. The skill of attorneys, the tardiness of some judges, and the creaking machinery of the legal system would prolong the agony for years.

But for the sake of those who had already waited more than eight years for compensation, for their own injuries or for the death of their loved ones, it seemed important that the story be told.

So here we go.

BOOK ONE

CRASH

ONE

CHRISTMAS 1973, high summer in the South Pacific, and the Hemsley family was where they could usually be found on such occasions: taking the sun at their beach house on New Zealand's North Island. The Hemsley family boat swung gently at its moorings, Hemsley family cars nestled in the shade, and the Hemsleys themselves sprawled around the barbecue set up on the white sand. Not many of these things were paid for, a fact that worried the Hemsley family not at all.

They were rich. And then again, they were not rich. It all depended on how you looked at it, how you judged such things. Charles Hemsley, head of the family, was a teacher. Not the most lucrative of professions, but his father had been a leading doctor in Auckland and had left him a modest income from investments, which helped to maintain the family lifestyle. Charles and his wife Edith had raised four sons, the eldest of whom, Edward, had finished his studies and was now working for a local law firm. William, next in line, had dropped out of college after a year and was off to see the world. Roy was a varsity student. Desmond was still at school. But the darling of the family was Mary, a pretty child at eleven and growing prettier by the month. Dear Mary. Two doting parents, four protective brothers, and a world full of sunshine and lollipops. She had a lovely Christmas. Such a pity that it was destined to be her last.

The Hemsleys were not like other people. In an age of dissolving family ties, they were shackled one to the other by bonds of genuine love and affection. In material things they shared, lent, borrowed, and spent together with gay abandon. In times of doubt and tension, even in sleepy New Zealand, they had the effrontery to be happy.

The Hemsleys lived for the family, by the family, and with the family. Outsiders, like Edward's new wife and longtime girlfriend Bineta, were sucked into the loving maw and ever so gently digested. No television scriptwriter, desperate for soap opera material, would dare to invent the Hemsleys. He would not be believed for an instant.

They were all at the beach for that Christmas holiday. All, that is, except William. At twenty-one, William was roaming around the United States, working occasionally, taking a lot of pictures, and sending a lot of letters home. He had been away for nine months. There had been vague talk of setting up in business with his father when he got home, perhaps running a motel together, but no one was in much of a hurry to do anything about it. William was happy enough getting the travel bug out of his system. All the same, he missed his family and planned to take a cheap trip to Honolulu. His parents missed him, too. They had arranged to fly north for a holiday, taking Mary with them, and to meet up with

William in the Hawaiian Islands. It was the sort of thing the Hemsleys did.

The flight was all fixed, or so they thought. But then, over those Christmas days, there came a change of plan. Their party at the beach house was joined by a lawyer named Donald Pilkington who, with his wife Nina, owned an adjoining property. Pilkington was a friend. At least, he saw himself as such, touching the family circle at the narrowest of tangents, yet welcome enough at the party. He had, after all, recently taken young Edward into the firm of Auckland solicitors where he was senior partner, holding out to the lad a partnership in due course.

Pilkington somehow lacked the gravitas of the legal image. His taste in loud sports shirts, his plump, bespectacled figure, his extroverted nature, and his liking for a good time sat oddly with his position as vice president of the New Zealand Law Society. But the New Zealand legal world is small and fairly placid. Donald Pilkington was a big frog in such a tranquil pool. He also had a passion for traveling. As Edward Hemsley already knew, having been given the task of minding the office while he was away, it took the smallest excuse for a business trip to get him on an airplane to almost anywhere.

For a time, Pilkington had been the travel representative of the Law Society, and it was well known that he positively enjoyed making travel arrangements for others. There were rumors that he may also have obtained commission on the tickets, but what of it? There was nothing illegal or unethical in that.

When the Hemsleys told Pilkington of their plans to meet William in Honolulu, it was no surprise to them that he should come up with a better idea. He could save them money, he said, by booking them on a different flight, and the Hemsleys were not so rich that they could refuse such an offer. And so, it was arranged. The tickets were changed. Charles, Edith, and Mary Hemsley joined the passenger list of Pan American World Airways Flight 806 from Auckland to Honolulu via Pago Pago on January 30, 1974.

———

FOR MICHAEL AND SUSAN ROGERS, young and starry-eyed, Flight 806 was going to be a magic carpet to adventure. They were newly married, had never been outside New Zealand, and neither had ever flown before. Now, having scraped together every dollar they could lay their hands on and bought their tickets and their rucksacks, they were off to see the world.

The Rogerses were an oddly disparate couple, like two sides of a coin left lying on damp earth. At twenty-one, Susan was blonde, bright, pert, and bouncy, full of purpose and ambition. She wanted to be a ballet dancer and she knew, she just knew, she had the talent to make the grade if only she could reach the great wide world outside.

Michael, a year her senior, was dark and intense. He had just left law school and was working, unhappily, for an Auckland firm of solicitors. He had never wanted to go to university and admitted no sense of vocation whatever.

He had met Susan at a law school dance. They were engaged in July 1973 and married two months later. Like most couples, they set out to explore each other's interests together, but Michael's idea of recreation was to go off hunting in the bush. She loathed it. Susan dragged him to the ballet. He hated it. One thing they had in common was the desire to travel, she because she wanted to go to

England for the sake of her dancing career, and he as a source of adventure.

Their plans were ambitious. Michael had a brother who had emigrated to the United States and had become an American citizen. The Rogerses' idea was to fly in stages to San Francisco, spending a week in Pago Pago and a week in Hawaii, and then to join Michael's brother for a drive down through Mexico and back up the East Coast. The party would then fly to England, from where Susan and Michael intended to travel by bus to Asia and the USSR. After that they would play it by ear, perhaps working in London for a year or so before returning to New Zealand.

They were determined to make their pipe dream a reality. They were young and very excited. The normal tourist routine was not for them. There was to be no staying at hotels in Pago Pago: they would take their sleeping bags, wander down to the beach, and make a nest among the sand dunes. Then they would move on to the local villages, hoping that the natives would be friendly. In their packs were a ten-pound block of cheese and plenty of tinned sardines. They were going to be all right.

On January 30, 1974, at just after eight o'clock in the evening, they said goodbye to their parents in the departure lounge at Auckland airport and climbed on board the Boeing 707 that was Pan Am Flight 806 to Pago Pago and beyond.

———

LEON MARTIN CLAIMED to be able to hold his breath for four minutes—a minor vanity, and an unusual one for a man of fifty-seven, but Martin was no ordinary American in late middle age. He had devoted his whole life to sports, had coached the US Olympic diving teams in 1964 and 1968, and ran his own swimming gymnasium in Phoenix, Arizona.

Martin had been in New Zealand for the previous four weeks coaching the Kiwis' national team for the Commonwealth Games in Christchurch and had been intending to wander home via the Far East, looking at diving talent along the way. He had no intention of taking the short route back to the United States via Pago Pago and Honolulu.

However, while the games were in progress, something happened to make him change his mind. He learned he was to be given the Fred Katey Award—America's most prestigious swimming trophy—and that the presentation ceremony would be in Los Angeles on February 2. Martin, an extrovert not averse to publicity, decided this was more important than his projected jaunt around the Far East. He left Christchurch two days before the end of the games and flew to Auckland, where he exchanged his previous booking for a ticket on Flight 806.

———

NOT EVERYONE who climbed the steps of the plane that evening was in a happy frame of mind. John Carter was far from cheerful. He was on his way back to the Tokelau island of Nukunonu, a remote speck in the South Pacific that he shared with 370 islanders and one other European. For the next twelve months, his only link with civilization would be an unreliable radiotelephone and a mail boat that called every three months.

Carter's exile was self-imposed. A forty-three-year-old carpenter, he had gone to the islands to work as a building overseer for the New Zealand government after his twenty-year marriage had broken up in late 1971. This had been his first trip back to the mainland since, but it was no pleasure visit. Five days before the departure of Flight 806 he had filed for divorce to render the legal separation with Lucy Carter permanent. For a man like Carter, brought up in the Roman Catholic faith, it was a somber step. His state of mind was made no lighter by the knowledge that his nineteen-year-old son Richard, second youngest of the five Carter children, had had a motorcycle accident while he was overseas and was now a permanent paraplegic. Richard's accident had happened on Boxing Day 1972, only days after his father had left to work in the islands, and a pall of bitterness seemed to hang over the whole Carter family.

Financially, John Carter was poor. Not so Johannes van Heerden, who took his seat a few rows away. But the two men had something in common: neither saw much of their families. Van Heerden was fifty-seven, a self-employed shoe designer and manufacturer who had come to New Zealand from his native Holland with his wife and children in 1951.

They had left Europe because they feared nuclear war, and van Heerden had brought his machinery with him to set up a shoe factory in Wellington, thus neatly evading the post-war currency regulations.

The factory prospered, shops were acquired, and by the early 1970s, the van Heerdens owned three houses and a beach chalet. Their younger son was at an expensive private school, but they were not a close family. In fact, between 1968 and 1972, while she was living on the island of New Caledonia and he was living in Wellington, Grace van Heerden saw her husband only during rare visits.

Attracted by the prospect of cheap labor in Western Samoa, van Heerden sold his Wellington shoe factory in 1972 and opened another in Pago Pago. He wanted Grace to set up home with him in Samoa, but she decided it would be wrong to leave the children. As a diabetic with early indications of heart trouble, she also preferred the temperate climate of New Zealand.

Van Heerden went to Samoa on his own, returning occasionally to see his family and buy fresh supplies of leather. On January 30, 1974, he flew from Wellington to Auckland, where he rang Grace to say that he would be spending the night at the hotel in Pago Pago before going on to the factory. Neither had any premonition that they would never meet again.

The Hemsleys, the Rogerses, Van Heerden, Carter, and Martin, all human beings with their private thoughts, fears, desires, and ambitions, joined eighty-three other human beings and trooped across the tarmac to the waiting aircraft. Clutched in their hands, or stuffed into handbags and pockets, each carried a blue-and-white Pan American ticket. And the ticket, as required by international regulations, carried the following advice:

> Passengers on a journey involving an ultimate destination or a stop in a country other than the country of origin are advised that the provisions of a treaty known as the Warsaw Convention may be applicable to the entire journey, including any portion entirely within the country of origin or destination. For such passengers on a journey to, from, or with an agreed stopping place in the United States of America, the Convention and special contracts of carriage embodied in applicable tariffs provide that the liability of certain carriers,

parties to such special contracts, for death of or personal injury to passengers is limited in most cases to proven damages not to exceed US Dollars 75,000 per passenger, and that this liability up to such limit shall not depend on negligence on the part of the carrier. For such passengers traveling by a carrier not a party to such special contracts or on a journey not to, from, or having an agreed stopping place in the United States of America, liability of the carrier for death of or personal injury to passengers is limited in most cases to approximately US Dollars 10,000 or US Dollars 20,000.

The names of carriers, parties to such special contracts, are available at all ticket offices of such carriers and may be inspected on request. Additional protection can usually be obtained by purchasing insurance from a private company. Such insurance is not affected by any limitation of the carrier's liability under the Warsaw Convention or such special contracts of carriage. For further information, please consult your airline or insurance company representative.

Note: The limit of liability of US Dollars 75,000 above is inclusive of legal fees and costs except that in the case of a claim brought in a state where provision is made for separate award of legal fees and costs, the limit shall be in the sum of US Dollars 58,000 exclusive of legal fees and costs.

This classic piece of small print, which few passengers have ever bothered to read, left out one important feature of the Warsaw Convention: it would cease to apply, and that damages would be unlimited, should the airline be found guilty of willful misconduct. But what of it? Up to that point in time no airline had ever been found guilty of willful misconduct.

The passengers who boarded Flight 806 that evening could have no idea that these dull phrases were to dominate their lives and the lives of their families for the next eight years.

TWO

THE EARLY 1970S were a bad time for Pan American. Their worldwide route structure, so long a source of pride, had become increasingly expensive to maintain. In 1970, the airline lost $48,400,000, and there were talks, which never came to fruition, of seeking aid from the Shah of Iran. Drastic economies, coupled with increased effort on the marketing side, slowly restored their position, and in 1973 Pan Am made an operating profit of $6,700,000—though it still lost $18,400,000 overall.

But then came the first of the OPEC fuel crises, when the oil-producing countries finally banded together to demonstrate their economic ability to hold the rest of the world to ransom. The price of jet fuel shot through the roof, and with it went all hopes of profit for Pan American. The company's 1974 operating loss was $98,200,000; their total loss for the year was a record $81,700,000.

None of this can excuse what happened; the primary duty of an air carrier is, and must always be, to carry its passengers from point to point in safety. But it must have been galling for Pan American executives to watch virtually all of their international competitors being cozily shielded by government subsidies during this period, while they had to operate by the harsh realities of the free enterprise balance sheet. The staff was cut from 40,000 to 30,000; 37 jet aircraft were sold. Still the losses mounted, and the banks grew more and more reluctant to bail out a ship that was sinking. Congress, too, refused to help.

Meanwhile the aircraft were still flying, and most of them were reaching their destinations. But in the nine months between July 1973 and April 1974, three Pan American Boeing 707s were lost. The value of the wrecked jets was perhaps $30,000,000; the price of the 282 lives was beyond calculation. Something was obviously wrong, and on April 27, 1974, a team of eight full-time investigators from the Federal Aviation Administration began an intensive inspection of Pan American's operations.

For six weeks, with the willing cooperation of Pan Am staff, they turned the airline inside out. They flew on the routes and observed that 43 percent of crews were failing to carry out established cockpit procedures. They watched captains going through proficiency checks in the simulator, and while they were watching, 36.8 percent failed. They noted, ominously, that some of these would have been passed by the examiners if the investigators had not been present.

"It is common gossip among the airmen, and in some cases cabin staff," said the final report, "that Pan Am has captains and first officers that are considered substandard by their peers and have been carried by the company and need the help of strong co-pilots. Further, efforts were made by certain first officers, second officers, and flight engineers to specifically avoid having a flight schedule assignment, if at all possible, with some substandard captains."

In other words, Pan Am was employing pilots with whom other pilots were scared to fly. The passengers, of course, had no knowledge and therefore no option but to fly with them.

The official Pan Am reaction to their accusation was to deny that substandard pilots had ever been employed by the airline. The contention was hardly borne out by the fact that "early retirements" from the flight line in 1974—after the investigators had submitted a list of names—totaled more than forty. In 1971 and 1972, the figure had been about five per year. In addition, within six months after the team's departure, no fewer than 146 captains, first officers, flight engineers, second officers, and instructors were removed from the seniority list. Six were fired.

Would any action have been taken had the enquiry not been carried out? Perhaps it is a question better left unasked.

Among the pilots themselves, there was no reluctance to cooperate. There had been growing unease for a long time, brought into sharp focus by the three crashes. On May 6, 1974, eight of them met with the investigating team at the Pan Am training school in San Francisco to air their anxieties. One of the most outspoken was Captain Frank Metlick, a 707 pilot, who later wrote an account for the confidential record:

> Long and onerous flight crew patterns, as produced by
> Pan American Airways, with their utter disregard of the
> human physiological factors, have contributed towards
> our series of accidents. Examination of our series of

tragedies shows a definite pattern in which accumulative fatigue is one of the factors. The company has been continually informed that flight crews were having a difficult time with a great number of our crew patterns. In fact, in a letter to the Director of Flight Operations dated April 4, 1973, it was pointed out that if these long duty periods and patterns of daylight rest were not dealt with, we would have a catastrophe. Since that time, we have had more than one catastrophe.

The history of our deteriorating patterns started with the introduction of a new operations management concept, wherein no pilots were utilized. This concept was a disaster, and has since proven to be just that.

Coupled with this new concept was the austerity program with which Pan Am is attempting to "cut" itself into prosperity. An airline cannot "cut" itself into prosperity.

At the root of Metlick's complaint was the provision in the pilots' working agreement with Pan Am that there should be a minimum nine-and-a-half-hour rest period between flights. "It was never intended to be used," Metlick said, "to construct patterns with this minimum rest to enable the company to save money, at the utter disregard for a crew member's health and morale." Metlick suggested the reestablishment of overseas crew bases by Pan Am to ease the problem. "This becomes a costly item," he admitted, "but any catastrophe is one hundred times more expensive."

Thus far, the FAA team had established that Pan American crews were often tired, frequently careless, and sometimes below standard. They now turned to the question of whether they really knew the routes they were flying. As a passenger sitting in the back, traveling to strange places while sipping a gin and tonic, it is often comforting to think that the men in the cockpit have been there before, many times. As the investigators discovered, in the case of Pan American in 1974, it was not necessarily so.

It transpired that under the company's system, pilots were allowed to "bid" for routes over the whole network on a month-to-month basis. A man could be flying to Europe one month and to Alaska or the South Pacific the next. Pan Am's route and airport qualification procedures were so broad that any airman could fly anywhere merely by reviewing films of the airports. These films were out of date.

All this required a complex schedule to be drawn up each month, and as these things will, it sometimes went wrong. Pilots would be diverted from the routes they had been assigned after they left home base. When that happened, it was anyone's guess as to whether they had even seen a film of the airport where they would have to land.

However, there was a reasonable chance that most captains would have some knowledge of the place where they were going. Not so the first officer, which could place an added burden on the pilot. "If neither pilot is thoroughly familiar," the team's report noted sourly, "confusion reigns." They recommended that crews be assigned to each operational area for not less than a year rather than dart about the globe. It is not known whether Pan Am took the advice.

By this time, it was becoming plain that Pan American was running a pretty sloppy airline. Just how sloppy, the investigators were to discover when they took a close look at the training program. There was no question but that Pan Am was conforming to the FAA regulations and subjecting its pilots to six-monthly checks of their proficiency. That was not the point. The question was: Who was doing the checking? How thoroughly were they doing it? And were they making any effort to give training in order to improve substandard performance in the cockpit?

The answers were staggering. Unlike other airlines, which use regular line captains to make checks on their fellow pilots, Pan American was employing pilots of such low seniority to do the job that if they had not held the position of check airman they would have had to be laid off. In other words, these men not only had the job of passing judgment on pilots vastly senior to themselves, but they lived with the nagging fear that if they failed them their own jobs might be threatened. Not surprisingly, most captains passed their checks, whether they deserved to or not.

The pilots themselves were perfectly aware of what was going on. Captain Donald Stubbs told the team of investigators, "Sometimes, most of the time, the captain gets by when the other crew members are harassed beyond belief. Many times, I have seen a simulator check where a captain shoots a bad approach and maybe gets his wrist slapped. The engineer or first officer then fouls something as bad, and he gets a 'down' or 'incomplete.' We are in the Clipper Skipper syndrome where he can do no wrong, and this is wrong because all humans have failures."

Captain Charles Banfe, who flew a 747, went further. He alleged that Pan Am's check pilots were often selected on the basis of "friendship and loyalty," that they had no formal training, and that each checked to his own standard.

Pilots, he said, were being allowed to deteriorate until their performance was marginal or below tolerable limits.

At this time there were forty-eight check airmen employed by Pan American who were not qualified line captains. They may still be doing the job. Though the inquiry team recommended that all check airmen should have this qualification, Pan American refused to fire its "professional instructors" or to transfer them to other assignments. It also did nothing to implement one of the team's other major recommendations: that there should be a centralized training organization for the airline instead of one divided between three locations.

In all, the FAA team came up with fifty-eight recommendations for Pan American to change its ways. A second check six months later showed that some had been heeded, some not. There was no enforcement action by the FAA and no attempt whatever to employ the toughest sanction of all: public opinion.

Every effort was made to keep the findings of the inquiry, and even its existence, a secret from the public. For after all, what right has the man in the street to know that a scheduled air carrier is liable to kill him through incompetence? Such knowledge might damage the commercial interests of the airline, and that would never do. It was a classic example of the contradictions posed by the FAA's joint responsibility for safety and the financial welfare of the airline industry.

On the tarmac in Auckland, on the evening of January 30, 1974, there were ninety-one people who might not have been there, had they known what the reader knows now.

THREE

THOUGH ITS PASSENGER load was well below capacity, the Boeing 707-321B sat heavy on the tarmac at Auckland on that late summer evening. Of its gross weight, 40 percent consisted of 52.23 tons of A1 jet fuel, which had been loaded into tanks within the wings and in the center section of the fuselage. The four Pratt and Whitney jets, slung in their dangling pods, were thirsty engines by modern standards. But even they were not thirsty enough to use that much fuel for the three-and-a-half-hour flight to Pago Pago. In fact, at their average consumption of 235 pounds per minute, they would burn up only 40 percent of it. Some of the remainder was needed for a possible diversion to the next available airfield at Nandi, but even if that had to be used, there would still be 37,900 pounds—17 tons—remaining in the tanks, sufficient for almost three hours of flying. Flight 806 was an aerial tanker.

There was nothing unusual about this for a Pan American aircraft at this moment in history. It was all part of the company's economy drive. During the oil crisis, fuel was in short supply and more expensive at some airfields than at others. It was Pan American policy to pick up excess fuel at the cheaper locations, so that less would be needed when the aircraft landed at more expensive points. It is doubtful how much economy was achieved; because the fuel consumption of an aircraft depends partly upon its weight, it costs fuel to carry fuel. However, it is possible that the accountants did not even know this, and the move must certainly have looked good on their books.

The amount of stored fuel to be carried had to be nicely calculated so that the aircraft would not arrive at its destination weighing more than its maximum permissible landing weight. In the case of Flight 806, that weight would be 245,000 pounds, and the captain had worked out that the Boeing would weight just 100 pounds less than that when it reached Pago Pago. It was cutting things a little fine, but it was perfectly legal.

There was one other precaution taken by Pan American when this money-saving operation began. Knowing that there were some airfields where landing at the maximum weight might prejudice safety, they published a list of the route stages, or sectors, on which stored fuel should be carried, and those on which it should not. The list also excluded, of course, those sectors that flew from a more expensive loading point to a cheaper one. It is not known whether Captain Leroy A. Petersen of Flight 806, known as Pete to his friends, had seen that list.

Captain Petersen was fifty-two and had spent his entire professional flying career in the service of Pan American. He had joined the company in March 1951 as a navigator and radio operator, working his way up to reserve co-pilot/navigator in 1960, when he was awarded his Air Transport Pilot Certificate. After that, progress was relatively swift. Petersen became a master co-pilot in 1965, and a Boeing 707 captain in November 1967. In all, he had flown 17,414 hours, of which 7,414 were in the 707.

In early September 1973, Captain Petersen had had a health problem that had prevented him from flying. It persisted until January 15, 1974, and after such a long layoff he was required to take a simulator check and perform three actual takeoffs and landings (Flight sections) before he could take charge of a line aircraft again. He passed these tests, but the flight section was carried out in daylight under visual meteorological conditions. These conditions were very different from those he would face on the night of January 30, 1974, when he guided Flight 806 toward an airfield on which he had only landed once before, in May 1972. Petersen had not flown an instrument approach for 132 days.

This was virtually all the information about Petersen that appeared in the official report on the accident. It was also all the jury was allowed to hear in the subsequent trial, aside from the fact that he had been given a satisfactory flight check from San Francisco to Anchorage, Alaska in the summer of 1973 and had once been asked to repeat an instrument landing system (ILS) exercise.

But there was much more to know about the flying record of Leroy A. Petersen. As with all professional pilots, the results of every check he was ever given throughout his career were filed away and kept. The FAA and Pan American had no excuse for not knowing what kind of pilot was in charge of Flight 806.

These are extracts from Captain Petersen's training records:

December 20, 1951: "Thinking and judgment of a professional and intelligent airman were marginal."

July 2, 1957: "ILS work with the ZR [navigational instrument] very poor. Lacks planning on initial intercept. Set up ZR wrong on second approach and failed to turn on additional radio aids while maneuvering at outer marker. Threshold speeds fast on crosswind approach and landings. Needs additional ILS work and landing practice."

August 29, 1963: "Repeated four-engine ILS approach too fast—20 knots too fast. Erratic bracketing [failing to maintain aircraft on glide slope]. Over-control on ailerons caused vertical bar excursions, with further over-control trying to chase movements."

June 1, 1965: "Failed FAA oral exam for 707 type rating."

June 21, 1965: "Failed FAA flight portion of the exam required for issuance of a Boeing 707-20 rating. Unsatisfactory landing technique. Maneuvering with engines out (2-engine en route climb). Maneuvering

for landing at weather minimums, and
landing with engine failure."

June 25, 1965: "Failed re-check for
FAA 707-20 rating. Unsatisfactory
landing and engine failure."

June 26, 1967: "Additional training
for holding entry and circling
approach. Holding entry was nonstandard and tolerances were
exceeded. First circling approach was
poorly planned; turned in too close
and very high on profile. Pilot
executed a go-round. Second attempt
resulted in a large over-shoot, with
an over-bank correcting back to final
approach. Touchdown was approximately
1100 feet long. Three-engine ILS
missed approach was very weak.
Airspeed, altitude and holding varied
considerably throughout the pattern.
Staggered throttles incorrectly on
two occasions.

Switched to approach mode too
early. Insufficient yaw control and
flight-directed interpretation on
final. Localizer minimums. Two-engine
approach was poorly planned and
executed. High on profile, he elected
to go to 50 degree of flaps very
early, and established deterioration
of profile and airspeed. Required

assistance as airspeed decreased to Vth [minimum speed required at runway threshold] minus five knots. Approached threshold and low on profile."

October 16, 1967/October 23, 1967: "Heading control not precise. Over-control of elevator and throttles on ILS, introducing yaw and roll. Approaches and landing phases unsatisfactory. Yaw and roll excessive in later stages of landings. Several landings had to be guarded by check pilot to avoid pod scraping."

It was immediately following these checks, on November 10, 1967, that Pan American promoted Leroy Petersen to the rank of captain in charge of the Boeing 707.

December 21, 1972: "Repeated three-engine ILS for glide-slope tracking. Over-control on elevators. Repeated ADF due to incorrect entry procedure; turnout exceeded limits. Also, high airspeed on final, and shallow sink rate. Did not get the minimums at missed approach point. Instrument cross check was slow, causing most of the problems."

> June 28, 1973: "He had to repeat
> three-engine ILS, due to being out of
> limits at decision height."

There was certainly no lack of warning that Captain Petersen was not the brightest and best pilot ever to fly the airways. Small wonder that he was one of the men with whom other Pan Am airmen preferred not to fly. Though much of the language in these reports may be too technical for the layperson to understand, the overall picture is clear enough. Captain Petersen was a man who had trouble with instrument landings, and he had suffered this deficiency throughout his career. Nonetheless, on January 30, 1974, he was still the man in charge of Flight 806, and in three and a half hours he was due to make an instrument approach into Pago Pago under the very conditions in which he had underperformed, to say the least, so often in the past.

Petersen, of course, was not alone on the flight deck. He had three others with him. They were First Officer Richard V. Gaines, Third Officer James S. Phillips, and Flight Engineer Gerry W. Green.

Gaines was not well that day. He was suffering from laryngitis, which was unfortunate because the first officer's duties included handling radio communications with the ground. It was also regrettable because Gaines, who had been to Pago Pago twelve times in the past year, had more experience there than anyone in the cockpit. Petersen's experience of the airport, since 1972, amounted to viewing Pan Am's out-of-date film and watching from his seat while another pilot made a landing there a few days before.

It was, therefore, James Phillips who sat in the co-pilot's seat as Flight 806 prepared for takeoff. Green was at the engineer's console, and Gaines sat on the jump seat behind the pilots.

Phillips, at forty-three, was perhaps a little old to be holding no more than a third officer's rating. He had possessed a commercial pilot's license since 1961 and had been employed by Pan Am since 1966. He had completed his training as a reserve co-pilot and navigator in January 1967 and had flown for 5,208 hours, 4,706 of them in the Boeing 707. He had passed checks in May and November of 1973, one of them observed by an FAA inspector, and he had made seven takeoffs and landings since October 1973. He had also flown into Pago Pago seven times in the previous seven months.

That was Phillips's public record, as recounted by the National Transportation Safety Board and relayed to the trial jury. Behind it lay a series of reports that were not revealed at the trial:

```
June 6, 1966: "Student a little slow.
Knows procedures but hesitates to
make corrections."
```

```
August 21, 1966: "Student unable to
execute ILS approach due to slow scan
resulting in poor airspeed control.
Did not stay on either glideslope or
localizer within prescribed minima.
Confused on holding pattern
procedure. Needs landings and
practice in maintaining profile. ILS
with flight director (600 feet) and
normal night landings graded
unsatisfactory."
```

August 23, 1966: "Quite a bit behind aircraft throughout, partially due to unfamiliarity with specific instrument and control locations. Needs improvement on air traffic control procedure. Consistently slow on getting correct holding entry. Needs to become more consistent on flying. Also needs much improvement on instrument failure recognition and corrected procedures."

August 16, 1967: "Lack of thinking is still causing difficulty. On the only missed approach attempted we would have crashed into the mountains due to letting the airplane turn 90 degrees to the left while climbing out. On the rudder-boost-off three-engine approach, after being vectored to a 60-degree intercept, due to poor thinking Phillips became so lost that he had to ask for vectoring to find himself. For the auto-coupled approach, the simulator was put in the freeze condition while still three minutes from the outer marker, and he was warned to plan ahead and review the procedure he was to use for this approach. After adequate time, the simulator was unfrozen. He failed to follow the planned approach

```
procedure, and could not complete the
approach."
```

```
November 12, 1968: "Sometimes slow in
planning.  Slow  following  approach
plate procedures."
```

```
May 18, 1972: "Repeated holding to
review operational entry procedure."
```

These, then, were the two men at the controls as Flight 806 began its journey. First officer Richard Gaines had no direct part to play, but he was still, according to company regulations, supposed to be monitoring the performance of the pilot and co-pilot.

Gaines was thirty-seven and had worked for Pan American for the past ten years. He had been upgraded to master co-pilot in June 1967, and all his 5,107 flight hours had been spent on the Boeing 707. Like Petersen, he held an Airline Transport Pilot rating. According to the National Transportation Safety Board (NTSB) report: "Numerous routine co-pilot reports were reviewed from his file, and no adverse comments were noted."

No adverse comments? A more diligent review of Gaines's training record reveals the following:

```
September 22, 1964: "Slow reaction to
corrections  on  power.  Airspeed  and
heading control slow."
```

```
October  20,  1964:  "Instrument
scanning a little slow."
```

April 27, 1965: "Slow scanning and erratic altitude control."

November 30, 1965: "Altitude control was ragged, and there was little or no use of vertical speed. Landing pattern work and landing were inconsistent. Cannot recommend line landings."

December 18, 1966: "Pilot continually behind the aircraft. Seems to lack confidence. He is unable to see objective of minima. Only concerned with procedures and details. Use of checklist, crew coordination, judgment, holding pattern, entry and two engine landings found unsatisfactory. He did not use the landing lights twice on night landings—simply forgot. Two engine approach was considerably below Vmc at 400 feet, and the 45-degree approach to mid runway. Pull-up was impossible. Landing patterns and touchdowns inconsistent. Recoveries from landing bounces unsatisfactory. Holding pattern entry was in opposite direction, 500 feet high, and too fast on speed. It is recommended that he receive a non-rated MCO [master co-pilot] check."

December 23, 1966: "Due to the unsatisfactory rating he received on many items, it is recommended that the type rating training be discontinued, and he should be re-scheduled to a two-hour flight to requalify as a reserve co-pilot."

January 13, 1967: "Pre-rating check incomplete and unsatisfactory. Trainee wanted to discontinue as he felt he was wasting time and already judged unsatisfactory."

May 8, 1967: "This pilot is slow and indecisive about almost everything he does. Spent almost ten minutes getting airplane into landing configuration with jammed stabilizer. Does not seem to be able to follow simple instructions unless repeated several times. Frequently changes power for no apparent reason. Very slow to trim stabilizer, with large altimeter errors as a result."

July 6, 1967: "Due to his inability to consistently demonstrate satisfactory proficiency of type rating maneuvers after extensive training, it is recommended that type training be discontinued."

Only eight days after this last recommendation, on July 14, 1967, Richard V. Gaines was awarded Airline Transport Pilot Certificate No. 1578652, with a type rating on, or qualification to fly, the Boeing 707-720.

When the training records of these three men were discovered by attorneys, long after the crash but before the trial, Pan American made strenuous efforts to prevent them from being introduced in evidence and thus made public.

Government attorney Mark Dombroff argued, "Where the competence, intelligence, ability to fly ILS approaches, scanning ability, cross-checking ability, and overall level of performance of the crew members of Flight 806 is in question, both individually and collectively, we can hardly think of more relevant and material evidence in this case than what Pan Am said about its own crew members."

But Dombroff's plea fell on deaf ears. Judge Matthew William Byrne Jr. ordered the records of Petersen, Phillips, and Gaines to be kept from the jury and put under seal, and he consigned them to room 64G. Which is where I found them.

It has taken a long time for them to emerge into the light.

FOUR

DOCILE AND TRUSTING as any band of airline passengers anywhere, ninety-one souls filed across the tarmac and climbed on board Flight 806. There were several Samoans and, to judge from the rucksacks, quite a few young New Zealanders with plans similar to those of the Rogerses. Young Mary Hemsley clutched her mother's hand as they mounted the steep steps.

The usual confusion ensued as seat belts were fastened, hand luggage stowed, and the aircraft sorted into general order by the six stewardesses. Some of the cabin bags and sports equipment were stowed on the floor, in an empty aisle beside one of the central emergency exits.

The Rogerses were having a ball. "We were like two kids at the circus," Michael recalled later. "As a boy I had always read war books, and I had always known a certain amount about aviation. Sure, I was interested. What was a 707 like? What was it going to be like up there? What did you see? All this was tremendously interesting. It was very exciting."

They settled themselves in row 16 on the port side of the aircraft, with Susan in the window seat and Michael in the center of the row of three. The aisle seat was occupied by David Pontiff, an American oceanographer who was returning to the States after working in the South Pacific. The Rogerses, bubbling over with the novelty of their experience, tried to engage him in conversation. But Pontiff proved reserved and taciturn, and they soon abandoned the attempt. Instead, they thumbed through the safety leaflets in the seat pockets in front of them and listened—with more rapt attention than most of the seasoned travelers on board—to the emergency briefing from one of the flight attendants. They noted casually, as the stewardess waved her arms in the usual vague indication, that they were two rows behind an escape exit over the wing. Unconsciously, the Rogerses filed the knowledge away. It would save their lives.

Flight 806 accelerated down the runway and pulled its heavy load into the air as it banked away to the north and east, leaving behind a pall of acrid kerosene smoke on the translucent New Zealand evening. The Boeing climbed steadily to its cruising altitude of 33,000 feet while the sun sizzled its way into the Pacific on their left-hand side, and Captain Petersen and his crew set the autopilot and relaxed. Behind them, drinks and meals passed up and down the gangway. It was an ordinary, normal flight. For the next three and a half hours, virtually nothing happened.

At twelve minutes past eleven in the evening, Pago Pago time, Phillips contacted approach control. They were 160 miles out from their destination. Control reported a light rain shower at the airport, with an overcast sky and a 15-knot wind out of the northwest. Visibility was ten miles.

There was nothing to worry about. Five minutes later, Petersen eased back the throttles and began his descent. As they passed through 20,000 feet, approach control cleared Flight 806 to make an instrument landing on runway 5.

Pago Pago International Airport has a single runway that is 9,000 feet long and 150 feet wide, paved with asphalt. The northern end extends into the sea, but the southern, toward which Flight 806 was approaching, has a hill 399 feet high just 1.7 nautical miles from the runway threshold. Because of this hill, known as Logotala Hill, the instrument landing system glide slope has had to be made a little steeper than is usual in order to give safe clearance. The difference in angle is not great, but it does mean that aircraft landing at Pago Pago on runway 5 have to adopt a slightly faster rate of descent.

There is one other minor peculiarity about the airport: it has no control tower. Instead, there is a splendidly titled Combined Approach Control/International Station (CAP/IS), believed to be the only one of its kind in the world. The CAP/IS is a sort of inferior control tower, from which the operators cannot see the end of the runway and which offers limited services. Frank Bateman, the controller on duty that night, had no authority to tell Captain Petersen to abort his landing or to pass detailed weather information on his own initiative. If problems arose, he could only do his best to help. And that he did.

But there were no problems. At least, there appeared to be no problems in the cockpit of Flight 806. The Boeing 707 continued to descend, picking up the radial beam of the airport's navigation beacon as it passed through 5,500 feet, and then finding the glide slope that would guide them down to the runway. They were now eight miles from their destination, and Phillips called out that he had the runway in sight.

A mile farther, and Phillips reported 2,000 feet registering on the radio altimeter. They were about 200 feet below the glide slope, and Petersen pushed the throttles forward to increase power and cut the rate of descent.

"Get down here you—" said Petersen (according to the cockpit voice recorder transcription), talking to the bars on his glide slope instrument, which remained stubbornly above the little aircraft symbol representing his own position. When the two came together he would be on course. He put on some more power. The aircraft seemed heavy, sluggish. As Petersen well knew, the extra stored fuel on board had made it very close to its maximum landing weight at this point, and heavy aircraft are slower to respond.

As the needles came together, Flight 806 was rocked by slight turbulence. "A bit bouncy out here," said Petersen (cockpit voice recorder transcription), conversationally.

From the ground, Bateman butted in. "Clipper 806, it appears that we've had a power failure at the airport."

The crew peered through the windscreen. Everything appeared normal. They checked the instruments. They were still functioning as they should.

Phillips pressed the transmit button on his microphone. "806. We're still getting your VOR [still receiving the signal from the navigation beacon at the airport], [and] the ILS, and the lights are showing."

"See the runway lights?" queried Bateman.

Phillips confirmed. "That's Charlie," he said.

Bateman sounded relieved. "We have a bad rain shower here," he said. "I can't see them from my position."

Phillips replied that they still looked bright to him. They were now five miles from the runway, just above the glide path.

Petersen adjusted the throttles slightly as Bateman gave his final instructions: "Okay. No other reported traffic. The wind is 030 at 20, gusting to 25. Advise clear of the runway."

"806. Wilco," said Phillips. He seemed cool and unconcerned.

As they crossed the cliffs at the end of the island, heading for Logotala Hill, rain started to spot the windscreen. The wipers were turned on.

"Flaps fifty," ordered Petersen. The heavy flaps on the trailing edge of the wings, already at forty degrees, cranked down a further ten degrees into their final landing position.

In the cabin behind, seat belts had been fastened and the "No smoking" signs were on. Outside it was very dark, but the Rogerses could see the occasional light on the ground from a passing car.

The final hill slid by beneath them. "You're by Logotala," Phillips reported.

Petersen said, "Let me know when you got the runway."

Phillips said, "You have the runway." And then, "You're a little high." At this point, Flight 806 was indeed above the glide path, but only just, and it was descending quite fast. Petersen thumbed the trim button on his control column to ease the load on the elevators caused by the increased flap setting.

"One hundred and fifty knots," called Phillips. One hundred fifty knots was the scheduled approach speed for a Boeing 707 in these conditions. Then he reported to Petersen, "You're at minimums."

This was the height at which Petersen had to decide whether to continue with the approach or to abandon it and go around again. The call should have been made at 280 feet. Actually, Phillips made it at 400 feet. In any event, there was no response from the captain, who had evidently decided to land.

"Field in sight," called Phillips. Now they were below the glide slope, falling fast. "Turn to your right." A pause. "One hundred forty knots," Phillips said. His voice was calm and steady, not a hint of anxiety.

And then, without warning, Flight 806 crashed. There were no further words from the cockpit.

It came down almost gently, scything the tops from the waving palms and cutting the trunks through lower and lower until the undercarriage tore away and the four screaming engines were ripped from their mountings to choke and fall silent. Only the fuselage remained intact, skidding between the obstacles with a charmed life until it vaulted a final gully, struck a low wall made of lava rocks, and came to rest.

A searing blossom of flame pushed back the night.

FIVE

THERE WAS NO SCREAMING, no panic in the crowded cabin. Strapped in their seats, the passengers were either motionless with shock or had simply failed to realize what had happened. Some said later that the impact was no worse than a rough landing.

They had crashed, and they were still alive. Indeed, hardly anyone was even injured. They had flown into the ground at 140 miles an hour, their proud aircraft lay scattered in pieces over a quarter of a mile of jungle, and yet they had survived.

"The thought went through my head," Michael Rogers said later, "that if this is the way an airplane crashes, it is not really too bad. What do people get excited about?" He was soon to know.

As the Boeing 707 had plowed through the trees, gaping holes had been torn in the fuel tanks within the wings. Impact with the wall had ripped out the belly of the plane, and with it, the rubber bladders of the center fuel container. The kerosene held for a moment, and then, carried forward by its own momentum as the aircraft decelerated, it gushed from the holes in a fine explosive spray. Contact with the hot engines or ruptured electrical circuits did the rest. The initial flash fire lasted only seconds as the vapor burned away, but then the remainder of the thirty tons of fuel on board began pouring into the gully over which the fuselage rested, eating into the thin metal shell above with flames of terrible intensity.

The Boeing's power supply had failed and the cabin was in darkness; now the raging inferno outside made it as light as day. A few passengers, a very few, acted swiftly. Leon Martin, on the starboard side of the aircraft where the fire was at its fiercest, flung open an emergency exit and slammed it shut again as the flames came bursting through to scorch his face and hands. His nose caught the first whiff of what he thought was chlorine gas, and he stopped breathing on the instant, dropping to the floor and crawling toward exits on the other side of the cabin.

———

MICHAEL ROGERS, two rows behind the nearest emergency exit on the port side, was up and running in a second. His one thought was to get clear before panic developed and he was trampled in the rush. Even so, he was beaten to the exit by another passenger, Thomas Hinton, who had been sitting in the row in front. Hinton wrestled with the exit door while Rogers tried frantically to move the pile of bags and equipment that covered the floor in the exit row.

The door came clear. Rogers had a fleeting image of Hinton, engulfed in flames and then tumbling out of the gaping hole into the fire beneath.

"At least I knew there was a way out," he said later. "Not a good way, but a way. I whipped round the seats in the aisle to get there."

Rogers flung himself through the exit, rolling over as he hit the ground and running straight through the burning fuel until he was clear of the flames. Unknown to him, Susan, his bride of three months, was still inside the aircraft. He had believed that she had gone out ahead of him. Actually, her seat had been dislodged from its mounting in the crash and she was having trouble unfastening her seat belt. Then, in an instinctive female reaction, she began to search for her handbag. It was trapped beneath the seat in front and she was unable to free it.

Finally abandoning the attempt, Susan Rogers looked up to find the cabin rapidly filling with smoke and her husband gone. She reached the exit door at the same moment as David Pontiff, and in a parody of civilized behavior, they wasted further seconds while each allowed the other to go first.

When Susan did escape through the emergency exit, she fell badly, tripping through a hole in the wing on to a patch of burning debris. Her hair caught fire, almost all her clothes burned off, and her nylon tights fused to her legs in the searing heat. Frantically, she beat at the flames with her hands, burning them severely in the process.

Hinton, who had left the aircraft as a human torch, had managed to extinguish the flames and was still alive. He, his wife, and Susan Rogers were found by Leon Martin. Martin had succeeded in opening the second emergency exit on the port side and had sprinted along the burning wing to safety with his eyes tightly shut. He helped the others clear and then encountered Michael Rogers, who was heading back toward the wreckage in search of his wife.

By now, it was raining hard, a sudden tropical storm that cooled their burns and soaked the undergrowth to stop the fire from spreading. They had no idea where they were, and there was no sign of any rescue services.

As they retreated to a safe distance and looked back at the remnants of Flight 806, the little band of survivors could see that the port side of the fuselage, from which they had escaped, seemed to be relatively intact. Flames were still leaping high on the far side of the aircraft, but under the port wing, they seemed diminished. Shocked and injured as they were, and incapable of doing anything to help, they were certain that many more passengers and crew would manage to escape. But they could see no one, and the main doors to the front and rear of the aircraft, though free of fire, remained firmly shut. The emergency exits over the wing gaped open, dark. There was no sign that anyone else was using the same route to safety.

In fact, though they did not know it at the time, four others had gotten clear of the burning plane, making a total of ten out of the 101 aboard. They were Herbert and Eunice Simpson, an elderly couple from Sun City, Arizona; a travel agent named Hans Richter; and third officer James Phillips. Phillips had suffered traumatic injuries in the crash itself, the only person to do so. A tree stump had torn a great hole in the nose of the Boeing, ripping away the rudder pedal assembly beneath his feet, and he had fallen through the gap to the ground when the mad slide came to an end. He was found there by firemen, badly burned but still alive. How the Simpsons and Richter got out has never been discovered. They too had suffered extreme burns.

Although a fire tender had been standing by for the arrival of Flight 806, and the crash took place less than a mile from the end of the runway, it was almost a quarter of an hour before Samoan firemen reached the scene. They had found their way blocked by heavy chains across the end of the access road that led directly to the crash site and had had to smash their way through with axes before their vehicles could get past.

Had they been quicker, it probably would have made little difference. Those still on board almost certainly died within the first two minutes, asphyxiated by smoke and gas and seared by the intense heat. Their bodies, charred beyond recognition, were later found scattered throughout the remains of the aircraft.

Slowly, painfully, the few survivors dragged themselves away from the scene, fearful that the Boeing might explode. They found a clearing and sat down, then Leon Martin and Michael Rogers, the least injured, went off in different directions to seek help.

Martin, having noticed the direction in which the plane was facing, went that way in hope of finding the airport and meeting the rescue services that surely, he reasoned, must be on their way. But it was Rogers who struck lucky, stumbling into the path of a local taxi that was careering down the dirt road through the forest. He guided the driver and two Samoan friends back to the clearing, and between them they got the others into the car, later picking up Martin on the road.

It was a terrifying drive. The Samoan behind the wheel, anxious to get them to the hospital as soon as possible, flung his vehicle around the bends at terminal velocity. The survivors, their burns growing more agonizing as the initial shock wore off, were tossed around inside the cab like dice in a shaker. At one point, Martin, who was riding in the front, reached across and snatched the ignition key in a bid to make the driver slow down. After one narrow escape from death, the last thing any of them wanted was to die senselessly in a car accident. But it made no difference. The wild ride went on until they arrived at the Lyndon B. Johnson Hospital for Tropical Diseases, eight miles from the scene of the crash.

Despite its imposing title, the Lyndon B. Johnson Hospital at Pago Pago was not quite the splendid institution it appeared to be from the outside. For all its two fine operating theaters, intensive care unit, and staff of nine doctors, it was a fine example of native custom triumphant over the mighty dollar.

———

WHEN SAMOANS WENT to the mission hospital that had stood there before the kindly Americans put up the new building, they took along the rest of the family and often their animals as well. The family cooked and slept in the ward along with the patient. And if they could get away with it, so did the animals. That was the way it had always been, and the charming islanders saw no reason to change things just because a new hospital had been erected. It was homey, but not necessarily the kind of place you would want to go if you were sick. More seriously, it had no burns unit nor any doctors specializing in the treatment of burns.

But it was all they had that night—that, plus some good physicians and a band of nurses who showed a tremendous degree of loving care. Susan Rogers was to say later that in all her long fight back to health, she never again had such tender treatment as she received from the Samoan nurses on Pago Pago.

It was not, and it could not be, enough. Though the hospital had been warned immediately after the crash to expect up to a hundred patients, and in the event had only ten—one of whom, Martin, was a walking case—the facilities were still overtaxed. In the intensive care unit, nine people were put in a room intended for four, male and female together, all naked because of their burns.

Co-pilot Phillips, who had broken both arms and legs and most of his fingers, in addition to having been seriously burned, was clearly in hopeless condition. But he was conscious, and when the National Transportation Safety Board team arrived the next day to investigate the accident, Phillips gave a statement to their leader, Richard Notte.

On the face of it, this was a great stroke of luck. There are few fatal airliner crashes in which the investigators can have the benefit of an eyewitness account from a man in the cockpit. If anyone alive knew why Flight 806 had crashed, it must have been Phillips. Yet his evidence was never used at the subsequent trial. The reason was quite simple: Notte forgot to use a tape recorder, and there were no witnesses present at the interview. Phillips's testimony, whatever it was, immediately became worthless. He died shortly afterward, in spite of an emergency operation to save his life, and his story was lost forever. It was not the first act of baffling incompetence surrounding Flight 806. Nor was it to be the last.

Of the other survivors, Susan Rogers seemed to be in the most critical state. She had severe burns over 55 percent of her body, and her scorched face and lips would not permit her to eat or speak. She lay there, a helpless broken doll, and she worried about washing her hair. She had been very proud of her hair. The nurses were too kind to tell her that there was none left.

Around her, the other patients seemed to be sitting up and talking. She wished that they would shut up and let her rest, and one by one they did. One by one, they died, and each time it happened she heard the blip of the heart monitor change to a steady tone, and she knew what it meant. Phillips, the Simpsons, and Mrs. Hinton died beside her. Thomas Hinton died while being taken to Hawaii eight days later. Pontiff survived.

There were four of them left. Just four.

SIX

HERBERT B. SIMPSON JR., eldest son of Herbert and Eunice, was a practicing lawyer in Chicago. Because of the time difference, it was late in the day of January 31 before he heard of the accident, and then only through a telephone call from a local newspaper reporter. He learned that his parents had survived the crash, that they had suffered burns, and that was all. Pan American could not, or would not, tell him anything further.

Simpson was a man of action who was not without connections. After contacting his two younger sisters, both married and living elsewhere in the United States, he set to work to garner information. At a nearby reference library, he researched the hospital at Pago Pago. He found out how big it was, how large a staff it carried, and what facilities were available. The data was not encouraging.

Doctor friends told Simpson that there were specialist burn centers in the United States, and he promptly telephoned two of them: the Brook Army Hospital in San Antonio, Texas, and the University of Michigan at Ann

Arbor. It was late evening before he managed to track down Dr. Seymour Tretter at the latter center.

Dr. Tretter was one of the leading burn specialists in the world. He told Simpson that if his parents were severely burned, and there were no other serious injuries, they could and should be moved to a specialist burn center within forty-eight hours. Provided their fluid levels were maintained during transport, there would be no great problem during that period. After forty-eight hours, however, such cases developed problems. There would be a build-up of poisons in the system, a risk of infection, and the possibility of kidney shutdown and cardiac complications. It was these aftereffects of a burn injury that the burn centers were specially equipped to handle.

Armed with this information, Simpson got back on to the Pan American representative in Chicago, William Smuck. It was 10:45 p.m., and Smuck was at home. Simpson asked him for help in getting himself and his sisters to Pago Pago and said they might need Pan Am's assistance in evacuating his parents to a burn center. He relayed the opinion he had gotten from Dr. Tretter, stressing the importance of acting quickly.

Smuck stalled. That sort of thing, he said, was going to require an awful lot of decision-making. It would be "more expeditious" to make these decisions at the start of the next business day.

Simpson was appalled at the prospect of waiting at least another eight hours before anything was done. The time clock on his parents' lives was ticking away. He wanted action immediately.

Smuck finally agreed to telephone the Pan American command center in New York that had been set up to deal with the accident. He refused Simpson's offer to do this himself, saying that "company rules" dictated that all dealings should be through him. He would call Simpson back, he said, when he had spoken to New York.

Simpson sat by his telephone in frustrated anxiety. It remained stubbornly silent. Finally, at 1:15 a.m. on the morning of February 1, Simpson could stand it no longer. He telephoned Smuck again.

Smuck was awakened by the call. He said he had spoken to New York and that the Pan Am command center had told him they "didn't have the personnel available" to make any decisions before the start of the next business day.

That would be too late, Simpson insisted. He offered to contact the telephone company to arrange a conference call between himself and whatever Pan Am officials in New York could make the decision. "Let's get this decision made and get doing," he said, as quoted in his affidavit.

But Smuck refused, claiming that such a move was impossible. The best he could do, he said (according to the affidavit he swore), was to be at his office at 8 a.m., which was nine o'clock New York time, and explain the situation to those responsible. Please, please, he added, don't call me again. "I trust this is the last time I will be hearing from you tonight." And he went back to sleep.

There was no sleep for Simpson. He got busy with the airline schedules and discovered there was a Pan American flight leaving Hawaii for Pago Pago at 6 a.m., Chicago time. At 2:45 a.m. he woke Smuck again to pass along this information and urge that Pan Am make sure there were doctors on that flight who knew how to deal with burn casualties. Wearily, Smuck agreed to pass on the message to New York. Simpson asked him to call back when he had done so. Half an hour later, still sitting by a silent telephone, Simpson called again. Smuck assured him that the message had gone through.

Simpson spent the rest of the night trying to telephone the LBJ hospital in Pago Pago directly. He finally got through and spoke to Dr. Peter Foster, the physician in charge of the case, who told him that his parents' condition was critical. This did nothing to ease Simpson's state of mind.

At eight o'clock promptly, he rang Smuck's office. Smuck was not there, and his secretary refused to let Simpson contact New York directly. She promised to call on his behalf, and to call back. She never did.

Simpson called again at 8:30. Smuck was still not in, but his secretary reported that the command center in New York had decided that there would be no Pan Am assistance with the evacuation of casualties, and no help for the Simpson children to reach Pago Pago that day. The best they could do would be to provide transport in three days' time.

Distraught with rage and worry, Simpson said to hell with Pan Am regulations and tried to telephone the company's chief executive officer in New York. He spoke to a man named Jeff Grindler in the chairman's office, who said the matter was being handled by a Mr. Serrano. Serrano, he promised, would call Simpson back promptly. He never did, nor did anyone from the New York command center ever contact him.

By this time, Simpson was beginning to get the message.

He decided to bring some political clout to bear and contacted a lawyer friend, Leslie J. Goldman. Goldman at this time was working as special counsel to Senator Adlai Stevenson of Illinois, but he had no more success in prompting Pan Am into action than Simpson. Goldman made a lot of telephone calls, pulling strings wherever he could, but the most he could achieve was to arrange transport for the Simpson children from Hawaii to Pago Pago—if they could get to Hawaii.

At this point, Simpson had his only unprompted call from the Pan Am office in Chicago, though not from Smuck. They advised him that there was a Continental Airlines flight from Chicago to Los Angeles in a few hours, with an onward connection to Hawaii. Simpson rounded up the rest of the family and they caught the flight.

When they arrived at Los Angeles, they were met by a Pan American representative who said he had been instructed to see that they had "a good and relaxed time" while they waited. They were taken to a private Pan Am facility until the Continental flight to Hawaii left later that evening. Simpson made constant inquiries about the condition of his parents. No one could tell him anything. "We made some rather negative inferences at that point," he said later.

There was another Pan Am official waiting at Hawaii. He had no information either. At 2:00 a.m. the Simpsons were driven to an air force base somewhere on the island and boarded a military transport for Pago Pago. They were disturbed to discover that in spite of Smuck's assurance and Goldman's string-pulling, there were no doctors on board.

At 8:30 on the morning of February 2, 1974, the Simpsons finally landed at Pago Pago, their aircraft sweeping in over the blackened heap of wreckage that still sat astride the middle marker on the approach to runway 5. It was fifty-seven hours since the accident.

The Pan Am representative who met them this time was a Mr. Kindel, who had flown in from Honolulu. Kindel took Herbert Simpson aside and said he wanted a private word. When they were alone, Kindel suggested they get going as soon as possible. That was fine with Simpson; that was what he had come for. But if he thought he was being taken straight to the hospital to see his parents he was mistaken.

As they drove away from the airport, along the narrow island roads, Kindel began to tell him what a splendid place Pago Pago was to relax, and how silly he was to be wearing a suit. No one wore a suit on Pago Pago. There was a great hotel; he was going to enjoy it.

For Simpson it was a surreal experience. He asked once more about the condition of his parents, and Kindel said he had no idea. He had not been to the hospital to inquire. Suddenly Simpson realized that he was not going there now either.

Losing his patience, Simpson abruptly ordered Kindel to take him to the hospital immediately, and Kindel, clearly thinking he had some kind of a nut on board, turned the car around. His manner implied that no one in his right mind would go to view a lot of burned bodies when he could enjoy the South Sea delights of Pago Pago.

It was doubly unfortunate that Kindel had not only not been to the hospital, he had not bothered to find out where it was. They drove around aimlessly for a while, asking directions from passersby, and got to the hospital at 9:30. The rest of the Simpson family, who had stayed behind to organize the baggage, arrived by cab at the same time. Kindel left them all to it. He was not going to spoil his day.

As it happened, they were just in time. Herbert Simpson Sr.'s heart stopped just after they entered the ward. The doctors got it going again, but he died an hour later with his son beside his bed. Mrs. Simpson lasted a little longer. She hung on until 5:40 that afternoon and then she, too, died. It was her sixty-first birthday.

Simpson's grief was tinged with fury. Not only had Pan American caused his parents grievous injury and pain, but the company appeared to have made no effort whatever to find out the needs of the survivors, let alone transport them to where they could get specialized treatment. He had told them what needed to be done. He had sought the most expert opinion available and passed it on, and no one had listened. As Simpson and his sisters made their weary way from the hospital to the hotel, he resolved that Pan American should pay for this.

SIMPSON'S EXPERIENCE was not unique. Shortly before dawn in Hawaii on January 31, William Hemsley telephoned the airport at Honolulu to confirm that Flight 806 was on schedule before going out to meet his parents and sister. The girl at the information desk was quite bright for that time in the morning. She was happy to tell him that the flight was expected to be on time.

The crash had occurred some five hours before, and the charred bodies of his family still lay in the wreckage. But William knew nothing of this. He believed what he was told. At the airport, he bought three leis—the traditional Hawaiian garlands of welcome—to hang around their necks when they stepped from the plane. He sat down to wait.

Hemsley waited and waited. Then he noticed that Flight 806 was not on the arrivals board. There was no help from the inquiry desk, but ultimately William managed to rouse someone from the back of the Pan American office. They told him there had been an accident and that there were some survivors, his parents and sister not among them. That was all. He was not offered so much as a cup of coffee.

In a state of shock, William Hemsley went back to the house of friends with whom he was staying in Honolulu and began to organize a flight back to New Zealand. There seemed nothing else to do. He was short of money and Pan Am refused to help, but with the aid of another friend in the airline business he managed to get on a southbound aircraft two days later.

It turned out to be another Pan Am Boeing 707, flying the reverse sector to that of Flight 806, and it stopped at Pago Pago. Transit passengers were not supposed to leave the airport building, but William insisted that he wanted to see the wreckage in which his parents and sister had died. He felt he should take photographs to show the rest of the family what had happened. As an attractive young man, he soon found a stewardess willing to bend the rules.

The crash site lay just over half a mile from the end of the runway. It had been cordoned off, but no one stopped William Hemsley as he climbed over the ropes and began to make his grim record. By this time the bodies had been removed, and a jagged hole had been cut in the tail section to reach the flight data recorder. Otherwise the Boeing was as it had been when the last of the flames flickered and died.

He was struck by the contrast in the view from different sides of the fuselage. Seen from the port side the huge airliner looked remarkably intact, except for the damage to the nose and the grotesque angle of the tail. He saw that the main exit doors at front and rear were still shut. The other side of the aircraft, however, had been virtually obliterated; the entire starboard wall and roof of the fuselage had been burned away, exposing a charred tangle of metal seat frames inside the totally gutted cabin.

Hemsley put away his camera and rejoined his flight, still dazed by what had happened. As it turned out, he was the last independent witness to see the wreckage of Flight 806.

————

SIX DAYS AFTER THE ACCIDENT, Michael Rogers was released from the hospital. Susan was still very sick, and he was an angry young man. He was angry with Pan Am for their apparent lack of concern for the survivors, and angry at them for trying to extract a statement from his wife as soon as she woke up after an emergency operation. "It was the first time I had been allowed to see her," he said later. "People were dying around us in every direction, and all they could think of was getting a statement out of her the moment she regained consciousness, in order to prove their case.

"Subsequently at the NTSB hearing in Hawaii they tried to produce a transcript of her statement, and they produced it as if it had been made as a written document. I was there the entire time and she could not speak a word. The most she could do was grunt, either in approval or disapproval of what they were saying. She was 90 percent under anesthesia and critically injured, and they grilled her to no good purpose. I almost got to the point of physically planting one on them for even trying."

In spite of the Rogerses' protests, the "statement" was given in evidence at the NTSB public hearing. "Nobody would believe us when we said she had never made it," said Michael. "It was just typical of the way in which these people seem to be allowed to get away with anything they try to do."

————

THE FRIENDLY STRANGER in the bar was a big man—over six feet tall and built like a quarterback who forgot to leave his padding in the dressing room. He had a short collegiate haircut and a smooth, ageless face. His eyes were light, deep-set, and the smile that began at his small mouth never seemed to reach far.

The stranger's name was Robert Benedict, and he was vice president of the United States Aviation Insurance Group, which had carried the insurance cover for Flight 806. It was Benedict's job to see that his company paid out not one cent more than it had to. He was very good at it.

Benedict was pleased to see Michael Rogers. He bought him a beer—several beers—and introduced himself. "He did not really mislead me as to who he was," Michael said later, "but I certainly did not realize the proper implication of his position."

At midnight, well supplied with drink, they adjourned to Benedict's room, where the insurance man produced a tape recorder and encouraged Rogers to talk freely about the crash. Rogers needed little encouragement. By the time they parted, somewhere between four and five in the morning, they had reached a mutual agreement that the whole matter of a claim against Pan American by the Rogerses should be settled as quickly as possible.

Benedict must have been delighted. No figure had been mentioned at this stage, but he had a tape recording of Rogers minimizing his injuries. Rogers had said on the tape that he was not hurt at all—in fact, he was quite badly burned—and that he was quite all right.

Later, Michael explained this by saying that at the time, his injuries seemed insignificant beside those of Susan and the other victims in the hospital. What Benedict thought of it was revealed when he met Rogers again just as Susan and he were leaving the hospital later that morning. Benedict offered him $10,000 in full and final settlement, but by this time Rogers was a more sober man who remembered his own legal training. He told Benedict that he wanted to discuss the matter with a lawyer before reaching a decision but would be interested to hear from him when they got back to New Zealand. The Rogerses never did get a letter from Benedict.

When Susan Rogers was carried from the LBJ hospital, strapped naked on a stretcher, she had no wish to travel once more on the "World's Most Experienced Airline." She said so, loudly. The livid burns covering almost 55 percent of her once-beautiful face and body were matched by the mental scars of what had happened the last time she flew Pan American.

Her protests were ignored. Young people without money, without possessions, and without clothes—all of which had been incinerated in the wreck of Flight 806—have very little influence. Especially when they are strangers in a foreign land. Pan American could have flown them back via Air New Zealand, but that would have cost money, which was of much more importance than one sick girl's mordant fear of flying Pan Am. In fairness, however, the airline did not charge the Rogerses for returning them to New Zealand, though it did refuse to refund their fare for the first flight. After all, officials argued, they got them to their destination, didn't they? One way or another. And business is business.

Still protesting, Susan was loaded into an ancient ambulance, its doors tied up with string, for the trip to the airport. Halfway down the road the string broke and the stretcher, complete with Susan, came flying out of the back. The apologetic Samoan crew stopped, replaced their cargo, and secured the door. Luckily, she was unhurt.

Things got no better at the airport, where Michael's plea that they should be allowed to avoid the TV cameras and reporters by not passing through customs was rejected by Pan Am officials. As Michael pointed out, having lost all their possessions and all their money, what could they have to declare? But Pan Am remained adamant until Rogers, his scorched face doubly livid with fury, threatened to string the official concerned from the tallest coconut palm on the island.

The journey was a nightmare for Susan Rogers. By the end of it she was, in her own words, "a screaming mess." Her intravenous drip, vital to maintain the fluid level in her body, had been disconnected. Nobody had remembered that she could not drink through her burned lips, and as a result, she became badly dehydrated. "I was just a dreadful wreck," she recalled later. "The stewardess was so distressed. Every time she tried to put something in my mouth it would just spill out."

To make matters worse, the aircraft pressurization was faulty. Susan Rogers, strapped helpless on her stretcher, was convinced that it was all about to happen again.

SEVEN

DONALD PILKINGTON first heard of the disaster the day after it occurred, on New Zealand Radio's early morning news. He drove at once to Edward Hemsley's apartment, where the young attorney and his wife were still asleep. Then the three of them went to the family home to alert the younger brothers, Roy and Desmond. The Hemsleys were in a state of shock, and Pilkington could not forget the fact that but for him their parents and sister would not have been on the fatal flight.

In New Zealand at this point, there was total confusion. They could find no one who knew whether the Hemsleys were among the survivors or not. Neither the Pan American representatives in Auckland nor the local police had any information at all, and the uncertainty was hard for the young Hemsley men to cope with.

Pilkington took charge. He had discovered that Los Angeles was to be the center of operations and insisted that he and Edward go there as soon as possible. The others agreed. Using money from Pilkington's trust account, which would have to be repaid by the Hemsleys later, the two men flew to Los Angeles some three days after the accident.

By this time, the bodies had been cleared from the crash site and airlifted to the United States, and the unpleasant task of identification was being supervised by the Los Angeles coroner. It was a harrowing period, but within a week, Pilkington and Edward Hemsley had achieved their purpose, and the three bodies were flown back to New Zealand, at the family's expense, for burial.

They had also discovered something of the procedure from this point on. Though both were lawyers, neither had much experience with litigation, and where aviation cases were concerned, they were completely ignorant. There had never before been a major crash involving large numbers of New Zealand citizens, though this was not to be the last. The men who were experts in the field, they discovered, would all be at the NTSB public hearing, which would be held in Honolulu six weeks later. They resolved to be there.

The purpose of the NTSB inquiry was to establish the probable cause of the crash. Richard Notte and his team had spent a week on the island, interviewing witnesses and retrieving the flight data recorder and cockpit voice recorder for later transcription. They paid less attention than might have been expected, however, to the second major mystery of the disaster: it was not only a question of why Flight 806 hit the ground but why ninety-one people who survived the impact failed to get out of the aircraft. Why did the doors not open?

The NTSB report, issued in November 1974, shed very little light on the question. It said:

This was a survivable accident. The cabin remained intact; the crash forces were within human tolerances, and occupant restraint was maintained throughout the accident. The only traumatic injuries were those to the co-pilot. The survival problems stemmed from post-crash factors.

The three major post-crash survival problems were: (1) The cabin crews did not open the primary emergency exits. (2) The passenger reactions to the crash, and (3) passenger inattentiveness to the pre-takeoff briefing and the passenger information pamphlet.

It could not be determined why the primary emergency exits were not opened on the left side of the aircraft. The fire outside the aircraft on the right side or the press of passengers may explain why the doors on the right side were not opened.

The doors on the left side of the aircraft may have been damaged during the crash. In this event, the flight attendants would be expected to redirect the passengers to other exits.

The surviving passengers were all seated near the middle of the aircraft and did not hear instructions given by flight attendants after the crash. Since none of the flight attendants received traumatic injuries in the crash, it is possible that they were overcome by smoke or that they tried to open the exits and did not redirect passengers to alternate exits.

It is also possible that the passengers crowded against the doors, and for that reason the flight attendants were unable to open the exits. [In fact, the position of the bodies did not support this theory, but the NTSB failed to mention this.]

It is unlikely that all of the passengers could have escaped from the aircraft through the left over-wing exits. However, it is possible that there would have been more survivors had the passengers acted according to preflight instructions and proceeded to the nearest exit, instead of moving towards the main exits through which they had originally entered.

All the survivors reported that they listened to the pre-takeoff briefing and read the passenger information pamphlet. These actions prepared them for the evacuation by stressing the location of the nearest exit and the procedures to be followed in an emergency. The movement of most of the passengers, including many of the passengers in the over-wing area of the aircraft, to the front and rear exits, indicates that they either did not absorb the pre-takeoff briefing or they reacted to the emergency without thinking.

So, in the view of the NTSB, the occupants of Flight 806 died through their own fault or the inefficiency of the cabin crew. But what about the doors? On this, the report was silent, and for good reason: the NTSB investigators paid them no more than brief attention. In most aircraft accidents, there is a detailed examination of the wreckage. If necessary, the relevant parts are taken away for even closer inspection, and in many cases, the entire aircraft is reconstructed from the pieces.

The man in charge of this aspect of the NTSB investigation was Brian Smith, chairman of the Structure and Systems Group. Later, in court, Smith was asked what examination he had made of the left-hand forward door.

"Well," he said, "I tried to move it, and it would not move."

"Did you ascertain what physically was preventing it from moving?" asked counsel.

"No sir, I didn't. There was too much deformation in there at that time. The door had been subjected to an awful heat, and the only thing we gave it was a cursory examination."

This might not have mattered. The NTSB had no monopoly on aviation experts, and with the amount of money at stake in claims for compensation, there were plenty who could have conducted a full investigation on behalf of their clients.

They were never to get the chance. The moment the NTSB had finished with the wreckage it was destroyed beyond hope of recall. A local contractor, operating a D9 Caterpillar bulldozer, pushed the remnants of the Boeing 707 down into the gully over which it lay, ran over it repeatedly, and finally covered it with earth. The evidence was well and truly buried.

The contractor was acting on the instructions of Robert Benedict, Pan Am's friendly insurer. Benedict has always denied, and denies to this day, that he buried the wreckage deliberately so that no outside experts could get to look at it. He claims that it was done at the request of the FAA, who considered the wreckage a hazard to navigation and who needed to restore the middle marker navigation beacon that had been destroyed in the crash.

Benedict's account is not supported by the evidence of Dennis P. Venuti, a young attorney working for Pan American who arrived at Pago Pago on the day after the disaster. Venuti made a sworn statement that Benedict had discussed the burial of the wreckage with him; that he, Venuti, had solicited the approval of the FAA for doing this, but that at no time had the FAA or anyone else insisted that the remains of the aircraft be disposed of in this way.

Did it matter? Possibly not, but no one will ever be certain. The incident was to provoke a degree of bitterness and rancor, the effect of which would be felt for years.

The upshot of the NTSB inquiry was to find that the probable cause of the accident was "the failure of the pilot to correct an excessive rate of descent after the aircraft had passed decision height."

> The flight crew did not monitor adequately the flight instruments after they had transitioned to the visual portion of an ILS approach. The flight crew did not detect the increased rate of descent. Lack of crew coordination resulted in inadequate altitude call-outs, inadequate instrument checks by the pilot not flying the aircraft, and inadequate procedural monitoring by other flight crew members. Visual illusions produced by the environment may have caused the crew to perceive incorrectly their altitude above the ground and their distance to the airport. VASI [a system of lights used to gauge correct height] was available and operating, but apparently was not used by the crew to monitor the approach.

That was the verdict of the NTSB. It was not worth the paper it was written on—not only because federal rules prevented the use of the board's report in any subsequent court action but because the whole thing was later to be scrapped and rewritten.

At the time the public hearing opened its doors in the Princess Kaiulani Hotel, Honolulu on March 19, 1974, many of those present had more urgent matters than the

NTSB verdict on their minds. As Donald Pilkington had anticipated when he insisted that Edward Hemsley and himself attend the inquiry, it was not only the aviation experts and those directly involved in the crash who were present. The place was infested with lawyers.

They were mostly Americans, and they were engaging in their traditional forensic sport of ambulance chasing. The practice is frowned upon, but the device that enables American lawyers to do this successfully is known as the contingency fee system. This simply means that lawyers are paid by results. If they succeed in getting damages for their clients, they will claim an agreed percentage of the proceeds, plus expenses. If not, they will have spent their time for nothing.

In many ways, this is an admirable scheme. It enables less affluent clients to get redress against major corporations without the danger, which exists elsewhere, that they will run out of money long before the case gets to court. But in the case of aviation disasters, the situation is somewhat different. Lawyers don't run the risk of total failure: the Warsaw Convention guarantees that damages will be paid whether liability is established or not. The sums involved are usually high, and most importantly, the majority of cases are settled out of court, minimizing the time and effort lawyers need to spend.

Air crashes, therefore, are happy hunting grounds for contingency fee lawyers. The number of potential clients is generally large, and they are easily identifiable. With luck, and speedy action after a crash, an enterprising operator can often pick up tens or even hundreds of clients from a single incident. Since they all involve the same basic set of circumstances and the lawyer is dealing with the same defendant for each one, the work is greatly simplified and the potential profit maximized.

The percentage demanded by the attorney for getting the utmost compensation out of an airline and its insurers is high. For cases settled out of court, it is generally between 30 and 40 percent; for those that go to court it can be 50 percent or more. Plus expenses, of course.

Simple arithmetic shows that this is not a bad business to be in. A lawyer who can garner fifty cases from a single crash and get them settled out of court for no more than the Warsaw Convention limit of $75,000 each will collect $1,125,000 for a relatively small amount of effort. Since ninety-seven people died at Pago Pago, it was small wonder that attorneys were practically crawling out of the woodwork. Had they known what was to ensue, most of them would probably have saved the fare and stayed at home. But at that moment in time Pago Pago seemed like a pretty simple case, and Pan American World Airways was being viewed as a blue-and-silver goose just waiting to lay a golden egg.

Among those present was Daniel C. Cathcart of the Los Angeles law firm of Magana, Cathcart, McCarthy, and Pierry, whose office suite is in the Avenue of the Stars, a stone's throw from the 20th Century Fox studio. It was an appropriate address for Cathcart, who could probably have made a less profitable living as a film star if he had not taken to the law. He was tall and handsome, with piercing blue eyes, and he dressed with an air of immaculate prosperity—who wants to be represented by an unsuccessful lawyer?

Cathcart was, to boot, a very good attorney with a growing reputation in the field of aviation litigation. At the time of the Flight 806 inquiry, he had already been involved in at least nine major air disaster suits, and he was to go on to play a leading role in the wrangles that followed the Paris DC 10 crash; the fearful collision between two jumbo jets at Tenerife; and the worst ever US aviation accident: the DC 10 crash at Chicago in 1979. He was a qualified pilot who had his own aircraft, and in addition to a membership of a long list of legal associations, he belonged to the Society of Air Safety Investigators, the Ninth Circuit Judicial Conference Air Crash Legislation Committee, and the Aviation Committee of the American Bar Association.

It was hardly surprising that two young lawyers like Michael Rogers and Edward Hemsley, and a small-town attorney like Donald Pilkington, should be very impressed indeed by Daniel C. Cathcart.

Hemsley and Pilkington had gone to Honolulu in company with the Rogerses, who were to be called as witnesses at the inquiry along with Leon Martin. There had been disagreements even before they left New Zealand —one of the partners in Pilkington's firm, a man named Paul Morrison, had been insisting that he go, too. Morrison, it was true, handled most of the firm's litigation work (which was little), but he knew no more about United States aviation law than the other two (which was nothing). Edward Hemsley, who was bound to be a client in the case they wanted to bring against Pan American, felt Morrison would not have much to contribute, and he begrudged the extra expense that he suspected, rightly, he and his family would have to bear.

As a junior member of the firm, Hemsley was overruled. All three lawyers flew to Honolulu and stayed at the best hotel on the island. Cathcart, naturally, was staying there as well. The Rogerses were given less exalted accommodation, courtesy of the NTSB.

The public hearing lasted three days. It was on the second night after their arrival that Cathcart, having done his homework, knocked on the door of Pilkington's room. He was greeted, rather to his surprise, by a bizarre figure in a loud Hawaiian shirt and shorts, clutching a can of beer. Donald Pilkington and his partner were intent on having a good time.

For two such contrasting characters, Cathcart and Pilkington struck up an instant rapport. They had a common interest, and that interest was money. Cathcart told the New Zealander bluntly that there was no way he could handle the Hemsley action on his own. He would have to team up with some American attorney, and his own services were available. Pilkington had already been approached by many of the other lawyers at the hearing, but none of them had impressed him as much as Cathcart. The two men agreed to meet for lunch the next day.

Also present at the lunch was Edward Hemsley. In two days of solid propositioning by the ambulance chasers, Hemsley had become thoroughly skeptical. Such practices were totally foreign to the staid New Zealand legal system in which he had been trained. Now he found himself sitting down to eat with two men who had apparently decided to handle a case that he had not yet instigated and, what was more, to grab as many more of the New Zealand cases as they could.

Hemsley said later, "I felt very much as if Donald Pilkington was no longer there as a friend but was taking absolute control of the matter. He was suddenly dealing with my case and was evidently in very thick cahoots with somebody I didn't even know. I wanted to know about

Cathcart. I had seen enough going on around me—and met enough of these so-called lawyers in those few days—to want to be damn sure that if I did decide to instruct someone it would be the right person.

"They were talking about large sums of money and very slick operators; the possibility of being gypped was exceptionally strong. The thought of paying between one-third and half of whatever was recovered to an attorney was quite bewildering to both myself and Pilkington, especially as we were assured it would not possibly go to court.

"When a solicitor or a referring attorney provides a principal attorney with cases in the States, they generally get a third of what the principal attorney gets. That's a hell of a lot of money for simply providing names, which is effectively all they do. Donald Pilkington was not slow to pick this up. It was discussed in the first two or three meetings with Dan Cathcart, and concern was expressed that there would be considerable difficulty in justifying such a referral fee in New Zealand. According to various scales and systems of charging, there is no way that anything like that amount of money could be charged."

So, discussions took place between Cathcart and Pilkington in Hemsley's presence, with him feeling more and more uneasy by the minute about the direction the conversations were taking.

They discussed various means by which they could provide Donald Pilkington with this referral fee in ways that would not be embarrassing to him. One of them was instead of getting actual money to him at the end of the day —and they saw that day as being pretty close—Pilkington would perhaps visit the States and take it by means of air travel and accommodation, those things of which he was so fond.

Hemsley said, "There were also discussions as to how, in the context of New Zealand legal ethics, those various potential clients could be obtained. The New Zealand legal profession jealously guards the provisions in our code of ethics which prevent advertising or chasing clients. Donald Pilkington, being on the Law Society, would be particularly vulnerable to such criticism.

"So, it was decided, since these same considerations do not apply to American attorneys, that it would be done in a rather roundabout way. Dan Cathcart would contact the news media in Auckland and make it known that he was dealing with the Pago Pago case, and that the way to come to him was via Donald Pilkington. Such advertisements appeared throughout the country. In short, they concocted within the framework of the professional ethics in New Zealand a way to have Donald Pilkington represented as the only person through whom you could possibly attempt to achieve the sort of damages that were being quoted in the papers at the time.

"Pilkington worked on it very actively. He was up and down the country, and full time on the phone to prospective clients and various other solicitors who became involved. Since it had never happened in New Zealand before, there was no precedent for what should be done in a situation like this. In many cases, relatives and others concerned probably did not know that they had any rights or, if they did, what to do about them.

"Obviously there were those who went to see their own lawyers anyway. Pilkington was very active in drumming up business. He had calls from solicitors all over the country. They were told that unless they came to Dan Cathcart there would be extraordinary delays, and the chances of success would be negligible. It may well have been that Donald Pilkington genuinely believed it."

Pilkington's account of events at this time was guarded. "The newspapers wanted to know all about it, and he got tremendous publicity," he said. "The rest of it just came flowing in because of that." He was reticent about his own financial involvement.

One of Pilkington's exploits during this period, however, did come to light. It came to light because it went wrong.

Lila Mariko was the wife of Mani Tuela, one of the Samoan victims of the crash. She had gotten in touch with her local solicitor, a certain H.W. Clark, and through him on August 12, 1974, had signed a contingency fee agreement with Butler, Jefferson, and Fry of Los Angeles. Not long afterward, however, she was called to the office of another Samoan solicitor, a Mr. Phillips, where she met Donald Pilkington. Pilkington told her that he had checked with the courts in California, and she had no claim on file. If she did not do something quickly, he said, she would be out of time and the action would be barred.

Lila had no means of checking this; Clark was in Australia at the time. She believed what she was told. "I was very worried," she said later, "and very afraid of losing my rights against Pan Am. They gave me some papers to sign, authorizing them to present my claim."

In fact, what Pilkington had told her was untrue. Jefferson had filed an action in her name, and it was only discovered when he began settlement talks on her behalf with the insurance company that Cathcart had filed one as well. There was a brief battle between the two attorneys as to who was really representing her and who would get the contingency fee. Jefferson won and Cathcart withdrew, but poor Lila's case was not settled. She had been a bone between two hungry dogs. As always, the bone had gotten the worst of it.

For Edward Hemsley, the conversation in Hawaii with Cathcart and Pilkington was to be the start of another ugly and unhappy period. "The moment we came back from Honolulu I was very unnecessary," he said. "Right from the moment he decided to talk business, I was an embarrassment to Donald Pilkington. It was no longer my case, it was no longer our family, it was no longer anything but these enormous referral fees and the limelight; something that would probably surpass anything that any other solicitor in New Zealand had ever contemplated before. That was the magnitude of it.

"And so, he [Pilkington] went from town to town, and then from country to country. He was off to Australia before anyone knew it to get those victims' families living in Australia involved. And then his trips to America started.

"When these trips to America started, I had to express some serious concern," Hemsley said. "That is when money really started to be spent without specific instructions from the so-called clients. Pilkington would simply go.

"Being right up with the claim myself," Hemsley went on, "I had severe doubts as to whether it was necessary. None of the other clients or most of my partners knew anything about it, and so I questioned him and asked why his partner, Paul Morrison, should also be accompanying him. But there would always be, to his mind, sufficient justification to go. And he went. Time and time again. Now I was in his way. I was asking questions, and so it was arranged by Donald Pilkington that I should leave the employ of the firm."

Hemsley was fired. Politely, but he was fired. He left Pilkington's firm of Wynyard Wilson and Co. under a distinct cloud and took up with a small suburban firm of Auckland solicitors, where he still worked at the time of writing. Nor was he the only casualty at Wynyard Wilson to arise from the Pago Pago case. Within a few months, heated arguments had begun to develop between Pilkington and his partner, Paul Morrison, over the subject of the former's frequent and apparently unproductive trips to the United States. The partnership broke up and Morrison left the firm.

Hemsley said later, "There was no way that Donald Pilkington was going to let anything get in his way. He had come to an arrangement with Dan Cathcart as to how he was going to make a lot of money and have a very good time, and there was nothing going to get in his way. It seemed more important to him than anyone or anything else."

This was certainly not the public image being presented by Pilkington in the first few months after the accident. He and his wife Nina insisted that Desmond, the youngest Hemsley brother, go and live with them. Since the death of his parents, Desmond had been living with Edward and his new wife, Bineta. Pilkington persuaded him that this was unfair to the young couple, and Desmond moved against Edward's wishes. Edward thought this another public relations ploy, but the fact remains that the gesture was made. However, Desmond was unhappy living with the Pilkingtons for a variety of reasons and returned to Edward after a few weeks.

For his part, Pilkington dismisses Edward Hemsley as an unfortunate young man who was so deeply affected by the loss of his parents and sister that he became rootless and unable to settle down to his career. It is not a conclusion with which anyone who has met Hemsley will readily agree, though the intensity of his feelings after so many years is remarkable.

Others, too, were caught in the vortex of greed that began to gather around the public hearing in Honolulu like a nascent tropical storm. Dan Cathcart offered the Rogerses a preferential deal. Since Michael was a lawyer himself, able to do the routine legal work on his own case, Cathcart said he would take on their action against Pan Am at a contingency fee of 25 percent. Most of the other deals at this time were being struck on a $33^1/_3$ percent basis, rising to 40 percent if the case went to trial. No one expected that they would go to trial.

Michael Rogers was as much impressed by the money involved as by the implication that he, having only just finished his studies, was regarded by the great man as a member of the legal brotherhood. Though 8 percent of what might turn out to be a $500,000 claim was not to be lightly regarded.

However, before signing the necessary contract, Rogers was approached by Donald Pilkington. Pilkington offered him another special deal on the legal old-boy network. Since, Pilkington said, he was getting an 11 percent rake-off on the cases he passed to Cathcart, why didn't Michael do it through him instead? He would pass back to Rogers the 11 percent, and only charge him legal costs on the standard New Zealand scale. These would amount to hundreds of dollars rather than tens of thousands.

Rogers did his calculations. This way, Pilkington's way, he would pay only 22 percent of their damages in costs rather than 25 percent. He agreed to Pilkington's scheme, grabbing the extra 3 percent with both hands.

As a lawyer, albeit a young and inexperienced one, Rogers should have known better, a fact he now admits. There was no written agreement between himself and Pilkington, who subsequently denied that the arrangement was ever made. Having missed the chance to strike a bargain with Cathcart, Michael found himself stuck with a 33-1/3 percent contingency fee like most of the others.

"He has got us over a barrel," he says bitterly, referring to Pilkington. "It's a really stinking situation."

EIGHT

AND SO, during the early months of 1974, the cases were gathered, deals were made between lawyers, and the whole complex process of trying a lawsuit in which the plaintiffs came from many different states and countries began to grind into motion. It was ultimately settled that the case would be tried in Los Angeles and that the individual plaintiffs would be divided between three attorneys: Daniel Cathcart; James J. Jefferson Jr. of Butler, Jefferson, Fry, and Dan of Los Angeles; and Floyd A. Demanes of Burlingame, California. As chairman of the plaintiffs' discovery committee, the major burden would fall on Cathcart. Pan American was to be represented by William G. Tucker of the Los Angeles firm Tucker and Coddington, though in reality the strings were to be pulled by Robert Benedict of the United States Aviation Insurance Group (USAIG). It was Benedict, the sole arbiter of what settlement offers were to be made to whom and at what stage, who now effectively controlled the fortunes of those who had suffered through and in the aftermath of the crash of Flight 806. And Robert Benedict was in no mood to be generous.

The battle lines were drawn. For the plaintiffs, the most vital concern was to override the restrictions imposed by the Warsaw Convention, as modified by the later Montreal Agreement, limiting damages to a maximum of $75,000. This figure had been fixed in 1964 and never adjusted to allow for inflation. In 1971, meeting in Guatemala, twenty-one nations, including Britain and the United States, had signed a protocol that would more than double this limit and provide further automatic increases at five-year intervals to match the falling value of money. This protocol had not been ratified by the countries concerned and still has not been as of the writing of this book. Cathcart and his colleagues were therefore stuck with a limitation on their clients' claims which, however fair it may have been at the time it was fixed, was ten years out of date in 1974. Had they foreseen that it was to become eighteen years out of date in a time of raging inflation, and they still would have no recompense in 1982, they might have surrendered then and there. But their crystal balls were clouded.

Benedict, for his part, was determined to pay not a cent more than $75,000 to anyone, and a good deal less if he could get away with it. That was his job.

There were a number of ways around the Warsaw Convention limitation, and Cathcart resolved to try them all. First, he could try to have Pan Am found guilty of willful misconduct in causing the crash of Flight 806. This had never been achieved before against any airline in any previous disaster, but it was worth a try. And as the evidence came trickling in, Cathcart came to believe that he had a chance on this score.

Then there was the question of product liability, which certainly had a good track record in aviation cases. If Cathcart could prove that some defect in the aircraft or the equipment on board had been responsible for the deaths of the ninety-seven, then Boeing could be taken for unlimited damages. Unlike the airline, the manufacturer had no protection under the Warsaw Convention.

There was the possibility that the United States government could be held responsible on the grounds that the navigation equipment provided by the FAA at Pago Pago was in some way faulty and had caused the crash. This was the theory being pursued by Pan American, which was suing the government for the value of the lost aircraft and for indemnity against the claims being made by the victims. In fairness to Cathcart, he never really believed that this line of attack would succeed. He did not think the facts would support it. But he had to cover all the options, so he joined with Pan American in their action.

Finally, the plaintiffs tried to prove that the Warsaw Convention was unconstitutional anyway or, failing that, that its limit on damages should be changed to allow for inflation. These were bright ideas, but they proved to be dead horses that never made it beyond the starting gate.

The judge put in charge of the Pago Pago case was Peirson Hall, a stocky, cheerful old man with a bulbous red nose, rosy cheeks, and the wildest of bushy white eyebrows. He only needed a sack of presents and a sleigh to qualify as Santa Claus.

Judge Peirson Hall was eighty years old in 1974. On reaching the mandatory retirement age ten years before, he had simply refused to retire. Instead, this blunt graduate of a South Dakota orphanage had set out to carve a new career for himself as the arbiter of complex airline disaster cases.

By 1968 he had become the automatic choice to try all such cases to be heard in California. He was an innovative judge, noted for his fairness, his hatred of hypocrisy, and his refusal to compromise on matters of principle. These qualities brought him enemies by the truckload throughout his career, and in later years brought him into sharp conflict with the Ninth Circuit Court of Appeals. None of which disturbed him very much. By 1974, he had presided over eight major air crash cases and disposed of them all in short order. He was known for his dislike of legal delay and for his compassion toward widows and children.

In all, Cathcart and his team could not have hoped for a better judge to try their case, but they were soon to be disappointed. Even the redoubtable Judge Hall was not immortal. He already had an electronic pacemaker installed in his chest to overcome recurrent heart trouble, and he was soon to be told that he had cancer. There was a further complication that was to have a disastrous effect on the Pago Pago litigation: in early March 1974 a Turkish DC 10 crashed outside Paris, causing the loss of 345 lives, and that case, too, was assigned to Judge Peirson Hall.

By comparison with Pago Pago, which happened on the far side of the world and involved relatively few deaths, the Paris DC 10 case was huge and glamorous and involved a lot of tough legal decisions. Judge Hall gave it his utmost attention and made it the final triumph of his career. Pride, perhaps, would not allow him to surrender the case of Flight 806 to another judge, but inevitably it commanded less of his attention. It was too much for any man to handle both at once, let alone an octogenarian in poor health. Little by little, it slipped behind, and lawyers were able to introduce delays that an alert Judge Hall would never, on his past record, have permitted.

As the months went by, the Pago Pago survivors and the relatives of the victims were left in total darkness as to what was being done on their behalf. Then, in mid-October 1974, there came a letter from Cathcart reporting on progress so far. It was a long letter crammed with legal technicalities, well calculated to reassure the anxious client that his lawyers were working hard for their money. In fact, very little had been done beyond the filing of the suits, but it looked good. Cathcart spoke of the probability that he and his team would have to make "more than one trip" through the South Pacific in order to take depositions, and he opined that it was possible that the case might be ready for pretrial conference in April 1975, with the trial following soon after. He felt the prospects for settlement were excellent, but not before the eve of trial.

It was enough—just enough—to keep the troops reasonably happy. Not those, however, who were themselves versed in the law. Edward Hemsley was to describe this and later circular letters from Cathcart to all the victims as "continuous waffle."

The year turned, and it was March 1975 before they heard from Cathcart again. Nothing much seemed to have happened, save that he had been to New Zealand to take depositions from the Rogerses, and to Washington for statements from the FAA and the NTSB. Pan American was roundly accused of wasting time and money, and the trial date was now being forecast for the fall of that year. With incurable optimism, Cathcart "strongly suspected" that Judge Hall was going to declare the Warsaw Convention unconstitutional and that Boeing would want to participate in settlement negotiations.

Hope sprang eternal in Cathcart's breast. By the time they all heard from him again in December 1975, almost two years after the accident, it was beginning to dim perceptibly among his clients.

This time, however, he had more encouraging news. Yet more depositions had been taken, and both Pan American and Boeing had been forced to produce documents that would be damaging to their cause. Pan American had been compelled to acknowledge many safety deficiencies in their system; Boeing had to acknowledge that they had been dragging their feet on making their aircraft crashworthy. "I think our case against Boeing will have very definite jury appeal," Cathcart said, "and our case against Pan Am is extremely strong. On the issue of basic liability, however, we still face a formidable challenge in showing willful misconduct."

He spoke vaguely of motions for summary judgment against Pam Am on "technical grounds" and against the estates of deceased crew members. Like the many similar motions that were to be produced to raise hopes over the months and years to come, no mention was ever made of what happened to them.

"I am sure you will all be deeply concerned," Cathcart said, "over the length of time this litigation has been pending. I can assure you that we have been working on it constantly." Now he was forecasting that the discovery phase would be completed in the coming spring and that the trial would take place in the summer or early fall of 1976. "I feel we have reason to believe that the Pago Pago air crash litigation will be a matter of past history by this time next year."

If Cathcart really believed that, he was in for a sad surprise.

GRACE VAN HEERDEN was in dire straits. The shock of her husband's death had aggravated her heart condition and left her prostrate for some weeks, but her economic plight was even worse. Virtually all the family assets had been tied up in the new Samoan factory, but Johannes van Heerden had been secretive about his business affairs, and beyond the fact that there had been a net profit of about $30,000 in the past year, she knew little of them. With his death, the flow of money stopped immediately. The van Heerdens had spent or reinvested practically all they earned, and from enjoying a comfortable existence, she was left practically destitute overnight.

It was vital to get to Samoa, and her second son, Henk, then twenty-five, approached Pan American for assistance. It was refused. "They were terribly mean," Mrs. van Heerden said later. "No one from Pan Am came to ask if I was all right or to say they were sorry." Oddly, though, the airline had brought her two sisters from Holland for the funeral, for which she was unable to pay. "My family in Holland is very influential," she said. "It must have been that Pan Am did not want any bad publicity there."

Influential or not, the family was no help to Grace van Heerden in her financial distress. She was left to fend for herself and her youngest son, Jan, on a widow's pension of thirty-two dollars a week. Jan added to her problems by declaring, "If you don't let me stay at school, I will hate you for the rest of my life." She did her best to keep the fifteen-year-old at his expensive boarding school for as long as she could, but it was impossible.

By the time Henk van Heerden did manage to reach Samoa several weeks after his father's death, he found the factory in total chaos. Much of the machinery and stock had been stolen, and the local accountant had run off with the money before being killed himself in a car accident. There was nothing to recover.

Grace borrowed from the bank, using her expectation of compensation from Pan American as security, but as the months went by with no sign of the money being forthcoming, the bank manager became more and more aggressive in his demands for repayment.

She was at her wits' end. She sold what she could and moved from Wellington to Auckland, where she was given a basement apartment in the city by the local authority. It was a far cry from the lifestyle she was used to, but she still lives there, a proud, frail, erect woman, her graying hair scraped into a severe bun. There are a few traces of former affluence: one or two old paintings on the walls, which mostly bear evidence of her devout Catholicism, and a scattering of Persian rugs on the floor.

To ease the pressure from the bank manager, Dan Cathcart made her a personal loan of $5,000—about the only generous act to come to light in the whole Pago Pago affair. Now it was 1976; surely the compensation money could not be long delayed? But Pan American and Robert Benedict had not finished with Grace van Heerden yet. Not by a long shot. And nor had fate. Within twelve months, she was to lose her eldest son, Willem, who died tragically in Amsterdam at the age of thirty, as well as both her parents.

———

THE DAY he learned that his father had died, Richard Carter got very drunk. He rolled his wheelchair into the nearest pub and drank a half-bottle of rum. "I remember growling at Richard and saying, 'At least you could have

asked me to come with you. I would have done the same,'"
recalled his mother. "I could not see the sense in coming
home to sit around and do nothing, because what could you
do?" It took different people in different ways.

Lucy Carter, forty-five at the time, was small, determined,
and tough. She had to be. It was no joke being separated from
her husband, now dead, with a paraplegic son who needed
frequent medical attention and had become morose and
hostile to the world in general. They lived in Rotorua, in the
hot springs area of New Zealand's North Island, where the
fumes of sulfur catch the throat while driving down from the
green hills littered with sheep. It was a small, dark, dank
house, and it would to be years before Lucy Carter could
summon up the money or energy to make it any better.

She was a simple woman but nobody's fool. She knew
about the automatic compensation that should come to her
via the Warsaw Convention, but she also, unfortunately for
her, had touching faith in lawyers. When Dan Cathcart
offered his services by telephone direct from Los Angeles a
few days after the accident and advised her to go for a
higher settlement, she agreed quite happily. She put him in
touch with her local solicitor, Douglas Clemens, and then
found that she had acquired, willy-nilly, the services of
Donald Pilkington as well. Hers was one of the forty-eight
cases Pilkington would gather during his autumn roundup.

Years later, she could never recall having signed a
contingency fee agreement, though she must have done so.
"We signed so many things," she said. "I don't know what
we signed. I think one should be given the right of going
over these things in a saner period."

Lucy Carter found herself besieged by lawyers. There
was her own solicitor, Cathcart, Pilkington, Morrison, and a

Mrs. Rushton, who represented the South British Guardian Trust, executors of her husband's estate. "Everybody is in on this thing," she said bitterly. "That's why I get so irate. And as the children grow older they become more irate about it, too."

In early 1974, Lucy Carter was desperate. She could have claimed a widow's pension but was told she would have to pay it all back when her compensation came through. So, she continued to work for a tiny wage in Rotorua's social services department, looking after Richard and her young daughter Jane as best she could. She even refused promotion because she believed that it would cut her award of damages, and she kept hoping that one day soon the money would arrive.

She never heard a word from Pan American. The compensation that would have provided special care and facilities for Richard and enabled Jane, a brilliant student, to go on to college and become a doctor, never came. There were only the "status reports" from Cathcart, each of them adding to the tension of the long wait.

"We are calmer about it now," she said in 1981, "but earlier on when everybody was a bit younger and frustrations were more intense, it was pretty bad. Now we laugh when we get the reports, but in the early days we got very bitter with each other as a family, each one blaming the other for causing the delay."

These disputes within the family were an added worry for Lucy Carter, for she had discovered to her horror that the house in Rotorua had never been a joint family home and that under her husband's will half of it belonged to her children, three of whom were grown up. Her solicitor told her that any one of them could at any time sell the place out from under her. As the arguments raged on it seemed a distinct possibility.

The money would have solved everything, but the money never came, and the Carters were becoming increasingly disillusioned with the legal profession. "I think we feel all round that there has been a lot of wasted time," Mrs. Carter said. "And they have wasted an awful lot of what ultimately would be our money. How many trips has Pilkington made to the States and achieved absolutely nothing? And how many times has Cathcart been out here? This is our money. They are using us, the little people, to feather their nests and line their own pockets. I can't afford a trip to the States, but they can trip around on my money."

————

SUSAN ROGERS WAS TAKEN to the Middlemore Hospital on the outskirts of Auckland, where she was found to have burns over 55 percent of her body. She was not happy there, missing the friendly personal treatment she had gotten at Pago Pago, and she seemed to be treated by a different doctor every day. Michael, who was seriously concerned, began to ask questions and found himself in front of the hospital board, who felt he was accusing them of malpractice. It was a difficult time.

They were also being pestered by the press. "Right from the start," said Susan, "the hospital was being hounded by the newspapers. Then I got all these religious nuts coming out to see me. Anyone could walk in off the street and see me. They used to wait for me when I went to physiotherapy and tell me how I was the chosen one, and through me everything was going to happen, and there was a reason why I was alive. Really, I got quite turned off the whole thing. The hospital took it out on me. I didn't know what was going on. I was too sick to care."

Michael said, "I couldn't find out who was treating her. When I was in Pago Pago the doctors told me that she would quite possibly die around two weeks after the accident. She might die quite soon from shock, but if she survived that she would go through another crisis in three days, when she could die from dehydration. After that there would be a further crisis through infection after ten to fourteen days.

"The time of the third crisis, when I quite expected she would die, coincided with the Auckland hospital shifting her from a private room to a public ward. Even then, I didn't say anything to anybody. Eventually I asked if I could speak to the doctor who was treating her, and the hospital people got really peculiar."

Susan: "One surgeon would tell me one thing, and one another, and I never knew I was going into theater until they came and started shaving me or something. One day they would bandage one part of me, and then a sister would come in and say, 'Who did this?' and rip off all my bandages. That hurt. It was hopeless.

"They would not give me any pain killers. In Pago Pago, I was on morphine the whole time, and when I got back to New Zealand, I got nothing. I kept asking for something for the pain, and they kept saying they had children in there who were worse than me. It was dreadful."

Susan Rogers eventually discharged herself from the hospital against the advice of her own doctor, who tried to have her readmitted. She refused to go.

Helped by their parents because they had lost everything, the couple at first lived in a flat in Auckland

and then moved down to a small house in Waihi Beach on New Zealand's Bay of Plenty. It was a tranquil spot—a cluster of holiday homes and a few small shops, set on a white sand beach studded with silica that sparkled in the sunlight. They had gone there largely to get away from people, because Susan was acutely conscious of her scarred appearance. Years of plastic surgery lay ahead; for the moment she felt like something from *The Phantom of the Opera*, and she hated it.

The move was not a total success. People in small towns, as they rapidly discovered, are more inquisitive than those in cities. The Rogerses were living in a goldfish bowl and found, to their amazement, that they were even regarded with envy.

Newspaper stories of settlements mounting into millions of dollars had been circulating freely in New Zealand, and no one would believe that they had not received a penny.

Then the psychological problems started. It was hardly surprising. They were both afraid to get into an elevator in case the cable broke. They could not bear to be in any situation where they did not have control. Even riding on a bus was agony. Once they traveled on the Cook Strait ferry between the two islands, and they became so convinced that the ship was sinking when the siren blew that they almost jumped overboard.

And all the while, snippets of encouragement came from the attorneys to keep alive their hopes of being compensated. On June 4, 1975, Pilkington wrote to Michael to tell him that he and Morrison were going to Los Angeles for several days and "on the best advice we can obtain" it was not expected that any claims would go to a court hearing.

On August 15, Cathcart wrote forecasting damages for Michael between $100,000 and $150,000 for the fright, shock, and horror of the accident itself; fear for his life and that of his wife; and loss of his wife's services. Three days later he told Pilkington, in a letter passed on to Michael, that he anticipated damages for Susan of between $200,000 and $250,000.

That was fairly academic to the Rogerses. They were in the process of mortgaging their home to pay for Susan's latest plastic surgery operation.

NINE

THERE WAS a consistent sentiment running through the minds of Pago Pago victims and their heirs during the pretrial years. A naïve sentiment by strictly legal standards, but a very real one nonetheless. No one hated Pan American for the crash. Few at this stage even blamed the airline for causing it. What stuck in their collective craw was the insensitive and cavalier way in which they had been treated—in most cases, ignored.

They were not asking for the moon and sixpence in compensation. Most were relatively poor, with no great aspirations. They would have liked, it was true, for some financial burdens to be met: the Rogerses would have liked their medical bills to be paid and their ticket money refunded; the Hemsleys would have liked to have been spared the expense of flying three coffins home for burial; and Mrs. van Heerden would have liked a free trip to Samoa to sort out the business that had come crashing down when Pan Am killed her husband. Such things would have been small change to a major corporation.

Compared to the millions of dollars that Pan Am was about to spend in legal fees in a bid to keep down the payments it would have to make in the end, such sums could have been taken from the petty cash account of the public relations department.

But all the victims really wanted was for someone to say they were sorry. For some fellow human being from Pan American to knock on their door and say, "Look, Mrs. Smith, we are truly sorry that this has happened. Is there anything we can do to help?" But no one ever came. The aftermath of the Pago Pago crash must rank as one of the lousiest examples of public relations in history.

If Robert Benedict had come down from his mountain and knocked on a few doors, expressed condolence, and made reasonable offers, there would have been few poorer lawyers in the world. There would also have been much less pain, less bitterness, less resentment, and far less waste of money.

But Mr. Benedict, apparently, was not that kind of man, and big corporations never say they are sorry. From the moment that Flight 806 hit the jungle, it had become for him—and for Pan American—a matter of principle: they were not to blame, and anyone who tried to prove otherwise must be fought without quarter. There is no sign that it occurred to anyone that there were people, fellow human beings, on board that airplane.

Robert Benedict was certainly not coming down from his mountain in the late summer of 1976. A settlement conference was called by Judge Peirson Hall on September 13, but the good judge might just as well have saved his breath. There was no way Pan American was going to offer a cent to anyone in excess of the Warsaw Convention limit, nor any way the plaintiffs' attorneys were going to accept it.

Nonetheless, the conference was to mark a turning point in the Pago Pago litigation. Judge Hall's doctors had just told him that he was suffering from cancer, and he finally admitted that he could carry on no longer. The case would have to be transferred to another judge, who would clearly take time to assess the mountain of documents that had already accumulated. Everyone was back to square one.

Cathcart and his colleagues were not as downcast by this prospect of further delay as they might have been. Indeed, Cathcart was quite ecstatic in his status report to clients on September 24, 1976. He wrote:

> As soon as a new judge has been appointed, we will immediately file a motion for summary judgment against Pan American, predicated on their responses to some of the requests to admit.
>
> Surprisingly, their responses admitted all the facts necessary, not only to show that they were negligent, but also to strongly support a case for willful misconduct.
>
> From their responses in admitting such damning facts, it is indeed extraordinary and even shocking. I suspect that once the motion is made, they will claim their responses were made from inadvertence, and seek relief from the court. It is problematical as to whether or not the court will grant them such relief.
>
> The granting of this contemplated motion for summary judgment should bring about a prompt resolution of the litigation.

Cathcart had been very careful not to say exactly what he was talking about. What had happened was that a young attorney in William Tucker's (Pan American's lawyer) office had, for reasons that can only be guessed at, filed an admission that the crew of Flight 806 were intoxicated at the time of the accident. He also admitted that they were emotionally unstable and had not been operating the aircraft in a coordinated and professional manner, and that the operating procedures and manuals on board were outdated, incomplete, and inadequate. All these facts, the young attorney said, had led to the crash.

There it was, an open-and-shut case laid down in black and white by Pan American's own lawyers. There would be, could be, no need for a trial after such an admission. The airline's entire defense had been stripped naked and would surely stand shivering at the bench to await judgment.

There was only one snag: it was palpably untrue. At least, the primary admission that the crew was drunk was untrue. Cathcart knew that there was not a shred of evidence from the postmortem examinations to show that the crew had been drinking that night, but he was not about to let a little detail like that stand in his way. There was, he may have reasoned, a finer sort of justice. If Pan Am could use every legal stratagem to avoid its responsibilities to his clients, then let it perish by its own mistakes.

It was not a gentlemanly thing to do, and in other circumstances Cathcart would probably have pointed out the error and quietly forgotten it. But the personal animosity in the case, especially between Cathcart and Benedict, was already such that the normal rules of conduct had been thrown away. It was war.

Tucker was horrified when he found out what had happened, but until a new judge had been appointed the case was in legal limbo and there was nothing he could do about it. Nothing except fire the young attorney responsible. Which he did.

Cathcart had another, more substantial reason for confidence at this time. On January 20, 1976, in room 625 of the Federal Courthouse in Los Angeles, a deposition had been taken from Jack W. Hudson, who had headed the FAA investigation into the operation of Pan American World Airways eighteen months before. Hudson was not a willing witness. He had retired from the FAA not long after completing his investigation and had to be subpoenaed to appear. (The report was commissioned on April 27, 1974. It was presented to the FAA on June 13, 1975.) Hudson's testimony, taken over more than a month, filled six volumes of transcript. Much of it was in confirmation of his original report, placed under seal by Judge Peirson Hall on September 23, 1975 at the urgent request of Pan American's attorneys. But this time, with Hudson under oath and subject to cross-examination, the testimony would carry greater weight and could be submitted in evidence. At least, that was Cathcart's reasonable expectation.

Before the deposition hearing began, with lawyers from all sides of the case present, everyone in the room was sworn to secrecy by Judge Aubrey N. Irwin. Hudson was then examined at length by Floyd Demanes on behalf of the plaintiffs' discovery committee.

The name of Hudson had already become almost legendary to those most closely involved. He was a former bomber pilot who had learned to fly while at college and had gone on to see combat in England and Italy during World War II. On release from the United States Air Force (USAF) he had served with Braniff International Airlines as a co-pilot for three years and had then become an air carrier inspector with the Civil Aeronautics Administration

(CAA) in 1948. From then until his retirement in 1975, he had served continuously with the CAA and the FAA. He held an Air Transport Pilot's license, which included a rating for the Boeing 707.

Hudson declared that he had never had a written assignment to conduct the Pan American investigation. The matter had been so urgent that he had been recruited by telephone, first by Dave Switzer, head of the FAA's European Region, and then by Jim Rudolph, director of Flight Standards, and by Joe Ferrarese, chief of the operations division. The calls came to him in Fort Worth on a Thursday night. By Saturday, he was in Washington and starting work. It was then that he learned Pan Am had already had an inspection conducted by a consultant of their own, a Mr. Dave Thomas. Thomas's report, given to Hudson on a confidential basis, was highly critical of the airline. Hudson took its contents so seriously that he took it with him on retirement, refused to give it to Pan Am, and only surrendered it to the FAA after being threatened with legal action.

His brief was to take a hard look at Pan American in the light of the airline's three serious accidents in the past nine months. The FAA was vitally concerned about this accident record and told him to pick his own team of men who'd had no previous association with Pan American and try to find out where the problem areas were. He was given unlimited authority to inspect the carrier and its records.

Hudson said he had started his investigation with a review of the FAA's own reports on the airline for the past two years. At this point during the pretrial hearing, Demanes asked the judge to order that these papers be produced together with those going back to 1969. There was an immediate objection from William Tucker, who insisted that such papers should be kept under wraps. "I think this type of activity on behalf of the plaintiffs," he said indignantly, "is certainly destructive of the entire interface between the industry and those who regulate the industry. This type of production destroys that integrity and confidence as it now exists."

Whatever was in those reports, it was clear that Pan Am did not want it to get out, even before a deposition hearing sworn to total secrecy.

Judge Irwin refused to commit himself, but he warned Demanes, "I think you're getting so deeply involved in this case right now that you're never going to find your way out. Let's get a little realistic. We're trying to determine liability in this lawsuit." He asked the government counsel, Mark Dombroff, to make the reports available for him to inspect in private. The defense lawyers objected, even to the judge being allowed to see them. "Total candor and confidence," in the eyes of Pan American, had their limits.

What Hudson himself had to say, however, was damaging enough. Quoting the figure from his report that 36.8 percent of Pan American captains had failed their observed proficiency tests, he said that similar observations on three other leading United States airlines showed a failure rate of 3 percent. When Pan Am's own check pilots conducted the tests, only between 5 and 10 percent of captains failed to get through. He and his team had had "deep concern" that some of the Pan Am check airmen were not upholding high standards.

Some check airmen were "spoon-feeding" substandard pilots, helping them to get through their tests; others had ignored cases where pilots had breached air traffic control regulations instead of taking action to remove the captain from command of the aircraft or to see that he was given additional training. All airline pilots, Hudson said, became deficient from time to time, and the whole purpose of these checks was to stop the faults and correct them before they became dangerous.

Hudson's report on his findings had not been taken kindly. A letter from the airline's president, William Seawell, dated September 19, 1974 said:

> We take exception to your reference to "some substandard airmen in Pan Am." No airman that was to our knowledge not currently qualified and certified by the FAA has ever been used in line operations. Our operations have been under the close scrutiny of the FAA and its predecessor agencies since the inception of government inspection authority, and our aim has been to exceed government standards. Since all our airmen meet or exceed FAA and Pan Am standards, the term "substandard" is generally inappropriate, and particularly unfair to those who lost their lives in accidents, the causes of which have not yet been determined by the NTSB.

Within a month or two of that letter, of course, the NTSB was to rule that pilot error *had* been the cause of the Pago Pago crash. Even more telling in rebuttal of Seawell's claim was Hudson's revelation that when he and his colleagues went back six months later to check what had been done, they found that more than twenty of the pilots they had singled out as substandard had been fired or were no longer flying.

Demanes took Hudson through his allegation that 43 percent of the Pan Am crews observed in flight failed to follow some established cockpit procedures. "Is there comparison with other airlines as to that statistic?" he asked.

Hudson replied, "All the team members who were assigned to other major airlines were unaware of any major discrepancies on the airlines to which they were assigned. We were somewhat astounded at the very high percentage of Pan Am crews who failed to adhere to these established company procedures. It would be only fair to say that when inspecting any airline, you will occasionally find crews who do not adhere to all the procedures, but nothing of the magnitude that we observed at San Francisco."

Hudson said he had talked to hundreds of Pan Am employees during his inspection. Many had wanted to talk because of their deep concern about the airline's safety record. They were aware of certain airmen whose "proficiency was questionable," and they did their best not to fly with them.

Much to the indignation of Tucker, Hudson was asked by Demanes to name names. He said that not only Captain Petersen of Flight 806 but Captain Zinke of the Boeing that crashed at Bali and Captain Everts, who crashed at Tahiti, were all on the "won't fly" list.

There had been, Hudson admitted, some improvements made when he and his team went back for their second look at Pan Am at the end of 1974. The airline had, for instance, made considerable efforts to improve the standards of its check airmen, though it had refused to replace them all with qualified line captains, as Hudson had recommended.

Nor had the airline introduced a centralized training program, which the team had also said should be done. At the end of their follow-up check on February 3, 1975, they had told the Pan Am management: "The team is still concerned that Pan Am's overall recurrent training may not be sufficient to overcome the lack of on-the-job proficiency and operational experience obtained in the airline's long-range operations. This was once again revealed when 26 percent of the pilot-in-charge checks, 16 percent of the flight officer checks, and 20 percent of the flight engineer checks which the team observed were considered unsatisfactory."

It was, as Hudson said, somewhat better than the first time around, but the failure rate was still very high by industry standards.

By way of explanation, he said they had been told during their investigation that in prior years there had been reductions made by Pan Am for economic reasons. The airline had reduced the amount of training and the number of check pilots. They had made a number of other cuts as well. "In our report," he added, "we were making recommendations to bring the airline back up to an acceptable level. All these recommendations would, in some measure, have cost money."

And money was at the root of the problem. Demanes, having sniffed out in the Thomas report that Pan Am had been putting its emphasis on marketing and thereby sacrificing both maintenance and operations, made a formal request that the company produce its finance statements and the minutes of relevant board meetings.

The reaction to this demand from the assembled Pan Am lawyers was one of shock and horror. Demanes might have been asking to see a videotape of the chairman's sex life. But Mark Dombroff joined in to support him.

"These documents," Dombroff said, "would open the way to an argument that a deliberate and willful management decision, based on the state of airline finances back in 1970 or earlier, may have been made to shift funds from the operations, maintenance, and training side to the marketing side. Over the years, this may have created a condition which produced as its symptoms the accident record of Pan Am and brought about the special inspection, the findings, the Thomas report, the FAA report, and the follow-up report. Pago Pago would not be an isolated instance, but simply one of a pattern."

The judge was unimpressed. If he made an order to produce so much material, he said, it would take years to process the case. He was reluctant to do so, though he did admit that if the minutes of a meeting recording these decisions could be found, it would be "an entirely different breed of cat."

The cat stayed in the bag, much to the disgust of Floyd Demanes, who said, "Your Honor, we have experienced time and time throughout this case the production of documents in the courtroom when the witness is already in the middle of his testimony or has concluded. It has seriously prejudiced the plaintiffs' preparation of the case." It got him nowhere.

Still, with the Hudson report, the Thomas report, and now the Hudson deposition in their possession—albeit under wraps for the time being—the plaintiffs' lawyers felt they had sufficient ammunition in their locker to blow Pan American out of the sky.

They had reckoned without Judge William Matthew Byrne, Jr.

———

JUDGE BYRNE TOOK over the Pago Pago litigation on November 18, 1976. He was forty-six at the time, a fair-haired, sturdily built bachelor who had been appointed to the bench by President Richard Nixon in 1971. The son of a judge and cousin of two others, Byrne's progress through the legal ranks had been swift. He had been admitted to the Bar in 1956, served for a short time as clerk to Judge Peirson Hall, and became an assistant United States attorney in 1958 after two years as a lieutenant in the USAF. From 1967 to 1970 he was United States attorney for the central district of Los Angeles, handling criminal prosecutions with such success that he was nominated as "outstanding law enforcement officer of the year" in 1969 by the California Trial Lawyers Association.

There was a spell in private practice, specializing in defense of insurance cases, and a leading role on the Presidential Commission on Campus Unrest, which did his chances of advancement no harm at all. President Nixon may have regretted his decision two years later, when Byrne acquitted Daniel Ellsberg in the Pentagon Papers case, but by then his position was secure.

Judge Byrne was known for running his court efficiently and standing for no nonsense. He was not renowned, however, for speedy decision-making.

In words that he was later to regret, Dan Cathcart announced the appointment to his clients. "I know Judge Byrne very well," he said, "and am very happy that he was given this assignment." Actually, they played golf together occasionally and had graduated from law school at the same time.

Cathcart promised to get his motions before Judge Byrne with the utmost speed, forecasting intense pressure on Pan Am to settle out of court. He wrote:

The evidence which we have accumulated against Pan
Am is so damning of their entire operation that it is
inconceivable to me that their management would ever
permit this case to be tried. At the moment, we are
under a court order not to reveal this evidence to anyone
other than our clients and experts. Once the case goes to
trial, this information will become public knowledge
and will undoubtedly receive worldwide publicity. This
is not the kind of information that any air carrier can
afford.

This was rousing encouragement indeed and, as it
turned out, total claptrap.

At first, it did seem that the new broom wielded by
Judge Byrne was sweeping clean. Within two months,
which is the speed of light by legal standards, Cathcart was
able to tell his clients that the trial to determine legal
responsibility for the crash would be scheduled for mid-
July 1977, to be followed by separate trials on the issue of
damages in each case. Settlement conferences were
imminent, and he was sure that Judge Byrne was going to
put pressure on Pan Am. Meanwhile, Boeing was making
noises to indicate that it wanted to buy its way out of the
litigation.

"I sense," wrote Cathcart, "that we are in a pivotal
position in this case, and that some significant changes in
the defendants' settlement posture must be forthcoming
shortly."

He was whistling in the wind.

Three months later, he had good news and bad news
for his clients. The good news was that a date for the
liability trial had now been set: July 26, 1977 at 9.30 a.m.
Although the inclusion of the exact time seemed to give this

information impeccable authenticity, it was to prove inaccurate by almost six months.

There had also been a promise by Judge Byrne to hear the outstanding legal motions—some of them outstanding for more than two years—on May 24. Cathcart made no mention, however, of the fate of Tucker's plea for relief from the infamous false admissions (that the pilot was drunk, etc.), or of his own motion for summary judgment that was to have brought the case to an end. Both issues had been disposed of some weeks before he wrote this status report on April 20. Tucker had won, and Cathcart had lost. Another mirage had faded from sight, and perhaps he felt it best not to mention it.

The bad news that Cathcart did pass on was serious. For some time, the three defendants in the case—Pan Am, Boeing, and the federal government—had been dickering among themselves as to whether they should make a joint settlement offer and get the whole thing off their backs. All three were anxious to avoid the bad publicity that would undoubtedly ensue from a public trial. Pan Am and Boeing were especially concerned. The airline had just suffered another bad crash in Tenerife, the worst in world aviation history, and two Boeing aircraft had been involved in that. Enough was enough.

The points at issue were how much should be offered and how the money should be split among the three of them. The trial was drawing closer, and the pressure to settle out of court was increasing. In February 1977, after long discussions, an agreement was reached on a joint offer. No details of this offer were ever disclosed, and the exact amount is not known, but it was almost certainly in the region of nine million dollars, to be spread among all the claimants.

It was agreed that Pan Am should pay 50 percent of the damages, the government 27 percent, and Boeing 23 percent. Since Pan American had already settled some claims out of court in the Pago Pago case totaling $944,000 at this stage, the government agreed that they would reimburse the airline 35 percent of this amount. But the offer was never made. Though the deal was signed by both Pan American and Boeing, it was ultimately turned down by Mark Dombroff, acting in consultation with the assistant attorney general. They had decided it was in the government's best interest to go ahead and fight the case.

It was certainly in Dombroff's best interest. He was an ambitious young lawyer with a reputation to make. He had never taken part in a jury trial before, but he felt that this one offered a tremendous opportunity to raise his profile. He was also convinced that the FAA was innocent of the charges being laid against it by Pan American. In the months to come, Dombroff was to become the wonder boy of the courtroom and to do great service for the claimants as well as for the government and himself. But he did the victims of Flight 806 no service in February 1977. Had the offer gone through the trial would have been called off, and they would have been spared years of frustration, anguish, and in some cases poverty. It did not, and from that moment, there was no turning back.

TEN

OUTSIDE THE AMBIT of the lawyers, more trouble was brewing. Even though their own representatives had taken part in the investigation, the NTSB report on the crash of Flight 806 had been received with scant enthusiasm by the Air Line Pilots Association (ALPA). Metaphorical smoke came seeping under the office door of ALPA president J. J. O'Donnell, high in the union's plush headquarters in Washington, D.C., as he read yet another accusation of pilot error.

O'Donnell was a formidable figure, a scourge of federal administrators who was not averse to picketing the White House if he felt his cause was just. On this occasion, his fuse burned slowly. It was not until May 1976, more than two years after the accident and a full eighteen months after the publication of the NTSB report, that a letter from O'Donnell dropped onto the desk of the Safety Board chairman, Webster B. Todd. The delay in O'Donnell's protest may have been explained by the thickness of the petition that accompanied it: a twenty-two-page, closely typed exculpation of the Pan American crew, which set out a host of new theories on the cause of the crash. These theories were similar, and in some cases identical, to those that were to be produced by Pan American's attorneys at the time of trial. Purely circumstantial evidence suggests that ALPA may not have acted independently: Pan Am had a considerable financial interest in getting the NTSB report toned down, but it could hardly succeed in doing so by approaching the board directly. There was, on the other hand, a well-established tradition that protests from the pilots' union could sometimes lead to the revision of accident reports.

Whatever the motivation, O'Donnell's letter was a sizzler. After a paragraph of mild preamble, he launched himself on the unfortunate Todd like an avenging fury:

The ALPA safety representatives have alerted me to the fact that not only was the Board's effort unsatisfactory on this particular investigation, but also that similar shortcomings are found with distressing regularity in other investigations.

Specifically, the superficial utilization of the data contained on both the flight and cockpit voice recorders regularly renders suspect both the findings and recommendations of the Board. If the Board it to be effective in the accident prevention field and do more than simply assess blame, superficiality must be eliminated from the final product. The attached petition clearly highlights the misapplication of the recorded data and illustrates a problem which recurs with far too great a regularity.

Of even greater urgency is the almost total lack of concern for the human factor involved in accidents, such as the one in Pago Pago. Clearly, if human performance is a factor in an accident, the relevant facts are what the crew perceived as related to the actual situation.

Only by exploration of these matters can there be any hope of arriving at recommendations which will prevent future accidents.

Absent meaningful study in this very complex area, the Board will be unable to do more than continue to point the finger of blame.

This makes it easy for the lawyers but a matter of despair for those dedicated to accident prevention. It is our hope that through your leadership we can see a major effort by both [the] Government and the industry to explore this largely uncharted area. Please be assured of ALPA's wholehearted support in any study efforts in the human factors field.

In other words, the board was failing in its duty to the public, and it was time Todd started doing his job properly.

The petition that followed, demanding a reopening of the investigation into the Pago Pago crash, was a finely honed piece of special pleading. No fewer than ten areas were listed in which it was claimed that the NTSB had been at fault.

1. Erroneous flight data recorder impact time;
2. Flight data recorder altitude trace not corrected for approximately 100-feet altitude error;
3. Omission in the board's report of a 400-foot altitude callout by either the first officer or flight engineer as recorded by the cockpit voice recorder (CVR);

4. Error in the time intervals attributed to each crew member's aural tone of their radio altimeters as recorded by the CVR;

5. No mention of a 10-knot discrepancy between the flight data recorder (FDR)-indicated airspeed and the first officer's airspeed callouts;

6. Erroneous interpretation of the first officer's statement regarding his "seeing" the VASI;

7. Failure of the board to complete analysis of the General Electric and Boeing data derived from the CVR and FDR respectively, which show the existence of wind shear during the approach;

8. NTSB's dismissal of the weather expert testimony obtained during the hearing;

9. Erroneous assessment of the captain's proficiency; and

10. Failure to mention the impact injuries of the captain that impaired his ability to direct the evacuation.

The petition went on to expand on these points in fine detail. Some of the argument was technical nit-picking, some was speculation, and some clashed head-on with the known facts. According to ALPA, for instance, when co-pilot Phillips said he could see the runway lights (which he said several times from as far as seven miles away) he must have meant the approach lights to the runway. Why? The two are quite distinct, and Phillips was emphatic, even on his deathbed, that he saw what he said he saw. But the approach lights are brighter, and it therefore fitted ALPA's theory that the crash was caused by bad weather if Phillips had been mistaken and the actual runway lights were obscured by rain.

ALPA claimed that their representatives on the spot had asked the NTSB to investigate the possibility that wind shear had caused the accident but that no investigation had been made.

They constructed a scenario in which Petersen had faced such impossible problems during the final stage of the flight (though there was no indication of such problems on the cockpit voice recorder) that he could have done nothing to prevent the crash. "Perhaps the instruments would have indicated the problem," said the petition, "but even if that were true, there would have been no way for the pilot to make timely use of the information. The Board cannot legitimately hold a human being responsible to perform a super-human task."

The "super-human task" referred to was to land the aircraft safely or, if that was impossible, to go somewhere else or wait until conditions improved. That is an airline pilot's job, a fact that ALPA chose to ignore.

It had certainly not been evident to co-pilot Phillips that conditions were fraught with difficulty that night. Just before he died, he was alleged to have told Notte that "just prior to impact everything looked normal." The petition skated around this inconvenient statement with breathtaking dexterity. "Clearly the crew was led to believe that the approach was normal. That it was not led to the conclusion that the tools available to the crew were not sufficient to do the job." It could also lead to the conclusion that the crew was incompetent, since other pilots had been handling the same aircraft with the same tools, often in the same conditions on the same airfield, for many years without any problems. ALPA did not wish to know that.

"We are haunted by the feeling," the petition went on, "that Captain Petersen, given timely advice on the onset of the rain squall, and with more than four hours of reserve fuel on board, would have discontinued his approach and held for the 15 or 20 minutes necessary for the weather to clear."

"Timely advice?" Captain Petersen was told by the controller that there was a bad rain shower at the airport, a rain shower so severe that the controller could no longer see the runway lights. That advice came through loud and clear on the cockpit voice recorder. It was given more than one and a half minutes before the accident, at which time Flight 806 was five miles from the runway at an altitude of 1,600 feet. How much warning did ALPA consider a pilot should need? It was the most arrant piece of nonsense in a farrago of misdirection, and the NTSB swallowed it whole.

There was one other canard, of particular interest because it gave a clue to the genesis of the whole petition:

ALPA representatives were assured after the FAA's flight inspection of the navigational facilities at Pago Pago that the ILS met the flight test inspection criteria; however, the recordings of the electronic signals were not distributed to the interested parties nor was this information made a part of the public record.

Recently, it has come to our attention that the ILS glide slope allegedly did not meet acceptable criteria in the vicinity of the middle marker. According to the information relayed to us, the ILS signal could present a fly-down indication in this area. This could easily explain the lack of concern regarding the descent rate experienced during the last few seconds of flight. If, in fact, the crew was following the ILS glide slope signal approaching the middle marker, a higher than normal descent rate would not have been apparent.

Much, much more was to be heard about that fly-down signal. It was to form the cornerstone of the Pan American case against the United States. So who had relayed this information to ALPA, and to what degree had they been responsible for the rest of the belated petition? We may never know.

On receipt of the ALPA petition, the NTSB had two options: it could tell the union, politely, to go play in the traffic, or it could accept the censure and do something about it. The board chose to do the latter.

Exactly how much reinvestigation went on in the months that followed is a matter for speculation. When the second NTSB report was finally produced on October 6, 1977, it contained radical changes from the original version. In length alone it had increased from twenty-eight pages to forty-five, and much emphasis was now placed on the phenomenon of wind shear, which had failed to rate a mention in the first report. Wind shear, which can be defined as any change in the vertical or horizontal movement of air, has been a known inconvenience to airplanes since man first started to fly. Yet the tone of the second report suggested that this was a new and startling discovery.

Comparison of the two documents reveals that many items critical of the crew's performance were deleted from the later version, and the "probable cause" finding had been considerably toned down. It now read:

The probable cause of the accident was the flight crew's late recognition and failure to correct in a timely manner an excessive descent rate which developed as a result of the aircraft's penetration through destabilizing wind changes. The winds consisted of horizontal and vertical components produced by a heavy rainstorm and influenced by uneven terrain close to the aircraft's approach path. The captain's recognition was hampered by restricted visibility, the illusory effects of a "black hole" approach, inadequate monitoring of flight instruments, and the failure of the crew to call out descent rate during the last 15 seconds of flight.

From the point of view of Pan American's lawyers, this was a huge improvement. Certainly, the crew had still been found at fault, but now there were excuses, possible reasons for their mistakes, of which much could be made in court. Yet all these factors had been in plain view at the time of the original investigation and the public hearing in Hawaii. Why had they not figured in the original NTSB report if they were now considered of such importance?

The first report of the board was a unanimous decision. The second was reached by a majority of the four members, only two of whom had sat on the original committee. The dissenting version was published by the acting chairman, Kay Bailey, who wrote:

I disagree with the probable cause in the majority decision. I think wind shear should be stated as a major factor in the cause of the accident. The probable cause should read: "The National Transportation Safety Board determines that the probable cause of the accident was the aircraft's penetration through destabilizing wind changes and the flight crew's late recognition and failure to correct in a timely manner the resulting excessive descent rate. The winds consisted of horizontal and vertical components produced by a heavy rainstorm and influenced by uneven terrain close to the aircraft's approach path.

The captain's recognition was hampered by restricted visibility, the illusory effects of a 'black hole' approach, inadequate monitoring of flight instruments, and the failure of the crew to call out descent rate during the last 15 seconds of flight." I believe we should look at the whole picture when determining probable cause.

Our vision becomes too narrow when we adhere to the "last possible chance to prevent the accident" as the only probable cause. In this case, the complete reasoning should begin with the fact that there was wind shear and then state the lack of proper reaction under the circumstances.

It was a shade of difference, but an important one. ALPA had done a good job, and O'Donnell must have been delighted. So were the Pan Am lawyers, whose case was now acquiring a degree of respectability of which they could hardly have dreamed.

What they had to do now was to go one step further and convince the jury that the wind shear, the visibility, and the alleged faulty glide slope had combined in such a way as to make the accident quite inevitable and no fault of the crew.

If they could also prevent the Hudson report and the training records of the crew, none of which had apparently been considered by the NTSB, from reaching the eyes of the jury, they were in with a good chance.

ELEVEN

THE TRIAL DATE WAS RECEDING. It seemed to be like an electric hare, forever just out of reach of its pursuers. By early June 1977, it was clear that the July 26 deadline could not be met, partly because Cathcart had been so convinced that a joint settlement was imminent that he had neglected to take certain depositions from Boeing employees in Seattle, Los Angeles, and Washington, D.C. These were depositions he had promised to take in January 1975, some two and a half years previously, but had somehow never gotten around to. The delays were not all on one side of the legal fence.

The new date for the trial was September 13. Cathcart told the faithful that in the meantime, he was trying to get Benedict to make financial advances to those in serious need. The sound of hollow laughter was heard all around the Pacific. "Prospects for settlement appear bleak at this time," wrote Cathcart, adding to the general aura of doom and gloom. But he added, "I feel certain that there will be no further postponement of the trial."

It was September 23 before they heard from him again. The opening words of this latest status report, "Trial of your action has not yet commenced," were received abroad with weary resignation. Cathcart reported that he and the other attorneys were meeting almost daily with Judge Byrne, thrashing out pretrial procedures that were aimed at shortening the trial itself. He estimated another two or three weeks before it could commence if, indeed, it was to commence at all. For the attorney was confident that new settlement negotiations then in progress could end the whole matter in a few days.

In fairness to Cathcart, however, he was having problems at this time, and so were the other lawyers involved in the case. At the root of their discontent was Judge Byrne and the seeming irrelevance that the Los Angeles Dodgers were involved in the playoffs for the World Series baseball tournament.

This was not irrelevant to Judge Byrne, who was an avid supporter of baseball and a great and good friend of one Peter O'Malley, owner of the Dodgers.

Under the rules of the Los Angeles District Court, where the action was to be tried, a pretrial conference had to be held, culminating in an order that would be signed by the judge and all the counsel involved. This order would settle the agreed issues in the case, which need not then be argued in court. The procedure saved time and money and was generally pretty much of a formality. "In a bad case," Cathcart said later, "it takes an hour."

Not, however, in the case of Flight 806, which continued to conform to Murphy's law: anything that can go wrong, will. All concerned now wanted to get the show on the road. All, that is, except Judge Byrne, who could not see himself being confined in a courtroom during the World Series. He ranted at the lawyers, accusing them of not having their briefs organized, and day after day they went back to work, cutting and pasting and rewording, only to find that next time they saw the judge he was still not satisfied. There was much puzzlement and frustration among a large section of the Los Angeles legal fraternity.

And then, one day, the penny dropped. Cathcart and some of the others were passing along a corridor in the courthouse, en route to sorting out one of Judge Byrne's latest demands, when they passed an open door and saw a television set. The occupants were watching one of the World Series playoffs in Philadelphia, and Cathcart slipped inside for a moment. As he watched, the camera cut away to a shot of the directors' box and there, having a great time, was Judge Byrne.

"While we were working ourselves silly," Cathcart said, "he was touring round the country watching baseball games. Then, of course, the Dodgers won the playoffs, and every time there was a game there was a problem with the pretrial order. We had to go back and meet by ourselves.

"After we got through listing hundreds of issues, Byrne then decided that he wanted an 'offer of proof' on many of these to see whether they would be a legitimate part of the case. This meant that we had to pull those elements out of great piles of documents and thousands of pages of deposition transcripts.

"For instance, we had to find out for him whether or not methyl ethyl kitone peroxide was on the plane, and if so what role it played. [It was, and it had nothing to do with it.] Then we would go down and argue that issue. But he would not decide it. Then we would argue some more, and submit some more, and this went on for six months. Then we would get through the factual issues and pass on to the legal issues.

"We had about a hundred issues of law which we had to brief. We would brief them, then the other side would respond, and then we would respond to that. Or they would brief and we would respond—it went on and on. Then we would argue the real points, and with very few exceptions Judge Byrne never decided on them as to whether or not they were genuine issues in the case. He didn't decide on the legal points either.

"The pretrial order is supposed to be signed at the pretrial conference before the trial starts. This one never was: we started the trial without it. And when the jury went out to retire seven months later, Byrne said, 'Now we are going to get this pretrial order signed.' And he ordered counsel to sign it. Pan Am did so under protest, with a great flurry, and that was the end of it. But he never signed it himself, and it was never part of the trial."

The significance of this remarkable episode, apart from the colossal waste of time and money, was that there would be no written record of any mistakes that might have been made by the judge during the pretrial conference and that could be brought up at the appeal stage.

"He is covering his ass on appeal from claims of errors made during the pretrial proceedings," Cathcart said bitterly. "It's terrible."

———

IT WAS EARLY NOVEMBER, 1977. The World Series was over, and Judge Byrne was now anxious to get on with it, pretrial order or no pretrial order. Jury selection was set to begin on November 11. But the strain was beginning to tell on all of them. Big, beefy William Tucker, an extrovert and workaholic who smoked about sixty cigarettes a day, suddenly fell ill with high blood pressure. There was a delay while Pan American decided whether or not they would have to instruct another attorney. If so, the postponement would be a long one while the new man briefed himself on the mounting complexity of the case. As it happened, Tucker recovered within three weeks, but by then the Christmas holidays were looming. It was decided to reschedule the trial for early in the new year.

Cathcart was still beavering away with motions aimed at upsetting the Warsaw Convention limitation on damages and circumventing the trial. Judge Byrne refused to rule on any of them.

The prospects of settlement, however, began to look a little more hopeful. Cathcart reported to everyone on November 4 that the government and Boeing had joined together to make an offer of $2,500,000. If this was added to the amount that Pan Am was willing to pay, within the Warsaw limits, then the total to be shared would be $6,775,000—or, actually, a little less because Pan Am was insisting that some cases were not worth $75,000.

Cathcart did not recommend these offers to his clients. He was nervous about releasing the government and Boeing from the action, because he would then have no one from whom to claim unlimited damages if his attempt to prove willful misconduct against Pan Am failed to succeed. As far as the airline was concerned, he felt he had found a way to have his cake and eat it by applying for summary judgment under the Warsaw Convention and then going ahead and suing for willful misconduct. He was also going to try to obtain interest of 7 percent dating from the time of the accident, which would bring the Pan American payment up to $5,152,000, and to have the Warsaw limit adjusted for inflation. If the latter move succeeded, it would almost double the amount of damages payable in each case.

"This is a novel approach which makes economic sense," wrote Cathcart, "but because it is new it may not be looked on with favor." He was right.

Edward Hemsley was to say later, "I respect Dan as a lawyer because he has a very progressive mind. He is an innovative lawyer, and such people are always exciting personalities for another lawyer. He has tried a lot of innovative things in this case, all of which could have been to our advantage.

"Unfortunately, it turns out that in many cases Dan's innovations in the cold, hard light of day in court were unsuccessful. I am convinced that Dan has been doing his very best for us, and that in a strictly legal sense he is a very interesting counsel, but I wonder sometimes how practical he is in expediting a conclusion to this case."

Six days later, on November 10, Cathcart reported fresh settlement negotiations. There had been a lump sum offer from all three defendants of $6,875,000, but once again he recommended that it should not be accepted. This time Cathcart's reason was that with an offer made in this form, it would be necessary for him and the other plaintiffs' lawyers to share it out fairly among the claimants. There would have to be help from the court—an arbitrator or a panel of judges. "The attorneys can't be involved in this area," Cathcart wrote, "since there would be an obvious conflict of interest in attempting to divide a fund among various clients." He also claimed that the offer only represented 60 percent of the potential value of the cases and was therefore inadequate.

On hearing this, Boeing and the government once again tried to settle on their own account, raising their offer to three million dollars. Again, Cathcart refused. He was sure they would go higher yet.

He was wrong. The government came up with an individual offer of $1,500,000, but this too was turned down.

Cathcart reported on November 23 that "those few people who have responded to the previous offers have all indicated that they have no desire to accept them at this time."

His report does not gel with the recollection of Edward Hemsley at the time. "I wanted it settled," he said. "It seemed to me that the global figure offered was an appropriate figure to disburse. We had got to a point where we could at least conclude the matter satisfactorily."

Hemsley claimed that there was no consultation with him as an individual client about the offer. He had only found out about it when he telephoned Cathcart from New Zealand. "I was concerned to get a result as quickly as possible," he said. "I could see it going on and on, with all the ramifications of appeals, etc., and I was not convinced with their very general statements as to what was happening.

"I asked: Why don't you accept this? What are the reasons? What will happen if we reject it? I asked some very specific questions, to which I only got very general answers. I was not getting the information voluntarily. They [Cathcart and Pilkington] made the decision to refuse the offer entirely of their own volition. But having told me they would have great difficulty in dividing it between the people involved, which horrified me, they said that in any event we were going to get a hell of a lot more out of it."

Hemsley refused to accept that it was impossible to apportion the money fairly. He said, "It could very easily have been distributed by agreement with all the claimants. I explored this very point with both Pilkington and Cathcart. In the event that one or more claimants would not agree on the amount suggested to them, it would have been well worth arbitrating. Being directly involved, it seemed to me that if all the claimants were brought together into one room to resolve the matter at that time, we would not have had a fight on our hands. But Pilkington and Cathcart were not even willing to embark on any investigation at all to find out whether that was feasible."

Hemsley's expensive telephone call to Los Angeles was not satisfactory. "Cathcart waffled," he said. "He could not be specific. He did not want to know about it. But I was assured that there was no merit in accepting this offer; it would be giving money away. There was absolutely no point in settling on this basis.

"As far as Cathcart was concerned, the question of distribution among the claimants was not the main issue. That was Pilkington's concern. Cathcart hardly mentioned it. He acknowledged it would be a difficulty, but that [the problem of apportionment] was not the reason why this [rejection of the offer] should happen. The reason was that there was much more in it, and it would be premature to accept such a settlement. We should proceed with the claim."

Hemsley blamed himself. "I am convinced," he went on, "that if I had taken a much stronger stand, if I had asserted myself, we could have concluded the matter. This is something that plagues me, because the figures involved were the sort of figures which had previously been quoted to us as a likely settlement. They were figures that as far back as Honolulu equated closely with the claims that everybody was realistically expecting.

"I called Dan with the purpose of giving instruction from this family to settle, on the basis being suggested. I was exceptionally concerned that the very conflict that I had foreseen right at the beginning was now being raised by the lawyers we had hired, in opposition to a settlement. To put it bluntly I was bloody upset. Our own lawyers would not settle because of possible conflicts within their own ranks."

Hemsley's younger brother, William, put it even more bluntly. "I believe we have been screwed," he said.

No such doubts clouded the mind of Dan Cathcart. He remained firmly convinced that the pressure of the coming trial would generate bigger offers that he could recommend.

In the meantime, in his final message for 1977, he wished everyone "a very happy and joyous holiday season, and a very prosperous New Year."

It was destined to be more prosperous for some than for others.

———

EDWARD HEMSLEY WAS NOT the only one who felt that a lump sum settlement could be shared fairly easily. Robert Benedict had the same idea. On January 4, 1978, he wrote a letter to Cathcart, Floyd Demanes, and James Jefferson, in which he repeated the joint offer of $6,875,000 that had been made in November.

This offer would be in full and final settlement of all the plaintiffs' claims against Pan Am, Boeing, and the government.

Benedict said:

You indicated concern over the manner of distribution of such a lump sum amount among your respective clients for settlement purposes. We do not believe such an allocation would be difficult to accomplish. On March 13, 1977, you submitted to Judge Byrne and each of the respective defendants a list of settlement demands for each of the outstanding claims. Obviously, you gave considerable thought to those demands, and their relationship to each other. By totaling those demands and dividing the total demand into any individual demand, one can mathematically compute the percentage which the individual claim represents to the whole. Each of the undersigned believes that the demands which you submitted on March 13 were greatly excessive, based upon the facts and circumstances surrounding each claim and the probable, applicable damage law. However, if you were to consider distribution in a manner similar to the relative percentage that of each of the said demands is of the total demand, and approximate that percentage as against the total offer of $6,875,000, you would arrive at a specific figure for each outstanding claim, and we believe a reasonable relationship and allocation with respect to the offer made herein.

It was a bold stroke. Cathcart had claimed that the offer could not be divided fairly, and Benedict was proving by simple arithmetic that it could be done. The insurance chief went on to set out, case by case, the awards that he suggested should be made. It was immediately apparent that he had conceded the principle of the Warsaw

Convention limitation. Though many of the offers worked out by Benedict were below $75,000, many were well in excess of this figure. Benedict's offers ranged from $15,000, which he proposed should be given to Michael Rogers and Leon Martin, to a combined settlement of $1,000,000 for two other victims of Flight 806: Robert Duran and his wife Glenda. He proposed $150,000 for Charles Hemsley, $125,000 for his wife Edith, and $25,000 for their daughter Mary. The Hemsley brothers would thus have received $300,000 had the offer been accepted at this stage.

The life of John Carter was valued at $150,000, and that of Johannes van Heerden at $250,000. The Simpsons were only offered $50,000 for each parent.

Benedict also offered small additional payments, ranging from $2,500 to $5,000, in cases where Pan Am had already reached a settlement. This may have been by way of conscience money, for the figures revealed were extremely low. Of the fifteen claims that Benedict had settled up to that point, only two had received the Warsaw Convention maximum of $75,000.

The settlements provided an interesting example of what the remaining claimants would actually get at the end of the day. The heirs of one of the victims, a Samoan named Rand Taol, had accepted an offer of $52,500. Of this, $16,166.66 was paid to Butler, Jefferson, and Fry as their $33^1/_3$ percent contingency fee, plus another $4,000 that the attorneys claimed as costs. The heirs therefore received $32,333.34.

Margaret Porter had two heirs, and the settlement in her case was $42,500. Once Butler, Jefferson, and Fry had taken their cut, however, plus $4,000 in costs, each of the heirs received a meager $12,833.33. The attorneys got $16,833.33.

Whatever the reason, Cathcart, Demanes, and Jefferson certainly failed to jump at Benedict's detailed offer as a way out of the impasse. They complained of several "ambiguities" in the letter that would have to be cleared up before they passed the offers on to their clients. The most important of these was the issue of whether the sums suggested were firm offers to each individual claimant, and whether all would have to be accepted before payment was made to any individual. Without slamming the door on Benedict, their reply was obtuse. They wrote:

> We are anxious to communicate any bona fide offers of settlement to our clients for acceptance or rejection. We cannot do so, however, until definite offers are made and the terms upon which they are made are clear. If it is necessary that each and every client accept whatever offers are made before any can be settled, it is almost a certainty that this approach to settlement will not work. It is also clear that the monies offered on the various cases are inadequate and cannot be recommended by the attorneys. Nevertheless, as soon as we know what the offers are and the ambiguities are resolved, we will of course communicate them to our clients and advise you of their response.

On January 18, Benedict replied. Though he still thought that Cathcart and company could work out the sums for themselves if they really put their minds to it, he was prepared "in order to alleviate your burden" to make firm offers of the specific amounts in his previous letter. In addition, although his offer had been intended to be a global one, he was prepared to consider settling cases individually on these figures.

Benedict wound up by imposing a deadline that, in view of the imminent start of the trial, may not have been unreasonable. He wrote:

> The offers were made in consideration of the fact that a settlement of these cases prior to trial would result in a substantial saving in legal fees, costs and expenses, to all parties. Accordingly, if these offers are not accepted prior to 9 a.m. Los Angeles time, on January 26, 1978, they will be withdrawn, and we will have no alternative but to try these cases to a conclusion.

A bare week was not too much time for Cathcart and the others to consult their scattered flock, though it could probably have been done. However, since they did not like the offer anyway, there was no real problem. The deadline passed, and the offer of settlement dropped away.

Perhaps the fact of the matter was that the Pago Pago case had acquired so much momentum and feelings were running so high between the lawyers concerned that there was no stopping it.

Cathcart did, however, go through the motions. He was ethically bound to do so. On January 20, 1978, he wrote to all the claimants setting out the procedure to be followed in the trial and adding, almost as an afterthought, the details of Benedict's offer.

Cathcart seized on the word "consider" in Benedict's letter of the 18th and wrote:

> I interpret that as meaning that if you do decide to accept the offer the defendants are not bound to pay it,

but will only consider it. Their decision on whether or not to pay it will be dependent, at least in part, on how many other people decide to settle their claims.

The defendants' apportionment of the fund has obviously not been carefully made. In some cases, the offers are well in excess of our evaluation of the potential verdict range in a particular case, even assuming we get around the damage limitation of Warsaw by showing willful misconduct. In other cases, the amounts being offered are grossly inadequate under all circumstances. In those cases where the offer is $75,000 or less, there is absolutely no incentive for those clients to accept those amounts, other than to avoid further delay.

Four years after the accident, with not a penny paid in compensation, the avoidance of further delay was no small consideration for many of the claimants. They already knew that the liability trial would take six months or more, to be followed by a huge procession of individual damage trials, and the near certainty of an appeal against the verdict, which could take years. And all the while inflation was marching on.

Perhaps sensing this, Cathcart went on to encourage the claimants by holding out the prospect of the Warsaw limit being increased to match inflation after the trial was over. Then he continued:

The defendant has indicated that these offers, if not accepted prior to 9.00 a.m. Los Angeles time on January 26, 1978, will be withdrawn and the case tried to conclusion. It is doubtful if all of you will even receive these offers by the expiration date, since many of them have to be communicated to distant parts of the world. The time limit is totally impracticable and unrealistic.

The vast majority of his clients could be reached by telephone, and the offer had been on the table since November 9. However, Cathcart went on:

Although I cannot guarantee it, I assume that if a desire to settle is shown after the expiration date, defendant's position will not change. I think the ultimatum contained in the letter was made for psychological purposes only. It is their fond hope that the threat of trying these cases to conclusion will cause many if not all the plaintiffs to capitulate.

He said he had been approached by the government with an offer of $1,500,000, which he had rejected. He had also seen the principals on the other side talking together. He said:

They must be talking about resolving the differences between them so that they can come to us and offer significantly more money.

It is inconceivable to me that the responsible representatives of the defendants, who are attempting to protect their principal financial interests, will not arrive at some agreement among themselves so that they can engage in meaningful settlement negotiations.

Because of the posture of the case, the position which we now enjoy as a result of Judge Byrne's order as to how the trial will be presented, I URGE YOU NOT TO ACCEPT THE ENCLOSED OFFER.

The capitals were Cathcart's. He seemed desperately anxious not to have the glory of the trial snatched from his grasp at this late stage. He added:

> Something towards settlement should happen soon. You have all been patient to this point, and I would hate to see us drown just as we are reaching shore. Though I cannot guarantee that we will win this case as to any defendant, nor whether they will indeed raise their offers, I feel we are in a very strong position factually and psychologically, and it is in the best interests of clients at this point not to accept these offers.
>
> Obviously, each of you must decide whether to accept or reject the enclosed offer relative to your own particular circumstances. Should any of you wish to accept, please tell me.

After that, no one dared.

BOOK TWO

TRIAL

TWELVE

MULTI-DISTRICT LITIGATION CASE No. 176 finally
began in the Los Angeles District Court on January 10,
1978 at 8:20 a.m., Judge William Matthew Byrne Jr.
presiding.

There had been a late setback for the victims of the
crash, although they were never to be told of it by their
attorneys: on January 6, after weeks of legal wrangling,
Judge Byrne had finally ruled that the Hudson report, the
Thomas report, and the written evidence on Pan Am's
misdeeds by the pilots in San Francisco would not be
allowed to be seen by the jury or even mentioned in their
presence. Nor would he allow discussion of the carriage of
excess fuel in relation to the intensity of the fire that
followed the crash, although its possible effect on the
performance of the aircraft would be allowed in.

At a single stroke of Judge Byrne's pen, a major part of
the case against Pan American, and the best hope of
achieving a verdict of "willful misconduct," had
disappeared.

There was a minor compensation. The judge had so structured the hearing of the case that the early stages would be taken up with the chief defendants fighting among each other and with the plaintiffs making their points by way of cross-examination. This was to help Cathcart greatly from an expense point of view: in essence the government would be calling (and paying for) most of the expert witnesses, virtually fighting the plaintiffs' case for them against Pan American. But the success of the ploy would depend hugely on the untried forensic skills of young Mark Dombroff. The immensely experienced lawyers from Boeing and Pan Am took one look at Dombroff and relaxed. They were going to eat this puppy for breakfast.

Though the crash itself had been relatively simple, the Pago Pago trial was to be extremely complex. No one was going to take the blame if they could avoid it, and in consequence, pretty well everyone involved sued everybody else. To simplify it as much as possible, Pan Am, the flight crew, and the passengers were all suing the United States government for allegedly causing the crash to happen through faulty navigation equipment. The passengers were suing Pan American for willful misconduct in causing the crash, and they were also suing both Pan American and Boeing for operating and building an aircraft that was not sufficiently crashworthy to preserve the lives of those on board.

The trial was to be divided into two parts: phase one would deal with the events leading up to the crash, and phase two with what happened after impact.

There was one added complication. Under United States law, a jury could not decide a case involving the government. Therefore, although the jury verdict would be final against Pan American and Boeing, the jury would only be acting in an advisory capacity to the judge in the cases against the United States. The jury would not be told this, however. As far as they knew, they would be deciding the whole thing.

Selection of the jury was not going to be easy. Not only would the trial last at least six months but the annual flu epidemic was not far away. It was decided that in addition to the primary jury of six who would have to make the decisions, there would be an alternate panel of twelve jurors standing by in reserve to take over in case illness or accident should knock out any of the six.

All would have to attend the whole trial, and none would know until the last day whether they would be called upon to reach a verdict. In addition, all eighteen would have to pass the criterion of complete ignorance about the crash of Flight 806 and any of the technical factors that surrounded it.

It was a tall order. At the end of the first day of jury selection, 155 people had been brought before the court and not one had been selected. The clerk's pool of potential jurors was now down to 250, and she was authorized to telephone them and see if they would be willing to serve. Most were not.

Nor was this the only minor hitch on the first day. One of the peripheral lawyers on the plaintiffs' side, a man named Morgan who worked for the New York office of Lee Kreindler, roundly astonished Judge Byrne by asking for the afternoon off. Well, asked Byrne, was he in the case or was he not?

Morgan prevaricated. The problem was, he said, that he and Cathcart had not yet reached an agreement on the division of fees.

Byrne reacted as though stung. "That is up to you," he said. "I am interested in the clients getting some representation. It appears that the only consideration is who is getting the fees. I don't care what arrangement you make about fees."

Morgan, a renowned aviation lawyer, replied cheekily, "What Your Honor doesn't care about is the *only* thing we care about at the moment," thus neatly exposing in a single sentence the attitude of the legal profession toward this case. He added that Kreindler had been corresponding with Cathcart over fees and said, "Now that we are down to the short strokes"—a phrase not often encountered in the Royal Courts of Justice—"there may be some reappraisal of the situation."

Byrne instructed all counsel to be back in court at 9:30 the next morning.

"Do I have to be here at 9:30?" asked Morgan.

"When you get into the swing of this," retorted the judge slyly, "you are really going to enjoy it." It seemed unlikely.

The days wore on, and the potential number of jurors dwindled. An extraordinary number of reasons emerged for disqualification. Some had read an article about dangerous airports, others were former pilots or had relatives who flew, and still more worked in the aviation industry. All were excused. One of the potential jurors examined by Judge Byrne was Michael Brent. Byrne had asked if anyone in the jury box had anything to do with aircraft and Brent, who had no desire to sit through a six-month trial, saw his chance to escape.

"I was in the navy down in San Diego," he said. "We would see nothing but smoke from the planes that would go down. I saw a plane go off the radar screen."

Byrne asked him, "Were you a radar operator?"

Brent replied, "No. I was a fire control technician."

Byrne said, "All right, we'll get to that. Do you think that experience in any way affects your ability to be a fair, impartial juror in this case?"

"No, sir," said Brent with reluctant honesty. He was a repairman with the local telephone company, studying business administration in his spare time. Ruefully, he reflected that his chance to avoid wasting six months in the jury box had just disappeared.

Later, much later, a great deal was to be made of these replies to Byrne's questions by Michael Brent. He felt at the time that he had given a simple, truthful answer. As he had. Michael Brent was, and is, a simple, truthful man. He would no more dream of perjuring himself to get on a jury than he would of setting fire to his house with his wife and two sons inside it. Anyway, he didn't want to be on the jury. He was far too busy.

The judge had asked him what his job had been, and he had told him. It was not for Brent to know that the attorneys in court had jumped to the conclusion that a fire control technician was a man who put out fires. In fact, as Brent would have told them if anyone had bothered to ask, the job was that of a radar mechanic working on fighter aircraft. It involved a knowledge of aircraft instrumentation, some of which would be relevant in the Pago Pago case. Since nobody did ask at that stage, Brent assumed they knew that. He sat down, disappointed that he had not been excused from service.

Brent made further attempts to escape. In fact, it seemed that every time Judge Byrne came up with a possible cause of disqualification, Michael Brent was the first on his feet to claim it as his own.

The judge asked if any of them had ever had an unpleasant experience on a commercial airline.

Brent had: he had once encountered a bad air pocket. It was not enough.

Had any of them any technical experience with aircraft? Brent was on his feet again. This looked like his best chance of escape.

Byrne asked, "What kind of work did you do on them?"

"On the radar," replied Brent.

"You were in the cockpits, then?"

"Every time I worked on the aircraft, right."

"Did you have any instruction at all on the navigational apparatus on the aircraft?"

"No, sir."

"Do you think what you may have seen or heard then you will be able to put out of your mind and decide this case solely on the basis of what you see and hear in this courtroom?"

Brent hesitated, but he had to tell the truth. "Yes, I can," he replied. "I don't remember what I used to work on."

"All right," said Byrne. "Fine."

Curses, thought Brent. Another chance gone. He was later to claim further acquaintance with radar, to have flown on Pan Am, and to have studied law briefly. None of it was sufficient to excuse him, and he found himself on the final short list for the jury.

Now it was the turn of the attorneys involved to make their challenges. Byrne had been chiefly concerned with making sure that there would be no undue bias and that no one person on the jury would be so knowledgeable as to dominate the rest. The lawyers wanted to see that they got the sort of jury that would be most favorable to their case.

They began with challenges for cause, of which there were thirty-one. Byrne granted four and denied twenty-seven. The name of Michael Brent was never challenged.

At this stage, there were sixty-nine jurors left on the panel, and fresh ones came in to fill up the empty spaces in the eighteen-person jury box. Michael Brent was now juror number 17.

With their challenges for cause exhausted, the attorneys began their peremptory challenges, of which they were each allowed four. They were now involved in the business of choosing the six jurors who would actually decide the case, provided they stayed the course. As each was rejected, another from the back of the box would move up to take his or her place in sequence, and another would be brought in to keep the jury box full.

Round and round went the series of challenges, and Michael Brent got closer and closer to the front. Finally, the stage was reached when each lawyer could have one more challenge. At this point Brent was juror number 7, just out of the running.

The prime jury now consisted of two men and four women: Renee Schwartz, Irma Lowd, Richard Fitzgerald, Jane Hard, Richard Hale, and Alexandra Hanna. Cathcart said he would accept that. So did Dombroff. So did Boyd Hight for Boeing. Tucker, however, had been the only attorney not to exercise all his challenges. He challenged Richard Hale, and Hale was excused.

This brought Brent on to the main jury as juror number 6. In the light of what was to happen later, William Tucker could have kicked himself all the way to Times Square. But he had no one to blame but himself.

The jury was now set; there could be no further challenges, except to the alternate jurors, and Brent was no longer among these. On the afternoon of Tuesday, January 17, jury selection was finally completed and battle could commence. At least, that was the theory. In practice, as with almost everything concerned with Flight 806, it did not quite work out that way.

THIRTEEN

BEFORE THE JURY could get into court on the morning of January 18, the counsel was involved in a furious argument among themselves and with the judge. Judge Byrne was angry, and it was small wonder why. The situation with which he was presented would have tried the patience of a saint, and Byrne, good Irishman though he was, was no candidate for canonization. He had walked into court that morning to find that the attorneys for Pan American, the flight crew, and the government had organized a fix among themselves behind his back. Overnight the trio had gone to another judge, Judge Lucas, and agreed that Pan American would drop its case against the government for the loss of their aircraft and the death of the crew, provided that they could bring it up again later if the parties failed to reach a settlement.

This was not only a flagrant breach of etiquette in Byrne's eyes, for which he roasted the young Dombroff like a sheep on a spit, but it would also destroy totally his intricate plan for the structure of the trial. To sort this out, the attorneys casually suggested an adjournment of up to three months.

Byrne blew his stack. Choosing Dombroff as the easiest target, he lambasted him for the colossal waste of money and judicial time that the dismissal of these cases would cause. Had he no concern for the millions of dollars that had been spent to bring this case to trial? Did he not realize that if the cases were not subsequently settled—and Byrne had a shrewd idea they would not be—then some other unfortunate judge was going to have to go back through the whole thing, start at the beginning, and try the case all over again?

Dombroff was on the spot. "I would have to stand here and lie to you," he said, "if I were to say that does not concern me. But there are reasons for our agreeing to do this that we have not told Pan Am, and I am sure that there are reasons which Pan Am has not told us, vis-à-vis the cases against the plaintiffs and the various legal defenses that the parties have. I think everyone sees himself as eliminating some very real legal risks by doing this. As I understand it, the greatest imposition that this might bring about would be upon the judicial system by virtue of the possibility of a second trial."

That was not a possibility, retorted Judge Byrne sourly; it was a certainty.

For Cathcart and the other claimants' lawyers, the sudden move on the part of Dombroff et al. was a potential disaster. Having structured their tactics on being able to allow the government to do most of the work in undermining Pan Am, they were now faced with the prospect of having to do it all themselves. This would be enormously expensive, adding still further to the costs that were whittling down the value of the claims every day, and it would mean yet more delay. Even worse, they would now be left to face the government and Boeing on their own. With the Hudson and Thomas reports already ruled out of the case by Judge Byrne, it was a bleak prospect.

Cathcart had had no prior warning of the application, another sign of the frigid relationship between the two sides. He was furious.

Floyd Demanes was stunned. He accepted that trials were often matters of strategy, but this was too much. The sole motivation, as he saw it, was to prejudice the plaintiffs' position.

There were adjournments, hurried consultations with New York and Washington, and still the jury sat outside and waited. Cathcart, agitated, insisted that the arrangement could not be made without his consent, and they were never going to get that.

It was 6:20 that evening before a weary Judge Byrne called it off for the day. They could reach what agreement they liked, he said, but they had better be ready to start the trial next morning.

They were not, of course. When the court reconvened, Robert Benedict, who had appointed himself as one of the Pan Am legal team, got up to tell the judge that they had not had time to put the deal together. Byrne brought out his big stick. He had no intention of getting the Pago Pago trial under way and then having to declare a mistrial and start all over again, simply to please Benedict. He had been doing his homework and discovered a legal ruling that read: "Any attorney or other person admitted to conduct cases in any court in the United States or any territory thereof, who so multiplies the proceedings in any case as to increase costs unreasonably and vexatiously, may be required by the court to satisfy personally such excess costs." That was the rule, and he would use it. If the defense attorneys were going to use his court as a public convenience, they could pay for the privilege. Personally. The move to drop the cases against the government was never heard of again.

In the late afternoon of Friday, January 20, 1978, after further legal wrangles and the opening statements of counsel, the jury finally got to hear the first witness in the case of Flight 806. He was Raymond Olin Hargis.

Hargis was the Pan American training captain who had given Petersen his flight check at San Francisco when the latter returned from sick leave. He had a flying record that at first sight seemed enormously impressive. Not only was he qualified on jets, right up to the 747, but he had flown an immense variety of piston engine aircraft and had licenses for seaplanes, gyroplanes, and even balloons. There was a feeling that if given half a chance, Hargis might grow feathers and fly around the courtroom.

Once he had testified that Petersen had passed his test satisfactorily, which was the sole reason for his presence, Hargis had to face cross-examination from Mark Dombroff. His record then began to look a little less impressive. He had been hired by Pan Am as a first officer in 1968 and had joined the airline's training department a year later. He had never flown as a line captain on jets for Pan American or any other air carrier. He did not have enough seniority.

In other words, Hargis was one of the Pan Am check pilots, mentioned in the Hudson report, who had the task of running checks on senior captains, with all that that implied. Naturally, no one was allowed to mention Hargis's link with the Hudson Report in court.

There were odder things to come. Questioned by Dombroff, Hargis said that although his signature was on the appropriate form, he had no actual recollection of

Petersen's check flight. In fact, he could not remember having worked with Petersen at all.

Judge Byrne began to get restless. He asked Tucker what had been the purpose of calling the witness. Tucker perhaps was beginning to wonder that himself. "You've got close to a can of worms that's been opened here now," warned Byrne. And he was right.

Dombroff's next question was nicely judged: "Was January 19, 1974 the date on which you administered these three takeoffs and landings to Captain Petersen in Oakland?"

"Yes, sir, that is correct," Hargis replied.

"Then why is there a date of February 4, 1974 on the front of this form, *five days after Captain Petersen died?*"

Hargis became vague. He assumed, he said, that the omission of his signature had been noticed when the training form passed through the administrative process and that the form had been passed back for him to sign. He didn't remember doing so, though he was "completely and entirely sure" that nothing else had been added to that form.

Hargis's sudden certainty after he had failed to remember anything at all about Petersen or the alleged training flight was not convincing. The doubt had been cast in the mind of the jury: had this check ever taken place? Dombroff let it rest there. He picked up Petersen's previous training record and got Hargis to admit that the captain of Flight 806 appeared to have had problems with three-engine instrument approaches and with flying glide slopes.

The record, or that small fraction of it that Dombroff was able to get before the court, showed that in January 1973 Petersen had been called in to discuss his difficulties with the flight training manager and had agreed to take voluntary sessions in the simulator. He had not done so, however, a year later. Hargis was forced to admit that he had not discussed Petersen's problems with other instructors. Nor had he checked to see why the simulator training had not been carried out.

The "can of worms" Byrne had forecast was now well and truly open. Dombroff had succeeded in showing, with Pan American's own first witness, that Captain Petersen was not all he might have been and that the airline's training procedures appeared to be lax. Tucker and Benedict began to reassess their opinion of this young man.

At the end of the day Dombroff got a mock caution from the judge. "You have a tendency to smile rather widely when things are going good," said Byrne. "Just watch it."

"I will control myself," Dombroff replied, suppressing an even wider grin. Things were indeed "going good," though not for Tucker and Benedict, who still had to endure Cathcart's cross-examination of the hapless Hargis.

Cathcart reinforced the doubt over Petersen's check flight and then went on to ask Hargis if Pan American pilots were trained to cope with wind shear. Yes, said Hargis, they were—and then he promptly contradicted himself by saying he could not remember any formal training program on the subject.

Tucker got up to salvage what he could from the Hargis disaster in re-examination. He had briefed the pilot overnight, in what must have been an interesting conversation, and now tried to get proof of the dubious flight check by producing Petersen's pay records for January 1974.

There were instant objections to this from Cathcart and Dombroff, anxious to see that their windfall was not lost. All three attorneys went up to talk to the judge, out of the hearing of the jury.

"Let me ask you," said Byrne, his voice carrying just far enough for the court reporter to catch, "is the government or the plaintiff contending that this check flight never took place?"

Dombroff dodged the question. "I think we are contending that we had the right to these records at the time," he said.

With growing impatience, Byrne repeated his question. Dombroff swallowed hard. "I think there is a clear inference that it never took place."

Byrne pounced like an Irish wolfhound confronted with a juicy bone.

"If this record shows that it did take place, would it be the government's position that the best way to achieve a fair resolution of that issue by the jury would be to keep this document from them so that you could insinuate that it didn't take place?"

Stung by the word "insinuate," Dombroff decided to stand on what was left of his dignity. The best way to achieve a fair result, he said, would be to make sure that he and Cathcart were given documents at the proper time.

Cathcart backed him up.

It was pretty low tactics for Pan Am to let Dombroff and him go out on a limb and discredit the witness, only to come in with fresh records to rescue him at this stage of the game.

Tom Smith, the attorney representing the dead flight crew, chimed in to say that Petersen's pay records had been available for inspection for the past three months.

"All right," said Byrne. "Objection overruled." Tucker sighed with relief.

The pay documents proved, as Dombroff and Cathcart knew they would, that Petersen had indeed made the three takeoffs and landings that were claimed.

Byrne stopped the case and called the lawyers to his bench. "I want the record to show," he said, "that, if not this time, the next time, I am going to start imposing sanctions in this case. You raised the issue as to whether Petersen had this flying experience on January 19. You have a stipulated fact that he did have those takeoffs and landings on that date. You bring in documents now and set up before this jury a totally false issue. I think it is offensive to this jury, and to the presentation of this court, to waste their time on this matter."

Totally false issue or not, the damage to Hargis's credibility had been done, and they all knew it.

DELAYED BY ADJOURNMENTS, the trial limped on until February 1 before the next witness of any substance was called. He was Frank McDermott, a self-employed air safety consultant who had been retained by Pan American in mid-1974 to make a thorough evaluation of the cockpit voice recorder tape from Flight 806.

McDermott was a stranger to the jury but not to the attorneys in court. They knew him as a professional witness, a man who had frequently given evidence against the government in aviation cases. Dombroff eyed him warily, debating whether to impeach him with his past record on the witness stand. He decided to wait and see what would happen, partly, perhaps, because he wished to avoid any further clashes with Judge Byrne. The judge was not in a good mood that day, having had his glasses broken when an airline stewardess trod on them. He had been forced to borrow a pair from another judge and was not seeing things too clearly.

McDermott's evidence, however, involved not sight but sound. He testified that by using specialized equipment to transcribe the cockpit tape, he had made about twenty amendments to the NTSB version of what the crew had said in the last minutes of the flight.

Before he could say what they were, Dombroff insisted on taking him through a lengthy voir dire examination designed to show that he lacked the technical qualifications to be regarded as an expert in this area. The young lawyer did a good job. He got McDermott to admit that he had had no training in electronics, that he belonged to no professional societies in the field of acoustics nor subscribed to any professional journals on sound engineering. Dombroff asked if he had ever been accepted as an expert on voice print analysis, sound spectrographic analysis, or acoustical engineering—all of which he intended to testify on. McDermott said he had not.

On the strength of this, Dombroff demanded with some confidence that McDermott should not be allowed to testify. At the very least, he said, he should be made to bring his fancy equipment into court so that the jury could hear the tape for themselves.

"What you are saying in effect," said Byrne, "is that he's a liar."

"Yes," said Dombroff cheerfully, having now learned that the safest course was to agree with Judge Byrne the first time around. It did him no good. Byrne said, "He can have good ears or bad ears and be a liar, but your thrust is, 'Don't let him testify to it because he experienced all his powers of hearing three years ago and couldn't hear anything, and now he says he's got a new tape recorder and all of a sudden either the tape recorder is better or his ears are better, and now he can testify to it.' I don't think that goes to admissibility. It goes to weight."

Byrne decided to hedge his bets. He would let McDermott testify, but he would also have him bring his machinery to court. Since most of it was heavy, and all of it was in Virginia, it was to be nine days before they got the apparatus screwed together in Los Angeles.

In the meantime, McDermott, who seemed to be a man of many parts, went on to give his views on the conduct of the air traffic controller on duty at Pago Pago on the night of the crash. Dombroff objected to that, too, and conducted yet another long voir dire examination. But he was overruled again. The impression was growing that Judge Byrne was not very smitten with the brash young government lawyer.

McDermott claimed that Bateman, the CAP/IS operator involved, should have advised Flight 806 that there was a heavy rain shower on the approach end of the runway and that his visibility was less than half a mile. He should also have contacted the weather station and asked them to pass more complete information to the pilot. Failure to do these things, he was sure, had contributed to the accident.

Dombroff objected to this answer, claiming it was wholly outside McDermott's scope. He was, of course, overruled, and it was the next day before he was able to tackle McDermott on cross-examination. When he did so the jury saw things in a rather different light.

McDermott was first forced to admit that whether or not a special weather report was passed to the captain, the pilot still had the right to descend to decision height and check the conditions for himself. He then had to agree with Dombroff that if the aircraft reached this point, and the first officer called "field in sight" (which is what had happened), there was no reason why the landing should not continue.

"Do you see any indication on this entire transcript [of the CVR]," asked Dombroff, "from the point that Flight 806 was eight miles from the end of the runway, that they ever lost sight of the runway or the approach lights?"

"No," replied McDermott. But he still maintained that the controller had a duty to warn the pilot of the rain shower.

"In fact, he did advise the pilot," Dombroff retorted. "He said, 'The rain is so bad that I can't see the lights, can you?'"

"He did say that, yes, sir," McDermott admitted, thus neatly contradicting most of his own testimony.

But the major point at issue in this section of the trial was what had been and had not been said in the cockpit on the final approach of Flight 806. It was the contention of the government and the plaintiffs that the crew had failed to conform to proper procedures, to make altitude callouts and so forth, as laid down in the book of rules. McDermott and his magic boxes had been brought in by Pan Am in a bid to prove that those callouts had been made, they were simply difficult to hear.

On Friday, February 10, the apparatus was assembled in the courtroom. It looked impressive. There were four large loudspeakers coupled to a four-channel tape deck, capable of playing the four tracks on the cockpit voice recorder separately or together. There was an amplifier with sophisticated filtering capacity to get rid of unwanted sound, and there was a strange green box covered with buttons, which was a portion of a voice print machine. This last device permitted any two and a half seconds of the tape to be played over and over again.

Judge Byrne and the lawyers listened to it first. They were quite unable to agree on what they heard. In two places, seventeen seconds apart, McDermott insisted that he could hear "eight hundred feet" and "five hundred feet." If those calls had in fact been made, then the crew had been doing their job properly. If they had not, then they were at fault.

It seemed a simple enough question: either the words were on the tape or they were not. Yet it was rather like the emperor's new clothes: in the face of one man's dogged insistence that he could hear these things, no one was too keen to admit that all they could hear was a high-pitched buzz.

At length the jury got a turn. They listened, first of all, to the entire thirty-minute cockpit voice recording—the last thirty minutes in the life of Captain Petersen and his crew. It was an oddly affecting experience, made the more dramatic by the very lack of drama they heard.

They listened to the calm, unhurried voices of Petersen and Phillips, punctuated by the extraneous noises of the aircraft. They heard Bateman's warning of the rain, the repeated assurances by Phillips that he could see the runway lights, and then, after a final call of "140 knots", silence. No one said they were coming down too fast; no one cried out that the plane was about to crash. There was nothing. It was eerie and, in its way, it told the whole story.

The sections of the tape in dispute were then played over and over. Cathcart asked McDermott whether he heard the alleged altitude calls. "Yes, I did," he replied. When Cathcart voiced disbelief, McDermott suggested that the tape might sound clearer through earphones.

Solemnly, a set of earphones was passed from juror to juror. Then McDermott discovered a rumble on the tape and fiddled with his machinery. The earphones went back and forth once more, with frequent pauses for de-rumbling, until Tucker and McDermott were satisfied that the jury had heard every last syllable.

It did them no good at all. Later, Michael Brent was to say, "You could make yourself believe anything, but I couldn't hear a thing. Afterward, when we talked about it in the jury room, I asked the others whether they heard any of the things that were supposed to be there, and they hadn't heard anything either."

FOURTEEN

IT WAS BECOMING hard to remember that Pan American was supposed to be on the offensive during this phase of the trial, making their case for alleged negligence against the government. Thus far their witnesses had been at best ineffective, and at worst positively harmful to their case.

Cathcart wrote to his clients on February 6:

Much of the evidence by Pan Am has been extremely helpful to our effort to show that Pan Am was not only negligent but guilty of willful misconduct. Some Pan Am captains who have testified have come very close to, and in many cases actually conceded, the multiple errors made by the cockpit crew on approach. The last witness to testify came very close to firmly establishing the elements we need to demonstrate willful misconduct. Accordingly, I believe our case against Pan Am is picking up substantial strength, while at the same time Pan Am's case against the government is being exposed as pitifully weak.

The particular witness who inspired this cry of joy from Dan Cathcart was Captain Frederick Ward Baggott, a former fighter pilot who had joined Pan Am in 1945 and had retired shortly before the trial. Though it is hard to match the transcript of his evidence with Cathcart's hyperbole, it was certainly not overly helpful to his former employers.

Baggott, a grizzled veteran of more than 23,000 flying hours, had become a line check captain in 1969 and had flown on a check flight with Captain Petersen in the summer of 1973. The flight had been from San Francisco to Anchorage, Alaska—a part of the world where the climate is somewhat different to that in Pago Pago—and Petersen had checked out as satisfactory. Baggott had some difficulty in remembering, however, whether the flight had involved an instrument landing approach.

Cathcart, cross-examining, persuaded Baggott to say that if a pilot had shown himself incapable of being trained to intercept and fly a glide slope, he should not be flying. This would have been an important admission had Captain Petersen's full training records come before the court. At this stage, Cathcart had no way of knowing that Judge Byrne was to keep them from the jury.

It transpired that Baggott had flown into Pago Pago as part of his duties as an area check pilot. It had been his responsibility to evaluate the airport, its weather, its terrain, and its navigation facilities as to its suitability for operation of the Boeing 707. Tucker objected to this line of questioning, and it was soon to become obvious why he had not drawn out this fact in his own examination of Baggott. The former Pan Am captain went on to tell Cathcart that although he had noticed there were no lights on the ground between Logotala Hill and the approach light system for the runway, he had not classified it as a "black hole" approach or mentioned it as a risk to safety.

This was the first mention the jury had heard of black holes. They were to hear much more, in support of Pan Am's contention that Pago Pago was under-equipped, but this admission by Baggott was to remove the wind from that particular sail before it had even been filled.

As Baggott described it, the Pan Am system for reporting defects at airports on its routes sounded a trifle casual. Though Baggott's job was to report back to the company if anything unusual or unsafe was discovered, there was no procedure for passing this information on to Pan Am pilots other than by word of mouth. In the case of Pago Pago, though Baggott had not experienced it himself, other pilots had told him of dramatic wind changes on the approach during thunderstorm activity and had emphasized the need for caution.

There being virtually no system, there was no way of telling whether information regarding the lack of lights was ever passed on to Captain Petersen.

Cathcart tried hard to establish from Baggott, who had actually flown the Boeing 707 that crashed on Pago Pago, whether the aircraft would have been capable of arresting its descent and climbing away with the load it was carrying on the day of the accident. But Tucker shouted "objection" and was sustained by Judge Byrne. The question was never answered.

———

ARTHUR MEREL SMITH was a unique character. Robert Benedict, who was masterminding the Pan American case, had reached deep into the scientific bran tub and brought him forth as an expert witness who could not only blind the jury with science (all Pan Am's expert witnesses did that) but who could not possibly be contradicted. The reason was that Mr. Smith did not merely profess a particular expertise, he had invented it. And what was more, no one in the whole wide world had ever done the same thing.

To put it in simple terms, which is like trying to write Einstein's theory of relativity on the head of a pin, Mr. Smith's specialty was to analyze the sound of an aircraft's engines, as heard on the cockpit voice recorder, and to deduce from that exactly what was happening just prior to the accident. He had developed this technique during twenty-three years of working in the aircraft engine division of General Electric.

It had been a process of trial and error. He had first tried to unravel the secrets of Flight 806 by processing the engine noises through the FBI's voice print machine, and then putting the results through a memory bank containing known engine signatures. It hadn't worked. Then he had come up with a new device involving the use of spectrograms, and this time, he was confident he had the answer.

The snag was that since Arthur Smith appeared to have been the only man on earth to have used this technique (or even to understand it), it was going to be extremely difficult to challenge his evidence. Normally one expert witness can be contradicted by another—and invariably is—but in this instance there was no one to do the contradicting. Would it be fair, puzzled Judge Byrne, to allow Pan Am to introduce such a witness when, for all anyone knew, his evidence might be unmitigated balderdash? Smith had never appeared as a witness in any court before, which did not make the decision any easier.

Byrne decided to listen to what Smith had to say, out of the jury's hearing, before ruling on whether or not he could give evidence.

Smith's opinion of what had happened during the last twenty seconds of Flight 806 was graphic and, if provable, of vital importance to Pan American. It could have gone a long way toward getting the airline off the hook by making it evident that some force outside the control of the crew had caused the Boeing to fall out of the sky.

Smith told Byrne that twenty seconds before the crash the sound of the engines had become "erratic." Since the post-crash investigation had not revealed anything wrong with the engines themselves, he saw two possible explanations. One was that a sudden pitch-up movement by the aircraft, such as might be caused by the pilot pulling back sharply on the control wheel, had caused the fan blades within the engine to stall; the other was that a similar blade stall might have been caused by a cross-wind component blowing across the face of the engines. In other words, wind shear.

It transpired that Smith was an altruist. He had not patented his process, preferring to say, "Here it is, world. Have at it and make a safer airplane." Nor had he taken any payment for helping the NTSB in the course of four accident investigations.

But none of this was much help to Byrne, who tried to find out if there was any expert anywhere on the globe who could challenge Smith's theory. The best Smith could suggest was his own assistant, and that got no one very far.

As Byrne summed up the problem facing him, it became clear to the Pan American lawyers that a vital ruling was about to be made against them. Tucker tried the desperate and somewhat unusual ploy of offering to scour the world for some other expert witness who could testify for his opponents, if only the judge would stay his hand.

Tom Smith, representing the crew, attempted to play down the technical aspects of the evidence while stressing its importance to the case. "What Mr. Smith is telling us about this engine is very limited," he said. "He's telling us the speed of the engine, knowing which it is possible to determine the power output. That is a crucial factor in this case because one of the things the plaintiffs and the government are contending here is that the crew sat in that airplane and did not do anything to prevent it hitting the ground.

"Mr. Smith will testify, as a result of his investigation, that this aircraft encountered a situation where the wind shifted rapidly and caused a change in the flow of air into the engine, which brought about a blade stall. That reduces the amount of air flowing through the engine, and it is the air, mixed with the fuel, which produces the power. If there is no air flowing through the engine, no power is produced. That testimony will directly refute the statement that is going to be made that this crew did nothing except sit there and watch the airplane crash.

"He will also testify that after that ten-second period there is evidence that power was being applied, which refutes the allegation that this crew did nothing about attempting a go-round. I think it is a crucial piece of evidence."

Byrne decided to put the problem aside until the following week, but he was clearly not in favor of allowing

Arthur Smith to take the stand. Cathcart and Dombroff, who had taken no part in the discussion, must have felt there was an element of rough justice here. So much of their own vital evidence had been ruled inadmissible by Judge Byrne. Now the other side was getting a taste of the same medicine. But Smith's testimony had been so truncated that it made very little impact.

————

THE DEFENSE LAWYERS were not about to give up on their wind shear theory. They were not so blessed with good angles on this case that they could afford to. Two days later, on February 14, after the court had heard an arcane deposition on the installation of instrument landing systems, Tucker and Tom Smith attacked the question again.

Their next witness was Billy Marion Hopper, who had been a naval flyer during World War II and, later, a flight engineer for United Airlines before joining the NTSB as an air safety inspector.

Hopper testified that he had made two analyses of the flight data recorder from Flight 806; the second, in September 1976, had been done with the aid of a computer. It transpired that the accuracy of the data-recording device, generally known as a "black box," was not all that marvelous. It was manufactured to record a tolerance of plus or minus 10 knots in airspeed, plus or minus 100 feet of altitude at sea level, and plus or minus .2G of acceleration forces.

It was all vaguely interesting, but Hopper had really been brought in to pave the way for another NTSB witness: William Giltz Laynor Jr.

Laynor had been brought into the case after the NTSB had been rocked back on its heels by the ALPA petition in 1976. He had been asked to evaluate the evidence from the flight data recorder to see whether the organization's claim that external forces had caused the crash had any substance. Among the tools he had used were thrust values taken from a sound spectrogram by General Electric.

At the first mention of these tools, Dombroff was on his feet. He scented an attempt by Tucker to introduce Smith's evidence by the back door and insisted on examining Laynor's credentials as an expert witness before things went any further. It emerged that Laynor did not have any credentials to speak of, that his only formal accident investigation training had been a four-week course at the NTSB school, and that he had no great knowledge of the aerodynamics of a Boeing 707 or of meteorology.

By the time Dombroff had gotten him to confess that he had no way of knowing whether the data he used for his calculations were accurate and that the results were pure speculation, there was not much left of Laynor's credibility.

Dombroff moved that Laynor's testimony should be ended then and there. Tom Smith objected, and Byrne brought the lawyers to his bench, where the jury could not hear them.

Laynor, said Smith, was going to testify that according to his calculations Flight 806 had encountered a decreasing head wind as well as a downdraft so strong that it would have required 8,000 pounds more thrust than the engines were capable of producing in order to maintain level flight.

Struggling against objections by Cathcart and Dombroff, who claimed that such evidence had never been accepted by any other court, Smith went on to say that

Laynor had written the NTSB report in which it was said that Flight 806 had encountered wind shear.

"But what in the world does that have to do with this?" Judge Byrne wanted to know.

"That is a very important part of this litigation, Your Honor," Smith replied. "Our contention is that this aircraft was caught in wind shear." And he claimed that since the NTSB report had found this to be so, that represented a legal admission by the government.

Smith neglected to say, of course, that the findings of the first NTSB report had been something quite different, or that the second one had been produced as a result of special pleading by ALPA. Nor did he choose to remember that NTSB reports could not, by statute, be used as evidence in a court of law.

Judge Byrne, who knew all these things perfectly well, decided to play with him a little. "If there's one thing I'm sure of," he said, "it is that in aircraft litigation around this country, when there has been a finding against the US by some investigator from the NTSB, then someone has attempted to get that into evidence."

Smith refused to give up, repeating the same point until Byrne, deciding that the grave had been dug to sufficient depth, pushed him gently into it.

"Then I think," he said, "that we should let the rest of the report in, so that the full document can be before the jury. In other words, the part about Pan American—"

Smith jumped in quickly before he could finish the sentence. "The problem with that, Your Honor, is that the board never considered the problem of the instrument landing system at Pago Pago."

"It all goes to weight," replied Byrne. He was enjoying Smith's discomfort. "If you think the document is admissible against the United States, then the entire document should be able to go in." Including, of course, the heavy criticism of the crew members, who were Smith's clients.

"Pan American had no part in writing that report," Smith said desperately.

"I know," said Byrne, "but just so the jury will be able to understand and be able to weigh the different findings of the board."

"I can't agree with the court there," said Smith.

"I'm sure you can't. I said it somewhat in jest. But what you're saying is that if some part of the NTSB report or some investigator of the NTSB makes some finding that is critical of the government, then that's admissible. Every other finding is not."

That was exactly what Smith was saying, and though Byrne ruled that most of Laynor's intended testimony would not be admissible, Smith continued to try to get the wind shear issue in front of the jury. He failed miserably.

―――――

THE TRIAL WAS MOVING into its second month, and things were going well for Cathcart and company. Pan Am seemed to be getting nowhere in its case against the government, and real points were being scored in favor of the plaintiffs along the way. On the other hand, if the government escaped paying damages to Pan American, it would probably escape paying them to Cathcart's clients, too.

It may have been this that persuaded Cathcart to ask his clients for permission to accept the latest settlement offer being made by Dombroff. The sum was only

$1,600,000—little more than the previous offer he had rejected out of hand—but Cathcart had another motive for acceptance. It appeared that the plaintiffs' lawyers were beginning to feel the financial pinch.

Cathcart was proposing that the money from the government be put into a trustee account, where it could draw interest until the case was decided. It would then be shared by the claimants in proportion to the sums they got from Pan American and/or Boeing. Well, most of the money would be going into the fund—$300,000 would be taken by the lawyers to defray their costs to date, including travel expenses incurred by Pilkington et al.

"A disbursement from this fund to the members of the plaintiffs' discovery committee would be of great assistance in easing the very significant financial burdens in advancing these costs," Cathcart wrote.

In New Zealand and other places where the claimants were doing their best to survive, this idea went down like a lead balloon. Other people had suffered costs: the Rogerses were having to pay for expensive plastic surgery, and the Hemsleys had laid out about $10,000 in connection with the case. But they and everyone else would have to wait for months or years before they saw a cent of the government money. Only the lawyers would get paid straight away.

As it happened, this settlement never came about. Two months later, having decided that the government might, after all, lose, Cathcart turned down the offer. "Certainly, hindsight may prove that this judgment was incorrect," he wrote to his clients on April 5. It was.

FIFTEEN

THE SAGA of the wet palm tree began on February 15, 1978. Its author and only begetter was a little man with a goatee, whose name was David Alexander Hodges.

Hodges was a self-employed consulting electrical engineer, another expert witness, and Dombroff followed his usual custom of attempting to get him thrown off the witness stand for not being expert enough. Judge Byrne would have none of it. His lip was beginning to curl with dislike whenever he looked at Mark Dombroff, and when the young man began to complain that he had never seen exhibits being presented by Hodges, Byrne snapped back, "It isn't the first time you've heard of them. They were filed, sir. I have asked counsel for the last four months to look at every exhibit that is going to be offered in this case. Day after day there are exhibits offered that no counsel has ever heard of before?"

Tucker twisted the knife by adding that these particular exhibits had been presented to Dombroff in December. The wonder boy grimaced beneath his heavy moustache, grown to make him look older than his thirty years, and sat down. He waited until he caught Tucker with an exhibit that had never been listed by anyone, and smiled again as the Pan Am lawyer got his knuckles rapped by Byrne. There was no keeping him down.

Hodges regarded this forensic byplay from the witness box with calm serenity. He went on to describe the electrical distribution system on Pago Pago, which he had visited at Pan Am's expense in September 1977, in graphic and boring detail.

In essence, Hodges was saying that electricity around the airfield was carried on overhead wires. Being a tropical island, Pago Pago had a lot of palm trees, which got wet when it rained. When the wind blew, said Hodges, these wet palm trees sometimes swayed against the electric cables, causing a short circuit. It was very interesting. The jury failed to see that it had much to do with the crash of Flight 806, but it was very interesting.

There was automatic circuit-breaking equipment, Hodges continued, which would turn the current back on when the trees swayed the other way. Unless, of course, it had been blowing so hard that the wet palm trees actually fell over on top of the cables, in which case the power would remain off until someone came out with an axe and the circuit breakers were reset. All this was liable to cause fluctuations in the electricity supply on Pago Pago. It sounded reasonable.

Tucker then launched into a hypothetical question of mind-boggling length and complexity. It went on for almost three thousand words and covered nine pages of court transcript before he came to the question mark at the end. Hodges, having been rehearsed, appeared to understand it. In this he was more fortunate than the jury.

"On the basis of your review," Tucker wound up breathlessly, "and as you have testified for the record, and your study on the island, have you formed an opinion as to whether there were any power fluctuations at the airport on the night of this accident as Flight 806 was approaching to land?"

"Yes," replied Hodges simply.

"What was that opinion, sir?" thundered Tucker.

It was to be some time before he could get a reply. Dombroff jumped to his feet with a barrage of objections. Not only, he said, had Tucker's hypothetical question been full of errors, but there was no evidence whatever that the circuit breakers had tripped that night. Nor was there anything to show that the emergency generators had started up, that any lights had gone out, or that the instrument landing system had ceased to function for a moment.

Byrne regarded him coldly. "Objection overruled," he said.

Hodges got to answer. "With the assumptions that you have given me," he said (an important qualification, since many of the assumptions seemed to be Tucker's own invention), "it appears obvious that there was a short circuit on circuit number two of a permanent nature that resulted in four distinct reductions in voltage to the receiver terminal area and put the transmitter site in the black."

The wet palm tree had struck.

Hodges was asked by Tucker what effect this would have had upon the VASI. The VASI was an important part of the approach lighting system. It consisted of two horizontal bars of lights, one above the other, both of which would appear white to a pilot who was above the glide slope. If he was below the glide slope, both would shine red, and if he was on course there would be one red bar and one white.

Hodges replied that the VASI would have gone "in the black" with the first reduction in voltage.

This was an important answer. One of the peculiarities of the VASI system was that once it had been put out of action by a power failure, it had to be manually reset before it could work again after the power was restored. No evidence was ever to be produced that anyone had had to reset the VASI after the crash of Flight 806, with the implication that it had continued to operate throughout the time of the accident.

The jury, however, was not to know that at this stage. They only had Hodges testifying under oath that the VASI lights had gone out. But Hodges was basing his answer on premises supplied by Tucker; he had not been to Pago Pago until nearly four years after the accident.

Everyone had to move into an adjoining courtroom at this stage. Hodges had prepared an elaborate model, complete with wet palm tree, to demonstrate his theory. By some miscalculation, however, it was too big to get through the doors of Judge Byrne's court.

Hodges tugged his palm tree against the wires, taking precautions not to black out the entire courthouse, to demonstrate what he meant.

He appeared to prove that if the voltage diminished by 25 to 50 percent, the VASI lights would go out and would not come on again when full power was restored. Dombroff made him run through the demonstration again, just for good measure.

Byrne wanted to be sure. "Do you have an opinion as to whether the VASI lights went out?"

"They did go out," said Hodges bravely.

"Then they would have to be manually turned on," said Byrne.

"That is correct," Hodges replied. He was full of confidence at this stage. Somebody should have told him about Dombroff.

The cross-examination began gently enough.

Dombroff merely established that Hodges had no experience with airport navigation systems and had never been to the Pago Pago transmitter site, the CAP/IS building, the receiver building, or to the VASI lights. Nor had he ever run any tests on actual VASI lights or glide slope systems.

He had not seen the transcript of the cockpit voice recorder (which disclosed that the crew could see the lights shining brightly throughout).

Hodges's credibility was beginning to slip, and he started to look nervous.

Dombroff put it to him that no one had turned the VASI lights back on after the accident, since they were still burning brightly. "Is there any technical explanation that you are aware of," he asked, "as to how the VASI would get on after the accident if nobody manually turned it back on?"

"No," replied Hodges.

"Well sir," said Dombroff, "isn't it fair then to state that the VASI was never off?"

"No," maintained Hodges. But the two answers were in total contradiction. He knew it, and so did the jury. The evening adjournment came to Hodges like the final bell to a fighter on the ropes, but next morning he was back in the witness box again, and Dombroff was still on his feet.

The young lawyer probed Hodges remorselessly. Item by item he dragged him through his testimony, converting certainty to doubt and doubt to recantation. For one who had never appeared before a jury in his life, Dombroff was doing pretty well.

"Are you aware, sir," he asked, "of any evidence in anything that you've looked at, or any record that you've looked at, which indicates that the glide slope went off the air during the approach of Flight 806?"

"No," replied Hodges.

"And isn't it true, sir, that all the evidence that you saw in this case indicates that the glide slope and the total ILS system was available for use and being used by Flight 806 during its approach?"

"Yes," said Hodges, cowed. And with that answer, any value that his testimony had to Pan American was utterly destroyed.

Still Dombroff had not finished with him.

He took another part of the Pago Pago navigation system: the non-directional beacon on Logotala Hill. Had that not been working perfectly when inspected after the accident?

"Aha," said Hodges, scenting an opportunity. "But during that period it could have shifted back from its emergency engine generator to commercial power."

Alas for Hodges, the non-directional beacon had no emergency generator.

Dombroff pursued him with vigor around the wet palm tree. If such a palm tree had indeed fallen down, would not a repairman have had to go out and clear the line?

Hodges agreed that it would be so.

"Did you see any single document in anything you looked at which indicated that a repairman went out to some site and either reset circuit breakers or cleared debris from power lines, or did anything?"

"We were unable to get any material on the operation of the distribution system in American Samoa," replied Hodges stiffly.

And so it went on, through cross-examination by Cathcart, re-examination by Tucker, and re-cross-examination by Dombroff. Hodges finally left the witness box late in the afternoon of Friday, February 17, grateful that a public holiday and a long weekend lay ahead.

He would be seeing wet palm trees in his dreams, which is where they properly belonged.

SIXTEEN

INCHWORMS MEASURE MARIGOLDS; Dr. Kenneth Reginald Hardy measured raindrops. Give Dr. Hardy a pocket calculator and a few reams of data, and he could work out the size and velocity of a raindrop falling in space over a tropical island thousands of miles away four years previously. Dr. Hardy was a whiz kid. That was why his testimony cost Pan American World Airways $20,000.

For a time, after he took the stand on the morning of February 21, 1978, it seemed that the money had been well spent. As he responded smoothly to the questioning of William Tucker, Dr. Hardy was the epitome of the expert witness. As a meteorologist his list of qualifications was so impressive that even Dombroff could not challenge it. The titles of his published works took up three and a half pages of court transcript, and he was young and handsome to boot —a fact that did not go unremarked by the female members of the jury.

Hardy gave his evidence in a soft Canadian drawl, and it soon became clear that the major plank on which Tucker would base his contention that Flight 806 had been blown into the ground by wind shear was that it had encountered forces no human crew could have survived.

The jury heard what wind shear was, and how these strong movements of air could be created in convective showers. They learned about thermals and the creation of clouds, and the way in which downdrafts were formed when rain began to fall. It was all very instructive, and even vaguely relevant.

Hardy had analyzed the weather conditions at Pago Pago on the night of the accident. He had used the surface weather observations of wind, rain, temperature, and humidity from the National Weather Service station on the island as well as data from two radiosonde balloons. One of these had been released from Pago Pago shortly after noon on the day of the crash, the other an hour after the accident. In addition, Hardy said he had employed satellite observations of the area and surface weather maps of the South Pacific. There was a long technical explanation of the way in which satellites could photograph cloud cover at night, which seemed to fascinate Judge Byrne.

Was there really any dispute, Byrne asked Tucker, that there were clouds over Pago Pago that night? No, replied Tucker, not really. Perhaps he was just determined to get his money's worth out of Hardy.

Hardy went on throughout that day and into the next to give a graphic description of the storm that had struck Pago Pago on the night of January 30, 1974. It had been circular in shape with a core 2,000 feet in diameter, and it moved across the island from the northeast at a speed of 23 knots. Just before the crash, between 23.38 and 23.39, it had dropped rain at the weather station for 45 seconds at a rate of 4 inches an hour. The total diameter of the storm, within which rain had fallen at half an inch per hour or more, was 25,000 feet.

The figures were impressive in their certainty. Hardy began to move toward the crunch, telling Tucker that the most intense portion of the storm would have been just off the end of runway 5 at the precise moment—to the second —when Flight 806 crashed. He had begun to spell out the updrafts and downdrafts at the runway threshold when a cloud no larger than a man's hand intervened. It was Mark Dombroff.

"This is a model of something several thousand feet from the end of the runway," Dombroff protested. "There is no measuring device out there. This man is relying on one rain gauge located in the middle of the airport, and he's relying on winds aloft taken hours before and hours after. He's trying to represent that this is weather existing at the time of the accident, several thousand feet from the measuring point of a rain gauge."

"Objection overruled," said Judge Byrne.

Encouraged by Tucker, Hardy proceeded to explain just how he had done it. He had used, he said, the measurements from the radiosonde balloon that was launched behind the storm. This had given him the approximate amount of rain in the air, and by knowing the humidity he could work out how much evaporation there was in the drier areas below the cloud base. Having established how much cooling was occurring, he could then compute the speed of the downdraft in the most intense portion of the storm. He had also worked out the downdraft for the time of 23.40.25 plus or minus ten seconds, at 510 feet above sea level, at a distance of 7,500 feet from the end of the runway. In fact, he had figures for the downdraft that would have affected Flight 806 at five-second intervals over its entire final approach.

The court was stunned by the fiendish ingenuity of it all, except Dombroff, of course. He waded in with objection after objection and was overruled each time.

Undeterred, Hardy asserted that at 23.40.40 plus or minus 10 seconds, at a height of 113 feet from above mean sea level and a distance of 3,700 feet from the end of the runway, the wind had been blowing from 40 degrees at 21 knots, there had been a downdraft of 100 feet per minute, and the rain had been falling at 2.6 inches per hour. Five seconds earlier, at a height of 260 feet, the wind had been blowing at 27 knots with a downdraft of 350 feet per minute.

Tucker took Hardy through calculation after calculation, building a mathematical mountain of such density that it seemed impregnable against any attempt at demolition by the other side. He was creating the impression of a witness so clever that he was bound to make a dunderhead of Dombroff.

How could you challenge a man who knew that a single raindrop, positioned 510 feet above the ground at Pago Pago at 23.40 and 25 seconds on the night of January 30, 1974 was 1.7 millimeters in diameter and falling at a velocity of 5.87 meters per second in a downdraft of 450 feet per minute? Tucker must have reckoned that Pan Am's $20,000 had been worth every cent.

But it was clear from the number of fruitless objections being made by the government attorney that he was not going to give up easily. Dombroff told Judge Byrne that he estimated his cross-examination of Hardy would take about four hours. Cathcart wanted about an hour and a half with the witness. On reversing the golfing principle that the man farthest from the hole goes first, Cathcart was allowed to take first crack at the meteorologist.

The American lawyer knew that he would have to destroy Hardy's exalted image if he was to make any dent in his credibility. He flicked through his long list of qualifications with some disdain.

"You're just a weatherman, aren't you?" he inquired blandly. Genius came down to earth with a bump. Just a weatherman? The effrontery of it! But Cathcart achieved his object. Michael Brent was to say later, "When he asked that question, all those degrees just faded away."

Cathcart began fairly gently. He established that Hardy had never been to Pago Pago and had never studied the local conditions there. He got him to admit that the crew of Flight 806 should certainly have seen the approaching line of thunderstorms on their weather radar screen and could have cruised around in fair weather until the squall line passed.

Hardy, it transpired, was an expert on radar as well. He had even written an article on the radar detection of flying insects. "I assume," said Cathcart, "that if you can see bugs on radar, you can see storm cells like the one over Pago Pago?" Hardy had to admit that was true. He also had to admit that he had not known that heavy rain was far from unusual on Pago Pago at that time of year. More than sixty-five inches had once been recorded in January, with twenty inches in a single day, said Cathcart. He was establishing that the crew of Flight 806 should have known what to expect.

"How long will you be now?" asked Judge Byrne as Hardy neared the end of his second day in the witness box. Cathcart estimated forty minutes; Dombroff still thought he would need four hours.

"It just goes to show what he thinks of your cross-examination," joked Byrne.

Cathcart replied, "I'm not doing much of a job," but he, too, was only joking. When Hardy returned to the stand the next morning, he found Cathcart had grown claws overnight.

The lawyer began by making Hardy pull out all the calculations on which he had based his evidence in chief. He seemed to nurture the unjust suspicion that the weatherman had really worked the whole thing out in his head. As it turned out, this was not far wrong.

Hardy admitted that those figures for the intensity of downdraft and the velocity of the wind, not to mention the size of the raindrops, were not the result of mathematical calculations at all. They were questions of interpretation or, as Cathcart put it, matters of opinion. He went on to agree that the local topography could have a big influence on wind speed and direction and then to admit that he had not taken this into account.

The weight of Hardy's evidence was now beginning to look very different. A few simple questions had transformed it from scientific certainty into inspired guesswork. He had to confess to Cathcart that his estimate of the movement of the storm could have been in error by 30 degrees in either direction and the speed of the wind by 25 percent. If those estimates had been in error, then the rest of his answers were also wrong.

While the rest of the court went off to enjoy lunch, Hardy sat hunched over a calculator and myriad pieces of paper, trying to figure it all out. It did him no good. The admitted margins of error were too great for any fresh assertions to carry the slightest credence.

Cathcart wound up for his final assault.

"This wind shear phenomenon," he said, "has been on this planet for as long as we have had weather, has it not?"

"Yes, sir," said Hardy.

"Is it also correct that ever since man learned to fly, ever since the Wright brothers, we have had wind shear?"

"Yes, sir."

"During all phases of flight?"

"Yes, sir."

"Is the amount of wind shear at all dependent upon topography?"

"Yes, sir."

"Did you allow for that in your evaluation of what the wind shear was at this particular place?"

"No, sir, it was not considered as a factor."

"Is there, in any case, anything extraordinary about the amount of wind shear that you calculated in this case?"

"No, sir."

"In fact," said Cathcart, "it is the sort of thing which could be commonly encountered on almost any flight, is it not?"

"Yes, sir," admitted Hardy.

So much for wind shear, and so much for the unfortunate Dr. Hardy. And Dombroff had not even started on him yet. The government attorney must have been impressed by Cathcart's performance, for he cut the estimated time for his own cross-examination by three hours.

There was to be no mercy. Dombroff waded straight in and caught Hardy with a sucker punch on the opening bell. He said innocently, "Isn't it correct, from the meteorological records that were available for your review, that it is not possible to derive any reliable estimates as to the degree of turbulence or wind shear which existed along the approach to runway 5 at the time of this flight?"

Hardy, suspicious, had the question re-read. Then he disagreed.

Dombroff invited him to read a paragraph from his own deposition, sworn on oath before the trial. Haltingly, Hardy read, "From the meteorological records available, it is not possible to derive reliable estimates as to the degree of turbulence and the change in wind speed [wind shear] which existed along the approach to runway 5 at the time of the flight."

"Did you write that, sir?" asked Dombroff.

"Yes," said Hardy.

There was to be no recovery. Having landed his first blow, Dombroff bounced Hardy around the witness box at will, forcing the scientist to admit that "neither the surface winds nor the downdrafts were exceptionally strong." He reinforced some of the points that Cathcart had already won and exposed Hardy's raindrop calculations as risible nonsense.

By the time the cross-examination ended, none too soon for his taste, Dr. Kenneth Reginald Hardy was a sadly diminished man.

For all that Tucker tried to undo the damage on his re-examination, filling the heads of the jury with yet more calculations, it was too late. "Meteorology," he said by way of exculpation, "is not an exact science."

The jury, one imagines, had gathered that.

SEVENTEEN

AS THE JURY sat in the courtroom day after day, it often seemed to them that they were living in a sort of legal limbo, that the world outside had ceased to exist. This was especially true in the week that carried them out of February and into March, a week spent listening to technical depositions of remarkably little interest or importance. Neither Judge Byrne nor any of the senior counsel bothered to be in court at all that week. The depositions were read into the record in front of a local magistrate. There were therefore few people on hand to react instantly when an event occurred that almost brought the trial to a premature end.

On Wednesday, March 1, a Continental Airlines DC 10 crashed while taking off from Los Angeles International Airport, less than ten miles from the courthouse where the Pago Pago trial was taking place. The DC 10, carrying 186 passengers on a trip to Honolulu, burst a number of tires in the final stages of its takeoff run, swerved off the runway, and erupted into flames. As with Flight 806, the fire made exits on one side of the aircraft virtually unusable, but resourceful action by the captain and crew on this occasion saved almost all the passengers. This was all the more remarkable since most of them were elderly. In all, two passengers died of smoke inhalation, and twenty-eight passengers and three crew members were injured during the escape. It was an outstanding example of what could be done to rescue people from a burning aircraft—even one with a great deal of fuel on board. The contrast with the fate of those on board the Pan American flight was striking.

It was a little too striking for the taste of William Tucker. He bustled his bulk into court on Monday, March 6 with metaphorical steam erupting from his ears. He wanted a mistrial. There had been TV and radio broadcasts about the crash, there had been a welter of press reports, and worst of all, members of the jury had been overheard discussing the Los Angeles disaster. Shock, horror. Tucker wanted the jury dismissed and the whole trial to be started over again.

He had a case, and Judge Byrne took it seriously. Throughout the trial the jury had been warned not to look at, read, or listen to anything to do with air crashes. But this one they could hardly have avoided. All the same, the thought of having to go through two months of testimony all over again was hardly appealing.

"Let me ask you frankly," said Byrne to Tucker, "do you really want this mistrial?"

"Are you asking me as a lawyer for Pan American," asked Tucker in reply, "or personally?"

"Obviously I'm asking you as a lawyer."

"Irrespective of my personal desires and wishes," replied Tucker unctuously, "I feel obligated as a lawyer to make this motion."

And this was only natural.

After all, he had been doing very badly up to that point. A fresh trial with a fresh jury would give him another chance.

Byrne was not satisfied with the answer.

What he wanted to know was whether Tucker was just making noises for the record or whether he genuinely wanted a mistrial to be declared.

Tucker said he did. "Notwithstanding the personal sacrifice it will create for me and others."

"Why do you think your clients will get a better trial?" he asked Tucker. They were out of the hearing of the jury.

"The thing that bothers me, Your Honor," said Tucker, "is the striking parallel between what happened at Pago Pago and what happened at Los Angeles airport. We've got fire, which is probably the worst way in the world to die. We've got vivid descriptions of the horrors the victims went through, and we have a captain who was praised to the highest by at least two of the print media. We've got a fire department that was superb in reaction time. According to some reports, that fire truck got to the fire before the aircraft quit rolling.

"Now we've got descriptions by the print media that the captain's heroics saved 196 people, and only two died. We've got criticism on the editorial page of a very well-respected newspaper of the interiors that go into these aircraft. Your Honor, if you were going to write a script for a crash you didn't want to happen during any trial, you could not have written a script with more striking parallels."

Byrne remarked dryly that he could think of a couple of differences: this had been a Douglas aircraft with a Continental crew, not a Boeing staffed by Pan American.

Exactly, said Tucker. That was the problem. It wasn't going to help Pan Am's case much to show that another airline could save 99 percent of its passengers when most of their own had been killed.

Dombroff was against a mistrial. So was Cathcart, who said quite reasonably that there was no way that air carriers could be barred from having accidents during the course of the trial, and that if they stopped proceedings each time there was a crash they would be there forever.

As for Tom Smith, he was in a difficult spot. He was in the anomalous position of representing both Pan American and the cabin crew. "Pan American as a plaintiff joins in the motion," he said. "The crew does not join in the motion."

"You mean half your clients join in it, and half your clients do not join in it?" asked Byrne incredulously.

"That's right," said Smith. He faced the problem of legal schizophrenia, arguing both sides of the case against himself. Byrne rejected Tucker's motion. The jury had sworn solemnly that they could remain fair and impartial, however many airplanes crashed around them.

Denied his reprieve, William Tucker carried on the case against the government. The task of proving that someone other than Pan American had caused the crash of Flight 806 had seemed an uphill struggle from the outset. Now two vital rungs of his ladder of proof—electrical power failure and wind shear—had been neatly sawed away from beneath his feet. Tucker sighed inwardly and began to reach for the next one: the black hole of Pago Pago.

The witness was Jess R. Speckart, a former FAA employee who, at the time of the accident, had been deputy chief of the Airports Division and responsible for the planning, development, and certification of airports in the Western Division. Pago Pago was in the Western Division. It emerged under cross-examination by Dombroff (Tucker had somehow forgotten to mention it) that Speckart had, since his retirement in 1975, joined a company called Aviation Systems Associates in Fairfax Station, Virginia. This was a firm that specialized in providing expert witnesses in aircraft accident litigation.

Tucker must have wondered whether Pan Am was going to get value for money this time.

The black hole about which Speckart was to testify was airman's jargon for an approach to an airport that contained no lighting on the ground that might help a pilot judge a plane's altitude.

Such approaches are not uncommon; they usually occur when a runway is on the edge of the water. In the case of runway 5 at Pago Pago, the last few miles of the approach were over uninhabited jungle, which produced the same effect.

Speckart's opinion was that five flashing lights should have been installed on the tallest trees beneath the glide path, which would have given the pilot of Flight 806 visual cues as to his distance from the ground.

Cross-examined by Cathcart, who found himself in the unusual position of joining forces with Tucker on this particular issue, Speckart claimed that obstructions on the approach should be lighted when they impinged on an imaginary fifty-to-one slope from the end of the runway.

He thought that six trees did so on Pago Pago (he had found one more since his evidence in chief), including the tree first struck by Flight 806. The lighting of such obstructions, he said, was an FAA regulation.

Then it was Dombroff's turn.

He went on to attack Speckman's competence and discovered that the witness had not only not been to Pago Pago but had not bothered to read the handbook from which he was quoting FAA regulations. Obligingly, Dombroff read it for him. The rule laid down that obstructions exceeding the fifty-to-one slope should be removed or lighted.

However, this applied to a standard glide slope angle of 2.5 degrees. In the case of Pago Pago, because of the height of Logotala Hill, the glide slope was set at 3.25 degrees—a much steeper angle of approach.

Because of this, Dombroff pointed out, the obstruction line would run at twenty-eight to one, clearing the trees and making them quite legal. It was like shooting fish in a barrel.

Dombroff produced a letter from Pan American to the FAA that recognized the nonstandard glide slope at Pago Pago, and in which the airline pointed out that its pilots were accustomed to flying steeper approaches than that into other airports. The letter had expressed no concerns about trees or black holes.

So, if the airline was happy and the regulations were satisfied, what was all the fuss about? Dombroff rested, content.

When Tom Smith, this time wearing his Pan Am hat, tried on re-examination to introduce fresh complications about the height of an aerial on Logotala Hill, Byrne lost his patience.

"I want to make it clear to all of you," he said, "that I've tried to stay out of this case to a certain extent. I'm about at the end of that role. This stuff is ridiculous."

Every now and then, Judge Byrne did have a knack for getting to the heart of the matter. But if he thought he was going to prevent Pan American from dragging technical red herrings across the noses of the jury at every conceivable opportunity, he was mistaken. The next witness was to be Mathew Rutherford Frampton, and Mr. Frampton had in his knapsack the most odiferous red herring of all.

EIGHTEEN

MATHEW FRAMPTON WAS a professional witness from the same stable as Speckart. A short, stocky man, he wore his receding hair cropped, so that it looked like a skullcap on the back of his head. He was blessed, or cursed, with an encyclopedic knowledge of electronics and an abrasive Irish temperament. Both qualities were to be much in evidence during the next thirteen days.

Like Speckart, Frampton was a former FAA employee who had joined Aviation Systems Associates on his retirement in 1973. His role with the federal agency had been as supervisory electronics engineer with the Airways Facility Division of the Western Region. In other words, he was an expert on instrument landing systems, and the first part of his testimony was devoted to explaining how these worked, in loving detail.

Whether Tucker judged it necessary for the jury to be given such an arcane gallimaufry of facts or whether he was trying to bludgeon them into submission can only be guessed at. Michael Brent probably understood most of it, but the remainder of the jury was largely composed of Californian housewives who were understandably baffled.

Presumably, Tucker was laying a foundation for what was to come, on the basis that no one with the expertise of Frampton could possibly be wrong about anything. In this he was to be sadly mistaken.

There was a storm coming. Its first feathery outriders appeared on the morning of Thursday, March 9, when Tucker began to ask Frampton if he knew of a phenomenon known as "incorrect signal sensing." Indeed he did, said Frampton, and he had found evidence of it on flight checks of the instrument landing system at Pago Pago made prior to the crash of Flight 806. The symptoms of this aberration were that an aircraft flying above the glide path would receive an instruction to climb rather than to reduce height. One already flying below it would be told by its instruments to descend still further.

This error, Frampton said, had been found on a flight check conducted on January 20, 1974, only ten days before the accident. With the aid of an enlarged recording chart from that test, pinned up in the well of the court by Tucker, he explained exactly what he meant.

Dombroff's demeanor in court was normally languid. Unless actively involved he appeared to pay little attention to what was going on. Now he leaped to attention as though stung by a hornet. This was potential disaster. If Tucker could prove that the glide slope portion of the instrument landing system on Pago Pago had been showing opposite indications, he need do nothing further to make his case against the government stick. From there it was a short step to showing that Captain Petersen had been an innocent victim of his instruments; that he had followed his glide path indicator and it had led him straight into the ground. Dombroff was not an electronics expert, but he could recognize the implication of what he was seeing and hearing. And so, he knew only too well, could the jury.

Tucker swelled with triumph as he carried Frampton through the damning evidence, tracing the lines on the graph paper that said "fly down" when they should have said "fly up."

As he did so, hurried consultations were taking place on the government bench. Sitting beside Dombroff was his own expert witness in the field of electronics, Dr. Richard McFarland. McFarland was being urgently pumped by Dombroff for a solution to the crisis.

To the young lawyer's surprise, McFarland seemed puzzled rather than worried. When Tucker switched his attention from the chart back to Frampton in the witness box, the government expert strolled across the court to examine it closely. With no change of expression he returned and sat down, putting a fatherly hand on Dombroff's shoulder.

"Don't worry," said McFarland. "Don't worry about a thing." He relaxed with a quiet smile.

But Dombroff continued to worry, as Tucker proceeded to get the maximum mileage out of his revelation. If he had stopped to think—if either of them had stopped to think— they would have realized that a fault of this nature, left uncorrected, would have carpeted the Samoan jungle with Boeing 707s, which had not happened. But until he could get McFarland on one side to discover what he meant, Dombroff was too worried to think. The case on which he had staked his reputation was about to be blown from under him.

Through that day and the next Frampton continued to testify, adding brick after brick to the solid wall over which

Dombroff had to climb to survive. He claimed that the glide slope facility appeared to have had a technical fault from the time of its installation in June 1973. He had found evidence of the false fly-down indication in records of tests conducted in August of that year.

Judge Byrne had a head cold and relieved his misery by overruling Dombroff every time the government attorney got up to make an objection, which was often. They broke for the weekend with the pall still hanging over Dombroff's head, and much of Monday, March 13 was spent looking at the cockpit of a Boeing 707 at Los Angeles airport. Cathcart had objected to this, saying that any layperson on seeing it would conclude that pilots had to be a special breed to understand such a confusion of instruments, and that this would hurt his case.

By the time the court reassembled with Frampton back in the witness box on the following day, Mark Dombroff was feeling much better. He ruined Judge Byrne's digestion by telling him that his cross-examination of Frampton would take at least two days and sat back to listen to further reams of abstruse technicality with renewed patience.

Byrne, his cold still lingering, grew increasingly testy and told Tucker he would rather be trying a railroad case. But the Pan Am attorney was not to be stopped from extracting every ounce of value from this, his star witness.

As the day wore on, Frampton was finding more and more faults with the Pago Pago glide slope system. Fluctuating voltage, he claimed, could cause it to send out a reversed signal, perhaps because of worn bearings in the mechanical modulator. They were almost, but not quite, back to the wet palm tree. Tucker must have winced at the memory. Frampton went on to criticize the siting of the glide slope transmitter, its lack of an uninterruptible power supply, and the fact that an emergency generator was not brought into operation each time an aircraft used the facility. In fact, if there was anything at all right with the instrument landing system on Pago Pago, it had totally escaped his notice. There grew a feeling that the pudding was being over-egged, that the jury might be swamped by a maze of technicality and forget the telling evidence of the reverse sensing, but Tucker plowed on.

By mid-morning on Wednesday, March 15, one person had certainly had enough: Judge Byrne. The air conditioning in the courtroom had broken down, not for the first time, and when Tucker began taking Frampton through the ramifications of some obscure FAA regulation, his patience finally snapped. He called counsel to his bench.

"I haven't said anything about the last four days of questions," Byrne said to Tucker, "because your style is probably far superior to any style I would attempt to use. But we've gone through tons of testimony, and until yesterday we never really got down to any opinion testimony. Now it may be true that they don't follow some FAA regulation—true or not true depending on the interpretation of the regulation—but I assume that what you're getting at is that some of these failures to follow these regulations had some effect on the flight of 806?"

That was so, said Tucker, on his dignity.

In that case, remarked Byrne, he might have noticed that his own witness was saying that it did no such thing.

"Well, it's hard to keep track," Tucker admitted. But lost in a maze of his own creation, he carried on. Dombroff, spying his chance, moved to strike that portion of Frampton's testimony, and Byrne was glad to oblige. If Tucker would not take the hint, he had to be taught a lesson. Finally, the Pan Am lawyer got the message and brought the marathon to a close.

Cathcart had first stab at cross-examination, but he was not about to do anything to save the government case from disaster. He was brief, but before Dombroff could step up to take his turn, for which he had been waiting with increasing impatience, Tucker approached the bench.

"I should have mentioned this earlier," he said, "but Mr. Frampton is hypertensive, and he does have a condition of arrhythmia. I don't know if I noticed any signs of distress at all, but I'm just wondering if we can leave a little early?"

It sounded odd coming from a man who had just kept Frampton in the witness box for nearly five days, but perhaps Tucker had a premonition that Dombroff's cross-examination was going to be bad for his witness's blood pressure. It was not destined to do Tucker's any good either.

The young lion licked his lips and waited for Frampton to be pronounced fit to continue.

———

EVER SINCE HIS talk with Richard McFarland, Mark Dombroff had been waiting for this moment. He had been involved with the Pago Pago case since September 1974, and since March 1977 it had occupied him full time. He had been commuting between Washington and Los Angeles on a weekly basis, spending so much time away from home that his marriage was coming under severe strain. The case of Flight 806 had taken up a large slice of his working career and had become his entire life. He was convinced that his future would depend on its outcome.

Dombroff was not a popular figure among the other lawyers in court, and he knew it. He lacked modesty, seeing no need for it, and was inclined to be less than respectful to his elders. He was brash, he was impetuous, and he thrived on the clash of personalities within the courtroom. He also—and this was his cardinal sin—made no effort to conceal his mirth when his peers fell over their feet. As often happened during the course of the trial.

Yet for all that, he was a likable young man with a winning smile. He was tall and he was handsome, with a shock of dark hair and a full mustache, and he had one telling advantage in court that set him aside from all the rest: he had done his homework. Though this was his first jury trial, and perhaps because of it, Dombroff had immersed himself totally in the case and planned his every move. Working entirely on his own with only a shared secretary, he had read every word and summarized every theory. All of it had gone down in an elaborate cross-index of his own invention. He was acting in self-defense, knowing the weight of legal talent ranged against him, and it paid off. Mark Dombroff was better prepared than any other lawyer in court, and it showed.

He had very clear ideas about what he wanted to do. Some of them were innovative, like the use of videotape, but others were things that he had learned at the knee of his lawyer father. He would present the maximum number of live witnesses, rather than rely on depositions, and most importantly, he would prepare them thoroughly for their cross-examinations.

Dombroff's witnesses, forewarned about what would be thrown at them, answered with frank assurance. Tucker's grew confused, contradicted themselves, and ended up by being exposed as incompetent or worse. This was certainly to be true of Mathew Frampton.

But then it seems probable that neither Frampton nor Tucker knew of the two great passions of Mark Dombroff's private life: his work as a semi-professional magician under the pseudonym of "Mark Andrew" and his obsession with the cases of Perry Mason. The combination was formidable. Dombroff was a man who delighted in pulling rabbits out of hats, and he had an insatiable taste for courtroom drama. When he stepped up to do battle with Frampton, he was to employ both talents fully.

Dombroff began by forcing Frampton to admit that he had never been to Pago Pago. For a man who had spent the past five days testifying in enormous depth about the facilities that existed on the island, it was a remarkable disclosure in itself. Pan American, it seemed, could cheerfully spend hundreds of thousands of dollars on lawyers' fees but would not give a free air ticket to their principal witness.

Then had he, asked Dombroff, conducted tests with the type of glide slope equipment installed on Pago Pago—the Wilcox Mk IC.

"No, sir," said Frampton.

But surely he had examined such equipment before formulating his opinions?

"No, sir," said Frampton.

While he was with the FAA, had he ever personally directed the installation of a glide slope facility?

"No," said Frampton. The "sir" had disappeared as he glared at Dombroff with a growing dislike.

Had he, then, supervised the on-site grading of such a facility?

"No," said Frampton.

The jury looked at the dumpy figure in the witness box with puzzlement shading into disbelief. Was this the same man who had been so confident in his technical criticism for the past five days? Did he really know what he had been talking about?

Dombroff, scenting blood and becoming lost in his Walter Mitty dream of Perry Mason, began to advance across the well of the court toward the witness box. Judge Byrne ordered him sharply back to the attorneys' podium.

"I'm sorry," said Dombroff, his reverie disrupted. Byrne, clearly thinking of Frampton's blood pressure, called time for the day.

Next morning, March 16, the storm broke. Dombroff, who had been freewheeling through an examination of Frampton's career, asked him whether he'd had any contact with the aviation authorities in New Zealand.

"No," said Frampton, puzzled.

Dombroff showed him a roll of paper from a flight test recording machine carried by Air New Zealand. Did Frampton know, he asked, why Air New Zealand made flight test recordings of FAA navigational facilities in the South Pacific?

At last it was a question Frampton could answer. Yes, he did know. There was an agreement between New Zealand and the FAA to share the inspection work. On Pago Pago, he believed, the two organizations made alternate checks.

Dombroff appeared satisfied. The jury, and Frampton, wondered what the devil he was getting at. Other than the difference in the type of machine and the format of the recording, Dombroff wanted to know, were there any differences between the FAA tests and the New Zealand tests?

He would hope, replied Frampton, that there were none.

For a while they talked almost amicably about the meaning of the markings on the graph paper and discussed whether one system was more accurate than the other. Frampton even began to congratulate Dombroff on his powers of observation and technical expertise. Cordially, Dombroff established with him that the fly-up signal from the glide slope transmitter was recorded on the left-hand side of the paper and the fly-down signal on the right side.

They looked at the lines on one of the recordings, which were rather like the trace on a barograph. "As I recall your earlier testimony," said Dombroff, "this is an example of what is known as reverse sensing. Is that right?"

"That is correct," said Frampton.

"So," continued Dombroff, getting the point firmly home, "if the airplane is below the glide slope and should get a fly-up signal, he actually gets a fly-down signal. Is that right?"

"That is what is indicated here," said Frampton.

"Okay," said Dombroff, seemingly unconcerned, "that's a New Zealand flight check recording, isn't it?"

Frampton agreed that it was.

"And I think you indicated to Mr. Tucker that exhibit 385, which is a roll of New Zealand flight check recordings, had additional examples of reverse sensing. Do you recall that testimony?"

"I do," said Frampton.

"Reverse sensing, sir, and correct me if I am wrong," Dombroff continued smoothly, "is a very dangerous condition, is it not?"

Frampton was only too happy to agree. "Highly so, yes," he said.

"In other words, if an airplane should be receiving a fly-up signal, he's actually going to be descending even further if he follows his glide slope instrumentation."

"That's absolutely correct," Frampton agreed. Together they went through all the New Zealand flight check recordings of the glide slope installation at Pago Pago. Frampton cheerfully identified reverse sensing in every one of them.

"Hmm," said Dombroff, reflectively. "Did you find reverse sensing in the FAA flight check recordings?"

"No, sir," Frampton replied. "Not on Pago Pago from the time we are talking about; from commissioning to immediately after the accident."

"Sir, did you ever wonder *why* you only found the reverse sensing in the New Zealand flight check recordings and not in those made by the FAA during the same six- or seven-month period?"

"Yes, I did," Frampton said, growing uneasy.

"Did you ever conclude why that was so?"

"No, I did not."

Dombroff struck. *"Isn't it so, sir, because Air New Zealand's flight check recordings are reversed?"*

Judge Byrne interrupted. "Mr. Dombroff..." he began, but Perry Mason was not to be deprived of his triumph by some interfering judge.

Dombroff went on: "And the right-hand side of a New Zealand flight check recording is the fly-up side, and the left-hand side is the fly-down side?"

Frampton was visibly shaken. "I can't accept that," he mumbled.

"Sir, you don't know, do you?" demanded Dombroff.

Frampton stalled. "I know what a standard crossover looks like in accordance with the FAA documents which

define it, and I know what reverse sensing is from having
seen this phenomenon, which takes place rarely, but when
it does take place it's usually at an installation prior to
commissioning, when it's recognized and the facility is
adjusted to correct that situation."

It was not an answer to the question, but Dombroff was
happy to let it go. He drew Frampton's attention to one of
the New Zealand charts and to one of the lines on the left-
hand side that Frampton had earlier pointed out as a fly-
down indication. Written on it were a few words in
green ink.

"What does that comment say?" asked Dombroff.

Frampton hesitated. "It says 'fly-up off meter,'" he said
finally.

Dombroff corrected him slightly. "It says '440 microamps fly-up off meter.' Is that right?"

"That's correct," Frampton admitted.

For good measure, Dombroff made him read what was
written on the graph paper again.

"Did you make any attempt at all to reconcile the
comment saying it's a full fly-up with your conclusion that
it was a full fly-down?"

"Yes, I did."

"What did you conclude after making that attempt,
sir?"

Frampton began to bluster. He said, "I couldn't accept
the nonstandard procedure, which is quite obviously a very
dangerous procedure. If we're going to accept this, Mr.
Dombroff, then the possibility that you are suggesting could
result in some very dangerous adjustments to existing
facilities."

It was not good enough. "Sir," said Dombroff,
dangerously polite, "it's not dangerous, is it, if the flight

inspectors and technicians involved with the New Zealand flight crews know that New Zealand reverses the side of its paper, is it?"

"I don't know," said Frampton. "I can interpret what is on the recording."

"Sir, you don't really know, as you sit here today, whether or not New Zealand does in fact reverse the sides of its paper, do you?"

Frampton waffled. Dombroff repeated the question. Frampton admitted that he did not know what New Zealand did.

"And if you are wrong, sir," continued Dombroff relentlessly, "about the way you interpret the New Zealand flight checks, then all your opinions about reverse sensing are also wrong. Isn't that true?"

Frampton would not admit it. He struggled through a long answer that meant nothing and got him nowhere. Dombroff waited patiently for him to finish and asked him to listen to the question again.

"No," said Frampton desperately. "That isn't true."

But it was true, and the whole court could sense it. Tucker's contention that the FAA had permitted a criminally dangerous fault to exist in the Pago Pago instrument landing system had come crashing down.

It had been founded on a cornerstone that was not only false but that the simplest of checks would have shown to be false. All the evidence was there, right in front of them. McFarland had spotted it immediately. New Zealand flight check recorders ran in the opposite direction to those used by the FAA; that was all there was to it. There was no reverse sensing at Pago Pago. There never had been any reverse sensing at Pago Pago. For Tucker, no less than for Frampton, it was a disaster. Pan American had been shown

to be incompetents at best—and liars at worst. They had
tried to gull the court on a vital issue with a stupid
fabrication. The jury would not easily forgive them.

Mark Dombroff had made his point, but he was not
finished with Frampton yet. He was enjoying himself too
much.

The unhappy Frampton was forced to admit that he
had never tried to contact Air New Zealand to find out why
the discrepancy existed between their recordings and those
of the FAA. By this time, he was fervently wishing he had.
Dombroff pinned him neatly with Morton's Fork. Was he
claiming that the New Zealand check pilots were not doing
their job properly, or had the FAA been incompetent?
Since on Frampton's interpretation one had found the
installation faulty and the other had not, yet neither had
reported the alleged reverse sensing, it had to be one or the
other. Frampton's gray thatch almost slipped beneath the
edge of the witness box as he withered before the semantic
assault.

By chance, Dombroff had chosen a good day for his
triumph. The Israeli Chief Justice, Mr. Justice Shamgar,
was visiting the court that morning and sat beside Judge
Byrne on the bench. Now Dombroff had an international
reputation.

Dombroff romped happily through the afternoon
session, adding to Tucker's discomfort by having Frampton
disclose that he, like Speckart, had worked for thousands of
hours on the case at twenty dollars an hour. Tucker must
have reflected that incompetence carried a high price tag in
these days of inflation.

———

NEXT DAY WAS FRIDAY, St. Patrick's Day. The jury had sent Judge Byrne a card to honor the occasion, and green ties had broken out in the courtroom like a sudden rash of verdigris. Everyone was happy except Frampton, who had to face another full day of grilling by Dombroff and, presumably, Tucker.

Dombroff pressed home his advantage from every conceivable angle, doing his best to make the electronics man look stupid, and frequently succeeding. But after a while even he began to strike the law of diminishing returns, scoring fewer points from the interminable exchanges. Judge Byrne began to interject, telling Dombroff to keep it short, something he had never done with Tucker. There was a feeling in the air that everyone had seen enough of Mathew Frampton, and when Dombroff announced at the end of the day that he might well be carrying on through Tuesday, Byrne's face was a study.

"It's not that I don't enjoy listening to Mr. Frampton," he said. "I don't mean that . . ." But he did mean that, exactly. It was Tuesday morning before a weary Tucker could start his re-examination, and there was nothing he could do to reverse the calamity. In a desultory fashion he tried to make light of Frampton's lack of paper qualifications, presenting him as a practical man who worked with his hands. This was a clear play for the jury's sympathy, but it failed to work. Practical man or not, Frampton had fouled up. The most important single element in Pan American's case had been lost beyond recall.

NINETEEN

TUCKER PERSEVERED. He had no other choice. He could console himself with the thought that even if his case against the government was looking distinctly shaky, it would still be up to the plaintiffs to prove Pan Am guilty of willful misconduct. With so much vital evidence already suppressed and with no precedent in their favor, that would not be an easy task.

His next witness was George Harry Saunders, a young Canadian aerodynamicist with a lengthy list of qualifications, who was a lecturer at the University of Southern California. Saunders was a likable man who made an instant impression on the jury. Tragically, he was destined to be dead within six months, killed in a mid-air collision over San Diego.

Saunders's task had been to set up a computer program simulating what might happen to a Boeing 707 on the approach to Pago Pago under varying wind conditions. There was one oddity about his experiment: though he had fed into the computer the same airspeed as Flight 806 as well as the same flap setting, he had chosen a weight for his hypothetical aircraft some 2,000 pounds lighter. Why he did this was never made clear. As Cathcart, himself a pilot, was swift to point out, the extra weight would make quite a different to the performance.

Both Cathcart and Dombroff objected violently to the admission of Saunders's evidence, claiming that it was immaterial, irrelevant, based on hearsay, and totally without foundation. They were overruled.

It was all a question of "if." Saunders had found that if there had been a sudden decrease in head wind of about 20 knots, the aircraft's rate of descent would have increased to 3,000 feet a minute after ten seconds. If there had been a wind shear of one-half knot per hundred feet combined with a down-draft of thirty feet per minute, it would have been sufficient to have caused the crash. If, if, if. The problem the jury had to decide, bearing in mind Hardy's shaken evidence, was whether such conditions had existed on Pago Pago that night. Hypotheses were poor substitutes for facts, however ably presented.

When Cathcart rose to cross-examine, Saunders told him that under the conditions he had been given to work with there had come a time, four and a half seconds before impact, when no action by the crew could possibly have avoided the crash. He had been assuming that Flight 806 had encountered wind shear seventeen seconds before the accident.

Cathcart seized on the point. Did that mean that in the intervening twelve and a half seconds there would have been things the crew could have done to avoid disaster?

"Yes," admitted Saunders.

"You will agree," Cathcart went on, "that captains of aircraft are not supposed to just sit there and let things happen. They are supposed to monitor the approach and keep the aircraft under control. Is that correct?"

"Yes, they are," Saunders said. The frank honesty of his answers almost compensated for the damage they were doing to Tucker's case. He agreed that if the crew of Flight 806 had recognized the need for action they could have applied more power. There had been sufficient power available to regain level flight and to start a climb. They could also have retracted the undercarriage and pulled up the flaps to improve performance.

As Cathcart hardly needed to point out, none of these things had been done. And he produced an interesting statistic from the Boeing manual, with which Saunders agreed. It appeared that at landing speeds, the difference in momentum between an aircraft weighing 247,000 pounds and one weighing 180,000 pounds was more than 22,000,000 foot pounds—an increase of 65 percent. The greater the momentum, the more time and control force would be needed to correct the flight path, but with the higher approach speed, less time would be available. Therefore, heavyweight landings required more attention to flight path and speed control.

These figures were not chosen by Cathcart at random. The actual landing weight of Flight 806 was 247,000 pounds, or a little more. It would have weighed 180,000 pounds without the fuel it still carried in its tanks. Nevertheless, this was a slightly low blow by Cathcart. It ignored the fact that 29,600 pounds of that fuel was a legally required reserve in case of diversion to another airfield.

The next testimony, a deposition from Anthony Murray, the Pan Am operations supervisor in Auckland, made this clear. Murray had been the man responsible for loading the fuel on board Flight 806. The decision to put the extra stored fuel on board, Murray said, had been made by a Mr. Harracks and a Mr. Chapman, who were Pan Am's manager of passenger services and manager of maintenance at Auckland. Captain Petersen had played no part in it.

Murray's deposition was brief and, apparently, routine —a reading into the record of essential but undramatic fact. There was no knowing at that stage that his inquisitors in Auckland had neglected to ask him one vital question, and that the answer to that question, when it finally emerged, was to decide the outcome of the trial.

———

IT WAS MARCH 23, the baseball season was fast approaching, and Judge Byrne announced that everyone could have a week off. They all needed the break. Before they could take it, however, Cathcart waded in with a powerful motion that he hoped would make his case against the government secure. It certainly needed some bolstering at that point. Having changed his mind and rejected Dombroff's offer of $1,600,000 in the hope of getting more, he now found himself facing the real possibility that there would be nothing from this source. Largely to save expense, the plaintiffs had been riding their opponents' mounts, relying on Pan Am's expert witnesses to make the case against the government, and on Dombroff to defeat Pan Am on their behalf. Now the first of those horses was almost at the end of its run and looking distinctly lame. Something had to be done.

At considerable length, Cathcart made a simple argument: because the FAA had assumed a duty to regulate the aviation industry, they should be held jointly liable when something went wrong and people were killed. It was a brave try.

"What you are saying," said Byrne, "is that there has been lousy training of pilots. Pan Am is negligent because of that lousy training, and the government is negligent for failing to upervise Pan American so that the pilots will be trained better."

He seemed to find that idea attractive. If the government was going to regulate an industry so closely, why should they not share the responsibility? But there was one mournful snag: Congress had not passed any bill to that effect. And if they ever did, the result would be so far-reaching that Washington would have to be rebuilt to accommodate all the extra lawyers.

Cathcart battled on. "The proof in this case," he said, "will be a history over a significant period of time when Pan American engaged in practices set forth in the ALPA report, the Thomas report, and the Hudson documents that the FAA knew or should have known about. When they did know about them, they had an affirmative responsibility to put a halt to it so as to protect the public from the very event which occurred here."

The jury might have pricked up their ears at this, having heard nothing of these intriguing reports. But the discussion was in private, and the jury members were in their back room, playing cards and doing needlepoint. The works of Hudson and Thomas were not for them.

What legal, moral, equitable, or philosophical reason could there be, asked Cathcart with a flourish, for a government agency to be given the responsibility of passing regulations and then to suffer no penalty for not enforcing them? "We can go back to the common law that the king can do no wrong, but even though that came over as a stowaway on the Mayflower, there is no reason to continue to perpetrate that doctrine."

"Except," Byrne reminded him gently, "that there *is* sovereign immunity."

Cathcart acknowledged the point. "There certainly is," he said. "Unfortunately."

But he would not give up. He quoted, ironically, from a judgment by Judge Peirson Hall, who had said, "If the repetitive emphasis by Congress on safety does not refer to the safety of individuals and does not impose a duty, the violation of which is an actionable wrong, then one is led to wonder just whose safety Congress is talking about, or if there is some safety that is in the public interest which does not include the saving of human lives. So often, unfortunately, lawyers and judges overlook the fundamentals."

Had Judge Hall been trying the case, would he have been moved by his own words? Judge Byrne was not. That judgment, he said, had nothing to do with what they were talking about. He rejected Cathcart's motion. The trial went on.

———

MARCH 24 WAS GOOD FRIDAY. The court sat anyway, making up for the time lost by Cathcart's motion and squeezing in two witnesses who had traveled from the East Coast.

The first of these was the elusive Arthur Merel Smith, whose testimony had caused such heated debate weeks before on the subject of spectrographic analysis of engine noise.

Smith was now allowed to testify, but each time his evidence veered toward a finding that wind shear had caused the fan blades to stall there was a barrage of sustained objections from Cathcart and Dombroff. The result was Hamlet without the Prince of Denmark, and the jury was left wondering what it all meant, if anything.

Charles O. Miller, known to his friends as Chuck, was a very different witness. A Falstaffian figure who had added a good few pounds since the days when he squeezed into the cockpit of a jet fighter as a test pilot, he was the founder, owner, and principal consultant of Systems Safety Incorporated. Miller was a man of many parts. His career had spanned flying with the Marine Corps, test piloting for Chance Vought, university lecturing in southern California, and directorship of the Bureau of Aviation Safety at the NTSB. He was also a professional safety engineer and was studying to become a lawyer. In the Pago Pago trial he testified on human factors, wind shear, and virtually anything else that William Tucker cared to ask him.

In soccer terms, Chuck Miller was a sweeper. He supported the opinions voiced by Pan Am expert witnesses on every subject, including the suspect fly-down signal. This he did with solid efficiency, to the annoyance of Mark Dombroff, who failed in an attempt to get his testimony stricken from the record. It was, said Dombroff, mere pyramiding of opinions. And so it was. But Miller got away with it and went happily on his way. Whether his evidence added anything to the credibility of the Pan American case was another question, but he was Tucker's last witness and he survived intact. With all that had gone before, this was no mean achievement.

TWENTY

AFTER TWO AND A HALF MONTHS, the Pan American case against the United States government finally closed. It had not been a roaring success. Cathcart, for his part, decided not to call any witnesses. He could see that the glide slope issue was a dead duck, wind shear appeared almost incapable of proof, and though it remained possible that the jury would be influenced by the FAA's failure to put lights in the black hole approach, he was not optimistic. In any case, there was nothing he could add to the evidence on this issue. He left the stage to Dombroff to mount his defense, hoping with expectation that yet more harm would come to Pan Am.

Dombroff could have made his opening statement at the start of the trial, but he had reserved it for this moment. He reasoned that the jury would have forgotten most of what he had to say in the intervening weeks, and though several of his advisors disagreed with this course, he overruled them. His plan was to be simple and direct, where Tucker had been complex and obscure, and he would pull dramatic visual aids out of his conjurer's hat and flourish them in front of the jury. He would give them basic issues that they could understand and not overburden them with technical jargon.

His plan started badly. Before the jury could even take their seats, Dombroff was involved in a heated argument with Judge Byrne over a large three-dimensional model of Pago Pago that he intended to use to illustrate his speech. Tucker objected, saying it was not to scale, and Byrne ruled that he must take it away and bring in a witness later to prove that it was accurate. Dombroff was furious. The model, he claimed, had been agreed as admissible in evidence a week before. Because of that he had sent his expert witness home, and now his opening speech would have to be redrafted and would take much longer. In any case, the model had never been represented as being totally to scale. It was purely for illustrative purposes.

Tucker seemed to be enjoying this piece of legal gamesmanship immensely. He was cutting the upstart Dombroff down to size, depriving him of one of his precious gimmicks, and he sensed that the judge was on his side. The model, he complained, looked more like Keokuk, Iowa (which is one of the flatter parts of America) than it did Pago Pago. Anyway, Dombroff had made a written claim that it was in scale both horizontally and vertically. So there.

Dombroff fought back. Byrne wavered, irritated by the waste of time, then finally ordered Dombroff to take the model away and get on with his speech. In cheeky reprisal, Dombroff moved that the whole case against the government should be dismissed there and then.

"Denied," said Byrne grimly. Dombroff shrugged and went to work.

But progress was not to be so simple. No sooner had Dombroff completed his opening statement in mid-afternoon than the jury members were sent back once again to their cards and their crocheting.

This time it seemed they might never come back, for Tucker stood up to reveal that he had uncovered the ultimate horror: a book on sale in Los Angeles that was devoted to the Pago Pago crash. It was entitled *Clipper 806: The Anatomy of an Air Disaster*.

That was bad enough, for how could the minds of the jury remain unsullied after reading a book with a title like that? Worse still, from Tucker's point of view, was the fact that the author, John Godson, had clearly taken the side of the passengers. He had engendered sympathy for those who had been killed. The effrontery of it had shaken Tucker to the core. "When I had finished it," he said, "I felt for the plaintiffs."

Tucker had a problem: he had already made one motion for a mistrial, over the DC 10 crash at Los Angeles, and he did not want to make a habit of it, but . . . "I think it is highly inflammatory and in favor of the plaintiffs."

Godson, he claimed, had clearly interviewed Michael Rogers (in fact they only exchanged letters) and several other witnesses.

He had included material that would not even be in the trial, some of which had been ruled out of order, and he had apparently had access to material that the attorneys had not seen.

"The only people that would be happy about this book being out are the plaintiffs," Tucker said. "He has a lot to say about the government, he has a little bit to say about Pan Am, and he has some words for Boeing. He didn't miss out anybody on the defense side of the table."

Tucker did not realize how lucky he was; Godson had made no mention of the Hudson report, the Thomas report, the pilots' training records, the statements by the Pan Am San Francisco captains, or several other items that would have destroyed the Pan American case.

Byrne, who feared jokingly that a rush to the bookshops by all the lawyers in court might turn *Clipper 806* into a best seller, had a dual problem. First, should he read the book himself, and second, and what could he tell the jury that would not inflame their curiosity?

In typical fashion, he decided to put off the decision to another day.

But the problem did not go away. Tucker was back on the following afternoon with a firm motion for a mistrial. Dombroff had now read the book, and he thought it was more damaging to Boeing than to Pan American. All the same, he urged Byrne not to read it, being mindful that the case against the government would finally be decided by the judge and not the jury. As for Byrne, he was reluctant to grant a mistrial on the possibility that one of the jurors might have read it. On the other hand, if he tried to find out whether or not they had, it might encourage them to do so. The fate of the Pago Pago trial teetered in the balance, placed there by the work of an author who may not have known that his book would be published in mid-action.

They argued and they argued. Dombroff wanted the jury warned about the book; Tucker did not want so much as the title mentioned. Byrne said he would think about it.

Next day he had reached a decision of sorts: he would not read *Clipper 806* himself. That still left the question of what to tell the jury, and Byrne was worried that the mere fact of telling the jury that a book had been written would indicate that there was something worth writing about, that someone was at fault. And so the wrangle continued, while the jury, all unknowing, amused themselves in the jury room as best they could. Cathcart had now read the book, and even he found it "highly prejudicial." Godson had achieved the feat of pleasing no one.

Byrne began to toy with the idea of using poetic license when describing the book to the jury, at which one of the Boeing attorneys, Sally Treweek, complained that there was too much poetic license in it already.

They fell to discussing the state of the courtroom air conditioning. Nothing was decided.

On Wednesday, April 5, the problem was finally solved when Byrne produced a form of words to read to the jury. Everyone was reasonably happy, except Sally Treweek, who objected to the name of the book being mentioned. Byrne overruled her. If he told them about the book and failed to mention the title, the jury would "bust their breeches" to find out what it was, he pointed out.

As it turned out, none of them had read it, seen it, or heard anything at all about it. Which must have been disappointing for Mr. Godson, but just as well for everyone else. In the meantime, hours of arguments and thousands of dollars had been wasted. Not that there was anything unusual about that.

―――――

HIDDEN in the interstices of this legal mess, like a vein of gold in a lump of purest dross, was the testimony of Dombroff's first witness, Dr. Richard McFarland. McFarland, the man who had saved the government attorney from disaster on the issue of the reverse-sensing glide slope, was an expert witness of an entirely different character from those who had gone before.

Unlike most of the others, McFarland had been to Pago Pago. An experienced pilot as well as an electronics wizard, he had spent five days testing the instrument landing facility himself. He not only knew about the Wilcox Mk IC glide slope transmitter installed there but he had acted as consultant to the company that made the device. In short, Dr. McFarland knew what he was talking about. From the moment he took the witness stand, it showed.

McFarland, at the age of forty-nine, was professor of electrical engineering and director of the Avionics Engineering Center at Ohio University. When Dombroff had hired him at a fee of $250 a day, he had insisted on getting first-hand experience of the Pago Pago facility because he had heard disturbing rumors about it. Dombroff gave him carte blanche. He was provided with an FAA aircraft complete with testing equipment and allowed to make as many flights as he wanted. It was striking evidence not only of McFarland's integrity but also of the effort and money that Dombroff was prepared to put into the case.

In contrast to Frampton, Hodges, and Hardy, McFarland testified in layperson's language. There was hardly a single mathematical calculation as he told the court that neither in his own tests nor in those of others that he had reviewed was there any sign of reverse sensing. He had, of course, talked to the New Zealand authorities and confirmed that their test instruments were set up in the reverse direction to those used by the FAA.

Dombroff questioned him about the effect on the glide slope of possible fluctuations in electrical power. With reducing voltage, McFarland replied, the strength of the signal would diminish, but it would still give the same information. This would be true down to about 60 volts from the standard operating current of 115 to 120. If the voltage dropped much lower than that, the glide slope would simply cease to operate and a warning flag would appear on the pilot's instrument panel.

All this he had tested personally. In fact, after hearing Hodges's evidence, he had gone back and done it again using the exact voltages Hodges predicted would cause the equipment to give a false reading. At no time did he get a hard fly-down signal.

At this point, Dombroff produced one of his gimmicks. Or, as he would have put it, innovations. The jury had already seen a glide slope instrument of the kind fitted to Flight 806, but the one shown them by Tucker was "dead." It gave no indication of the way in which the needles moved, of what Captain Petersen would actually have seen in the cockpit as he made his final approach.

Dombroff had come up with the idea of equipping the same instrument with batteries and switches so that his witnesses could demonstrate exactly what they were talking about in terms of fly-up and fly-down indications and all the rest. It was very simple, a classic example of a picture being worth a thousand words. Tucker, who had expended thousands of words in the same quest, now expressed a few more in violent protest against the device. Byrne seemed doubtful, listened to long arguments from each side, then relented and allowed it to be used. Dombroff, sensing that the tide of rulings might be turning his way, promptly asked for permission to have his model of Pago Pago brought back into court as well. With numerous caveats about its scale, the request was granted. Now the jury had a graphic presentation in front of them to match the words.

McFarland ran through his tests, aided by a videotape of an actual experimental run recorded in the FAA aircraft he was flying. It was becoming clear that Dombroff either had sufficient clout to get better facilities than his opponents or had more imagination. Perhaps it was a combination of both. At all events, as McFarland said repeatedly, "I saw no unsafe condition," he sounded eminently believable.

Tucker intervened to take McFarland through a voir dire examination of his credentials that began to sound suspiciously like a cross-examination. The questions and answers were tart, as though the two men had taken an instant dislike to one another. This was understandable on Tucker's part: he was facing the man who had stolen his metaphorical trousers.

The Pan Am attorney was at a disadvantage, because McFarland clearly knew the subject better than he did. At one point, he challenged the scientist to tell what he knew of an alleged "leaking cable" to the middle marker beacon.

"What type of leakage are you talking about?" asked McFarland.

Tucker replied portentously, "I am talking, sir, about power leakage of five-tenths of a megohm on that particular cable, and its effect on the glide slope transmitter, and particularly with respect to the reduction of voltage available to that transmitter."

The court tensed. Was this some new and vital issue? Would this be Tucker's revenge?

McFarland regarded the big lawyer with some scorn. "Mr. Tucker," he said, "we would not leak ohms." He went on to explain, as to a slightly dim five-year-old, that the leakage of current was expressed in microamperes, or milliamperes, or possibly even in amperes, all of which were measurements of electric current. But never, never in ohms.

Tucker glared at him, sparing a sideways glance for his own expert who had prompted the question and caused him to appear an idiot. He dropped the subject as though it had become too hot and asked McFarland if he had investigated the possibility that the glide slope unit had been struck by lightning. Lightning was simple. Let him play his fancy tricks with that.

"No, sir," said McFarland, slightly baffled. It was the first time anyone had mentioned lightning. Where had Tucker dredged that one up?

At length Dombroff, who had been dozing in contented reverie while his pet d'Artagnan fenced off Pan Am's Cardinal Richelieu with consummate ease, rose to protest that Tucker was going far beyond the bounds of a voir dire examination. Byrne overruled him, but finally even he lost patience. He sent the jury out in an attempt to discover in private just what Tucker was getting at.

It transpired that Tucker was trying to show that there had been radical changes in the Pago Pago glide slope installation between the time of the accident and the time McFarland made his tests. The device had been struck by lightning, certain parts had been changed, and an uninterruptible power supply had been installed. McFarland's experiments had therefore been meaningless in terms of the conditions that existed on the night of January 30, 1974.

Not so, contended Dombroff. He admitted that there had been a few changes but none that would have affected the result of the tests substantially, except the uninterruptible power supply. And that had been bypassed by McFarland when making his experiments. He added virtuously, "The FAA did not stop making what they considered improvements to the system just so that they could accommodate the Justice Department."

Byrne considered the point. All right, he said, changes had been made before McFarland made his tests in February 1976. "For whatever it is worth," he added. He supported Tucker's objection to the offer of proof, but the ruling did not seem to affect what the jury was hearing. McFarland continued to insist that the glide slope was perfectly in order and that it would not have been affected by any fluctuation in the power supply. He did admit, when Tucker began his cross-examination proper, that if the power supply was cut off altogether there would have been a momentary fly-down indication in the aircraft when the current was restored. But then there would have been a warning flag on the instrument to alert the pilot.

Tucker went on, with notable lack of success, to enmesh McFarland in the abstruse technicalities beloved of Frampton and Hodges. He put him through copious calculations, none of which seemed to lead anywhere. Then, at length, he turned to the vital question of reverse sensing.

"Sir," asked Tucker, "before you got involved in this case, have you ever seen any flight check recordings in which the cross pointer indicator, or the course deviation indicator, moved in a direction 180 degrees out of phase with the direction in which your flight recorder moves, and the direction on which the pen in the FAA type flight recorders move?"

"Yes, sir," said McFarland.

"You've seen those before?" Tucker could hardly believe his luck. Could it be that the great Dr. McFarland was going to support his theory? He followed up swiftly.

"And those were in cases, sir, where actual reverse sensing occurred. Isn't that correct?"

McFarland regarded him calmly. "No, sir. I said I have seen recordings when it went in opposite directions."

"You've seen FAA recordings where it went in the opposite direction?"

"That wasn't your question," McFarland replied. "I have seen them because I used to make them that way, Mr. Tucker."

Mr. Tucker was not amused.

The one point he did score during his cross-examination of McFarland was an admission from the scientist that the ground in front of the glide slope transmitter did not meet the criterion of flatness that he himself had laid down when drafting regulations for the FAA. However, McFarland said, he had since relaxed these standards in the light of the experience; it was not the ground that mattered but the behavior of the radio beam in space.

Tucker's cross-examination carried through until Friday, April 7, when Cathcart stepped up to try his luck. Cathcart had a double option: he could either try to break down McFarland's testimony, which would strengthen the case against the government but weaken it against Pan Am, or he could do the reverse. He took one look at the witness and decided on the latter course. It was safer.

What Cathcart established from McFarland was quite simple: because of the narrowing of the beam toward the transmitter, it took a smaller variation from the glide slope to register a large indication in the cockpit as an aircraft approached the runway. Captain Petersen would therefore have had a strong warning that he was flying too low and descending too fast as he flew toward the middle marker.

He would have had a full fly-up signal, McFarland said, from the time he slipped forty-six feet beneath the glide path to the time he hit the ground.

It was the end of the week and everyone was tired. Constant mistakes were being made in the technical calculations that Cathcart, like Tucker, seemed to regard as an essential part of the case. At length, Byrne called it a day before Tucker could get started on his re-cross-examination and confuse everyone further. Cathcart was moved to remark that the jury ought to get a medal for their perseverance.

McFarland had to fly off to Oklahoma City in his own aircraft that weekend and did not get back until Tuesday of the following week. When he returned, he scarcely endeared himself to Tucker by proclaiming that in his view the Pago Pago glide slope was an excellent facility and had been so on the night of the accident. "I think it's an outstanding example," he said, "of a glide slope performing in the role that we expect it to perform."

Tucker tried hard to shake him, pointing out that McFarland's own test measurements had sometimes varied by as much as .14 of a degree (hardly measurable under flying conditions). McFarland was not impressed. If you asked any twelve people to measure this courtroom, he said, no doubt they would all come up with slightly different measurements.

McFarland was not Tucker's favorite witness. More to his taste, however, was Donald Wilmer Beran: Dombroff's answer to Hardy, "the Rain Drop King."

Beran was a meteorologist with the usual list of exalted qualifications, though by this time the jury was learning to regard such things with less reverence. He had, it transpired, reviewed the same evidence as Dr. Hardy for the weather on Pago Pago that night but had come to a different conclusion. Asked by Dombroff whether it was possible to work out from this data what the weather had been during the last thirty seconds of the approach of Flight 806, Beran said simply, "I don't think you could do it."

There was, said Beran, just not enough information available to be able to state with accuracy what was happening to the weather at that place and time. It would certainly have been impossible for an observer on the ground to predict the location or timing of wind shear. What they were talking about was a mesoscale analysis—a study of weather conditions during a period of thirty seconds over a distance of a few thousand feet. It could only be done by experts using a dense array of surface observations, launching radiosonde balloons every few minutes, and probably using sensitive radar as well. None of these things was available at Pago Pago, ergo, it could not be done.

Dombroff had few questions, Cathcart had none, and it was left to Tucker to rub some salve on his bruises. It was time he got his own back.

"Have you," he asked casually, interrupting another line of questioning, "ever made a formal study of convective cells as they exist in the South Pacific?"

"No, sir," admitted Beran.

"Have you ever made a formal study of the weather patterns as they exist in the area surrounding Pago Pago by three hundred miles?"

"No, sir."

This was better. Just for a change, one of Dombroff's witnesses was being made to confess ignorance. It had happened often enough to his own. But before Tucker could capitalize on the advantage, Dombroff staged a diversion. He jumped up to tell Judge Byrne that he had found yet another book that might prejudice the jury. This one was called *Jet Roulette: Flying Is a Game of Chance*, and it contained a chapter on the Pago Pago crash that, Dombroff claimed, had more inaccuracies than the whole of *Clipper 806*.

Dombroff also decided to tell Byrne that he would be calling another witness, one whom Tucker had not been expecting. There was a cry of strangled fury from the Pan Am bench, and time was spent in heated arguments around the judge while Beran relaxed and collected his thoughts.

Byrne was perplexed. "I really don't understand," he said. "After four months of this case [in fact it was only three, but it certainly felt like more] I would have thought some of the gamesmanship would be out of it. It's this great desire to wait until the last minute. Let's at least extend courtesies to each other—after three years in this case—to give the other side an opportunity to know who they are going to have to examine."

"It was nothing to do with gamesmanship, Your Honor," protested Dombroff. Byrne gave him a long hard look. The argument continued fitfully until the lunch interval, by which time Beran had gotten his breath back.

Tucker returned to the attack in the afternoon, asking the meteorologist whether he had made any analysis at all from the data of the radiosonde balloons.

"No, sir," replied Beran.

Had he made any calculation of the wind direction or velocity?

"No, sir."

"Did you make any determination as to what the storm motion was at Pago Pago within the thirty minutes prior to and the thirty minutes subsequent to the crash?" asked Tucker.

"No, sir."

"Did you attempt to determine the velocity of the storm as it passed over Pago Pago weather station?"

"No, sir."

Tucker then asked Beran his opinion of Dr. Hardy's professional reputation. "He's an excellent radar meteorologist," was the reply.

It had been a short, effective, and destructive piece of cross-examination. Though Dombroff came back to have Beran say that the available information had been insufficient to do these calculations, the damage had been done. Tucker had succeeded in restoring a little of Hardy's shattered credibility.

Like any set of eyewitnesses, those who were present on Pago Pago that night had varying tales to tell. Many of the variations that were to come before the jury, causing no little confusion, concerned the power supply. Had there been an interruption, a flicker, a series of fluctuations, or had there been none of these things? Who could remember with certainty that the lights had dimmed a fraction seconds before a major catastrophe drove all else from their minds? Yet here they were, standing in a witness box four years and thousands of miles away, expected to dredge their memories on oath. It was hardly surprising that some tripped over their previous statements and were pounced on by lawyers eager for inconsistency.

One such was William Arnett.

Arnett was a radio maintenance man at Pago Pago airport, but he had a variety of duties. One of them had been to turn on the approach lights about half an hour before the arrival of Flight 806, at which time he noticed that the VASI lights were also working as they should. He had then gone to the transmitter building, a mile beyond the middle marker, which housed an array of communications equipment.

While he was there, Arnett told Dombroff, he noticed a brief power failure of about two seconds. The lights had gone out and then come on again. It had happened at 11:40 p.m., which was the time of the crash.

Arnett was Dombroff's witness, but he did not seem to be saying what the government attorney wanted to hear. Had he not told a Mr. Bracken, Dombroff wanted to know, that there had been no power failure that night?

Arnett simply could not remember. He could only recall seeing the fire about five minutes after the power failure, thinking it was a native hut ablaze, and driving down to see if he could help. By that time, he said, the rain had almost ceased and the wind had dropped. It was another piece of confusing evidence—if Hardy had been right, it should have been blowing a gale and pouring in torrents at that place and time.

But even the time seemed to be in doubt. When Tucker cross-examined, he showed Arnett an entry from his own log proving that he did not leave the transmitter building until midnight, twenty minutes after the crash.

There was really no profit in William Arnett to be gained by anyone. They all must have watched him leave the witness box with a certain relief.

TWENTY-ONE

MORTON M. BLOCK was a Pan American flight controller working out of San Francisco. The crash of Flight 806 had disturbed him deeply—so deeply that on February 12, 1974, he wrote a letter of protest to the vice president and general manager of Pam Am, James O. Leet.

Block wrote:

> Many of us in Flight Control were deeply saddened by the recent crash of 806 at Pago Pago and the deaths of Leroy Petersen and his crew, all good and close friends of many dispatchers in the San Francisco Flight Control Office. With the many burdens of your office already, we realize what crushing additional problems this adds. There are, however, some unique aspects of dispatching to Pago Pago that warrant your attention.
>
> San Francisco Flight Control is very much involved with Pago Pago International Airport. We dispatch Pago Pago-Honolulu trips as well as to other nearby stations,

and we know these facilities intimately. I quote from my
route check report of August 9, 1970:

"Pago Pago—of all the airports in the world that
need a tower and facilities for landing aircraft, Pago
Pago is perhaps the most in need. With the VOR [a
sophisticated navigation device] inoperative and one
NDB [non-directional beacon] very weak, we were
given a wind of 130/09 in a period of rain squalls and
2,000 ft. ceilings. The actual landing was a difficult one,
with gusty crosswinds shifting almost at the threshold,
crab of almost 20 degrees, ocean spray covering the
windshield from high waves adjoining the runway, and
no advice from operations PPG [Pago Pago airport].
This station needs accurate wind measuring equipment
near the runway, and an Operations Rep who can give
some visual data to the pilot.

"My conclusion is that this airport is an accident
waiting to happen. The winter weather is bad, over a
period of many weeks. The weather information is
inaccurate, and winds in the lee of the high mountains
are treacherous and changeable. There were two
diversions a few days after our transit due to un-forecast
low ceilings and poor landing conditions. Our own
aircraft came very close to scraping a pod on landing
due to winds gusting at touchdown point."

We now dispatch into this area without South
Pacific route checks of any kind, since the Air Transport
Association convinced the FAA to limit our yearly
checks to San Francisco-Los Angeles-San Francisco,
and a "trip" in the simulator. We have Pago Pago
terminal forecasts in the office, but dispatch without a
valid significant weather map of any kind, so we know
what the Weather Bureau anticipates but cannot tell

why, or from what direction the weather is moving. This also applies to Nandi, Nouméa and the area west of Tahiti. The maps are drawn in Honolulu weather office, but we are not privy to the data. We do get a printed enroute forecast, but this tells nothing of surface weather conditions, nor the general conditions to the west or east of the station. In other words, we dispatch "blind" and often do not see Pago Pago hourly weather for two hours, since it is mixed in with other reports and re-sent via Honolulu communications office.

The Flight Controller is in a unique position to look at all the safety aspects of such a station and area—the weather, the facilities, NOTAMS [notices to airmen from a civil aviation authority], runway conditions and local peculiarities. But without route checks, maps, and the tools to do the job we are indeed operating blind. Incidentally, our Flight Operations Department doesn't care enough about dispatcher judgments even to ask for a Flight Controller on the investigating team of the 806 accident. And, obviously, no one reads our route check reports. There is only one man left in Pan Am's meteorology department; yet we are intimately involved with weather all over the Pacific every day of our working lives. My own conclusion is that no one really cares, least of all the pilot group and the management. Yet it may very well be time for a change.

Block's letter sang of the desperation of a man who had lost friends because no one had heeded his past warning and because of the situation he saw around him in the Pan American operation. He sent it off to Leet at the Pan Am headquarters in New York. But if he thought anyone there was going to take any notice, he was grossly mistaken.

The reply came a month later, signed personally by Leet on March 12, 1974. Leet wrote:

> This will acknowledge your letter of February 12 concerning the Pago Pago accident. The interest and concern felt by yourself and other members of the San Francisco Flight Control office are sincerely appreciated.
>
> I can understand your desire to perform more route checks and found your observations on the Pago Pago airport most interesting. However, to send our Flight Controllers to all—or even a selected few—airports that Pan Am serves would require an investment in time and money that we cannot now afford. Our objective in scheduling route checks for Flight Controllers is to ensure your continuing familiarity with cockpit procedures and the flight deck environment. This can be accomplished on any flight segment.
>
> Our Operations Management is well aware of the professional knowledge and skills possessed by your group; we intend to utilize these assets wisely.

It was a brush-off. Morton M. Block did not like it, and he did the only thing he could: he passed a copy of his letter and its reply on to Jack Hudson and his team of investigators. That was how it came to be discovered by Dan Cathcart, and that was why, on April 11, 1978, Block became a controversial figure in the Pago Pago trial.

Block was no young hothead. He had worked as a flight controller for Pan Am for thirty-four years, and it was his responsibility to warn pilots of anything that might affect the safety of their flights. In the light of what he had to say in his letter, it cannot have been an easy task. While operating out of San Francisco he had had responsibility for outward-bound flights to Honolulu and Pago Pago, but the Auckland-Pago Pago leg on which Flight 806 crashed was the responsibility of his opposite number in Sydney, Australia. That fact did not lessen Block's concern.

By the time his letter had been discovered by the lawyers, Block had been transferred by Pan American to London, England. They traced him there in March 1976, and he willingly made a deposition that included the text of the letter and swore to the truth of what he had told Leet. It was this deposition that was now before the court and was the focus of a bitter dispute.

Incredibly, at this stage in the proceedings, they were still going through the pretrial procedure. There were long gaps in the evidence as the lawyers huddled around Judge Byrne and decided what should and what should not be allowed into the action. The jury was forced to wait around while they discussed the very things that the pretrial order was meant to resolve. With no such order, in spite of the six months spent discussing it, the trial had to proceed in fits and starts.

They needed to save time, and one of the ways to do it, they decided, was to summarize the depositions. Thus, instead of the jury being compelled to listen to long depositions by minor witnesses, often full of irrelevant details, they would merely be given a summary of the important parts. This sounded a fine idea. In practice, however, the snag was that no part of a deposition could be read to the jury unless all the lawyers had agreed on it. And not one of these attorneys was about to agree to something that might damage his own case or help that of the opposition. The result was that much vital evidence was suppressed, and as far as the depositions were concerned, the jury was fed a diet of pap.

The deposition of Morton M. Block was a case in point.

There was no way that Tucker wanted to see that letter to James O. Leet produced in court. For the jury to learn that Pan Am had been warned by one of their employees four years prior to the crash that Pago Pago was "an accident waiting to happen"—and had apparently ignored that warning—would do his cause no good at all. He argued that there had been changes made between 1970 and 1974, notably the installation of the ILS, which made the warning irrelevant.

Byrne seemed to agree with him. "I think it would be unduly prejudicial as to 1974," he said, "without some substantial foundation that everything was the same, and in fact we know it was not the same."

But as Cathcart pointed out, Block's letter went far beyond the instrument landing system. It went to the point that Pan American's economy measures were precluding pilots from knowing what conditions they were flying into.

He said, "In spite of Mr. Block's letter, their company continued to dispatch blind into this area. Not only that, they loaded their airplanes up as heavy as they could get them to go in there to cope with the prevailing conditions, which Mr. Block pointed out to them almost caused an accident on the airplane he was in when they almost scraped a pod on the runway.

"There was indeed notice to the company—from their own employee. Right or wrong, they had notice. Now the notice may have been of an incorrect fact, may have been a bad opinion, but that goes to the weight of the evidence. It is the company that is coming into this courtroom and talking about how difficult it is to land an airplane, even with the new systems which they have in there."

Technically, the Block deposition was being offered by Dombroff for the government. But he did not want all of it read to the jury either. Block's letter had been critical of the lack of control tower facilities at Pago Pago—an FAA responsibility—and Dombroff wanted that part cut out.

Cathcart wanted all of it. He failed. When they had all finished ripping out the aspects that they did not fancy, like hyenas tearing at a carcass, there was only one sentence of Morton Block's letter remaining: "The winter weather is bad, over a period of many weeks, the weather information is inaccurate, and winds in the lee of the high mountains are treacherous and changeable."

And that is all that the jury were allowed to hear. They were, however, permitted to hear a deposition by James Leet in which he swore that no reports had come to his attention dealing with the adequacy or inadequacy of the navigational aids at Pago Pago airport prior to the crash of Flight 806. Nor had any such reports come to his attention dealing with weather observations or their dissemination. His correspondence with Block was not, of course, mentioned.

The only man left alive who had played an active part in the last moments of Flight 806 was Frank David Bateman Jr. Bateman was the air traffic controller on duty in the CAP/IS facility as Captain Petersen began his final approach.

Since the court was not to be permitted to hear the deathbed statement made by co-pilot James Phillips (there was no recording of his statement nor were there any witnesses to it), Bateman's testimony would be the sole first-hand account available to the jury.

Bateman was forty-five at the time of the trial. He had been stationed at Pago Pago since 1972, and his experience as an air traffic control specialist went back to 1957. His duties in the CAP/IS facility, he told Dombroff, included passing on to pilots the reports from the National Weather Service and information about the wind speed and direction and the barometric pressure at the airport. He was not allowed to pass on his own estimates of visibility, being unqualified to do so.

When Flight 806 had first contacted him by radio, he had transmitted to Petersen the most recent report from the weather bureau. It spoke of broken clouds at 1,600 feet and 4,000 feet with an overcast sky at 11,000 feet. Visibility was ten miles with light rain showers, and the wind was blowing at 15 knots from 350 degrees. The temperature was 78°F.

It was at 10:39 and 21 seconds, when Flight 806 had begun its approach, Bateman said, that he warned Petersen that there was a bad rain shower at the airport and that he could no longer see the runway lights. He had no authority to instruct the pilot to make a missed approach—that was Petersen's responsibility.

For himself, he had felt that the weather conditions that night were fairly typical for Pago Pago. They were not severe. The CAP/IS facility was equipped with monitor alarms for the instrument landing system and the VASI lights, in case they should develop a fault. There had been no alarms that night.

Bateman went on to describe in detail the instructions given to Flight 806 from the moment he first made contact until the moment of the crash. Without radar facilities, he'd had no way of knowing the exact position of the aircraft, but there seemed nothing unusual about the approach. At

10:38 and 53 seconds, he had notified Petersen of a possible power failure at the airport because he had seen a red light come up on the tape recorder power supply. The recorders had continued working, however, and he had no idea what had caused the light to come on.

It was this, Bateman said, that made him look out of the window to see if he could see the runway lights, three or four of which were normally visible. He could not see them, but Phillips, from the cockpit of Flight 806, confirmed that they were in fact on. He then assumed that the rain shower was blocking his vision.

While he was talking to Phillips about the lights, Bateman said he heard the teletype machine from the weather bureau begin to rattle out a message. He waited until it had finished, pulled it off the machine, and read it.

"Did you transmit it to the aircraft?" asked Dombroff.

"No, sir."

"Why not?"

"Because I saw an explosion."

Dombroff sat down. Through Bateman he had achieved exactly what he wanted to impress on the jury: that nothing was done on the ground to cause the crash of Flight 806 and that nothing had been left undone that could possibly have prevented it. The responsibility had been in the cockpit.

Cathcart, in his cross-examination, took the theme further, establishing from the controller that Petersen was not being ordered to continue the approach, that he had complete freedom to abandon it and to hold or divert if he considered conditions unsafe to land. No permission for this was needed from the CAP/IS.

Tucker, however, was not happy. Why was it, he wanted to know, that Bateman had not contacted the weather bureau for a report on the visibility after he found he could not see the runway lights? There was an intercom facility; he could easily have done so.

Bateman replied that his main concern was whether there had been a power failure. Once Phillips had reported that everything was working and that he could see the lights, there had seemed no need. In any case, the weather bureau intercom was some ten feet away from his working position, and he would have had to leave his microphone with an aircraft on final approach.

It sounded reasonable enough to most people, though not to Tucker, who began attacking Bateman for not turning on emergency generators when a storm was in the vicinity. There were regulations, Tucker said while waving a piece of paper, which instructed him to do this and to monitor weather reports to check when storms were around.

This was news to Bateman, who had never seen any such regulation. It was news to Dombroff, too, who made violent objections to such a thing being produced without his prior knowledge. Judge Byrne, however, allowed it into evidence—though Tucker never disclosed by whom it was supposed to have been issued, or when.

———

THE MAN who had been at the other end of the teletype machine, sending the special report from the weather bureau that was too late to reach the ill-fated Captain Petersen, was Laauli Ifopo, a young Samoan.

Ifopo brought some color to the proceedings, appearing in court in Samoan national dress and wearing sandals on his bare feet. His command of English was not great, which made his answers simple and direct. He came across as a witness of transparent honesty, which was just what Dombroff wanted.

He had followed, he said, the normal procedure that night. His instructions were to make a special weather report when the visibility fell from ten miles to one mile. This he had done. As soon as it started raining he had gone outside, where he found that visibility was one mile with heavy rain showers and that the wind was from 40 at 22 knots, gusting to 35 knots. He had gone back inside and punched the information on to the teletype machine.

The special bulletin had gone out at 23:39, one minute before the crash and three minutes after he had made the observation. There had, Ifopo said, been no power failure or fluctuation at the weather station that evening.

Cross-examined by Cathcart, he confirmed that it was just normal rainy Pago Pago weather. He had seen the same conditions hundreds of times on the island, and it was quite possible to have strong winds and heavy rain in one spot and nothing at all a short distance away. Pago Pago weather was like that.

Tucker got nowhere with Ifopo. The Samoan was an ordinary man doing his job as he had been taught to do it. There was simply no way Tucker could prove otherwise.

TWENTY-TWO

IT WAS APRIL 18, 1978, the fifty-fifth day of the trial, and Pan American's discomfiture was made worse by a procession of their captains through the witness box to testify for the government. The pilots were not there in person; the nature of their job may have made that impossible. But their depositions did nothing to help the company for which they worked, even after emasculation by the summary process.

The first, Bruce Duncan Abbott, testified to the adverse effect of carrying excess weight in an aircraft subjected to a severe down-draft and said that Petersen had had the right to refuse to carry stored fuel. The co-pilot, he added, had a duty to call out any excessive sink rate; if he failed to do so, it marked a breakdown in crew coordination.

Captain William A. Brown, Pan Am's director of Flight Operations, Technical, said he could recall no reports of excessive wind shear or remarkable rates of descent from pilots flying into Pago Pago. Some pilots, he added, used the dangerous technique of flying below the glide slope in order to land as near the end of the runway as they could. It was a violation of Pan American regulations, but it happened.

This point made a great impression on Michael Brent in the jury box. Was Petersen, he wondered, trying to land as short as possible in order to get out of the rain?

Brown went on to say that if a pilot lost sight of the runway after reaching decision height he must execute a missed approach immediately. "You don't wait for anybody to tell you anything," he said. "The pilot must make that decision and do it."

Petersen, he added, should have realized from Bateman's warning of a heavy rain shower at the airport that his visibility on final approach was likely to be affected. He had listened to the cockpit voice recorder tape and had heard nothing to indicate that there was any power failure on the ground or any loss of runway lights or navigational equipment.

And he, too, confirmed that Phillips should have warned Petersen when the rate of descent of Flight 806 exceeded a thousand feet a minute.

Brown testified that he had been involved with Pan Am's fuel policy, which had started in the spring of 1973 with the object of conserving fuel and saving money. Dombroff took the opportunity to bring in the Pan Am document that laid that policy down.

It was an interesting piece of paper, instructing pilots to carry all the fuel they could when there was an economic advantage but saying, too, that they should allow a small margin to accommodate last-minute increases in payload or to avoid arriving at their destinations over the maximum landing weight. For a Boeing 707, such as Flight 806, that suggested margin was 2,000 pounds.

There was clearly much at stake, because in 1972 Pan Am's fuel bill had been $134,000,000, and the price was expected to increase by around 65 percent in 1974. A 3 to 4 percent saving, which the stored fuel policy and other measures were expected to achieve, would save the airline about $9,000,000.

Attached to this document was a schedule instructing pilots and dispatchers on which of Pan Am's routes they should carry stored fuel, and on which they should not. But that schedule, on which the whole trial was destined to turn, was not produced by Dombroff at this stage.

Like any good conjuror, Dombroff kept the ace up his sleeve, waiting until he had a live witness in the box to produce it with maximum effect. At least, that is the charitable explanation. It is also possible that he failed to realize the importance of this scrap of paper. It was only one among many thousands.

They moved on, this time to a deposition from Captain William Bacheler, who had been flying Boeing 707s for Pan American since 1965 and was chairman of the ALPA air safety committee at the time of the accident. Captain Bacheler had flown twenty approaches into Pago Pago without problems, but he went on to explain one of the hazards that Captain Petersen may have faced that night: visual illusions in rain.

"In rain," he said, "the tendency is for the horizon to appear to drop [making the aircraft appear higher than it really is], so the pilot tends to drop the nose with it. I've landed in rain at Tahiti, when I had to resist consciously the urge to drop the nose. I was thinking about it all the way in. I was telling myself to stay on the glide slope, stay on the gauges, stay on the glide slope, and just don't drop the nose at the last minute.

"In other words, when you've established your flight path along the glide slope, all you have to do is to hold it all the way in until the wheels touch, and you'll make a successful landing, and you'll stop before you get to the end of the runway. It's just human nature, when you get this effect in heavy rain, that you are high, to drop the nose. You have to resist it constantly."

Was Captain Petersen a victim of human nature that night? No one would ever know, but to the jury it began to look distinctly possible as an explanation for an otherwise inexplicable crash. Especially when they heard Captain Bacheler say that he knew of no training given by Pan American to their pilots to counter such visual illusions prior to the Pago Pago tragedy.

In Captain Bacheler's view, if an aircraft began to descend at more than 800 feet per minute on final approach, the crew should mention it to the pilot and keep on mentioning it until they got some response. This was a point that Dombroff and Cathcart drew from witness after witness, for they had clear evidence that Flight 806 had been coming down at a rate of 1,900 feet per minute and that nobody in the cockpit had said a word.

Dombroff had a deposition from George D. Richabaugh Jr., Pan Am's director of operations at Pago Pago, saying that he had no formal reports of problems with the ILS prior to the accident. He also had a statement from Daniel W. Frost, another Pan Am captain, who had been flying into Pago Pago for thirty-four years and had never experienced wind shear at the airport.

The depositions went on all day. It was impossible to tell what had been cut out of them during the legal horse trading behind the scenes, though if the example of Morton Block was anything to go by, it must have been a great deal.

The cumulative effect of what was left, however, was impressive. Here were Pan American's own pilots, men of great experience and proven loyalty, who were saying, though not in so many words, that the crew of Flight 806 had done a lousy job.

Next day, it was time for another red herring to be dragged from the seemingly bottomless barrel of stinking fish that pervaded the trial from start to finish. It was an issue so arcane, so lacking in substance, that many an attorney would have been embarrassed to mention it. There were no blushes, however, on the cheek of Dan Cathcart as he began his cross-examination of Harold Truitt Anderson. Cathcart was in a bind. He had rejected the government's settlement offer, and it was becoming clearer by the day that he was unlikely to recover any damages from that source. He had no witnesses of his own in this part of the case, and Tucker's had proved weak by comparison with those now being paraded by Dombroff. It was time for desperate measures.

Anderson had been the man responsible for the installation of the glide slope at Pago Pago. The point Cathcart was trying to make with him was this: that a whip aerial on the non-directional navigation beacon at the summit of Logotala Hill was six feet higher than it should have been. Therefore, Cathcart said, working from the standard obstruction clearance in FAA regulations, the decision height for the approach to Pago Pago should have been set at 700 feet instead of 280 feet. If such a decision height had been enforced, he argued, Captain Petersen would have had more time to recover from his excursion beneath the glide slope.

There was nothing wrong with Cathcart's arithmetic; it was logic that let him down. A 420-foot allowance for a little 6-foot aerial, which the aircraft could probably have brushed without noticing, made little sense. As Anderson pointed out patiently, the aircraft was still flying toward the runway on the same glide slope, no matter what the decision height was.

Byrne stopped the trial and called the lawyers to his side. "Is there an issue in this case that the decision height is wrong?" he asked.

It was news to Dombroff. Tucker, of course, thought there was and said he would like to be heard on it.

"I would like to be heard on a couple of things," Byrne retorted. "These things are just popping into your minds as the case goes on. It's very hard for me to believe that prior to this, or any other substantial time prior to this, it was believed that it was an issue that the decision height should have been 700 feet."

"Your Honor," protested Tom Smith with righteous indignation, "we believed that ever since we found out that Logotala Hill was—"

Byrne cut him off in mid-sentence. "You sure don't write what you believe," he said. "After the months that we spent on the pretrial in this case, I would think it might have been mentioned just one time. If you can find me one place in any of the transcripts where it was mentioned that the decision height should have been 700 feet, I will stand totally corrected."

No one could, of course. They stood slightly shamefaced, small boys caught in the act, while Dombroff smiled a quiet smile and Byrne threw the red herring back in the barrel and shut the lid. He would have no more of it. At the end of the day he complained bitterly that this had been the least organized section of the trial. Cathcart and Tucker had been going over and over material that witnesses could have no knowledge of, and he demanded that they write out for him a list of the pretrial issues they believed to be related to the 700-foot decision height and similar points.

Cathcart looked pained. He summoned his dignity and said, "The need to inquire into these areas with witnesses put on by others, Your Honor, has in part stemmed from the court's determination that I could not add a witness on the subject."

Byrne flushed angrily, his temper rising to the surface. Not even the eminent Mr. Cathcart was going to get away with criticizing the way in which he ran his court.

"Sir," he snapped, "the court's determination is based upon the decision that after three years of discovery, knowing that this issue was there, continually knowing it was there, with the plaintiffs having had the advantage of every other party in this case putting on their case for them, you don't go out and get a witness. You don't list a witness on the witness list, and the other parties rely upon there being no witness. Then, in the middle of the trial, you decide that you now want to call an expert. That was the basis of the court's determination. It's not upon any ruling of the court. It's upon the failure of the plaintiffs to have a witness set down at the proper time."

Byrne swept his papers together and got to his feet. "I will see you tomorrow at eight o'clock," he said.

"Thank you, Your Honor," Dombroff said. Nobody else said a word. Byrne had stabbed Cathcart at the weakest point in his armor. He was saving money by riding along on the backs of the government and Pan Am, changing sides whenever it suited his case, and it was beginning to show.

Nor was Cathcart the only attorney to suffer at the hands of Judge Byrne at this time. Robert Benedict had been sworn in as one of the counsel for Pan American at the outset of the case, but precious little had been seen of him since that time. He preferred to remain in the background, masterminding proceedings from afar. Now, on Friday, April 21, there came a message from Benedict in New York that he wanted to be released from the trial.

It was not the done thing. Byrne blew a gasket. "He allowed himself to sit at counsel table," he said. "He allowed himself to be introduced as counsel in this case, and he is not going to have a unilateral withdrawal without my permission. I intend to hear from him in the near future."

Tucker did his embarrassed best to defend the absent Benedict, explaining that the insurance lawyer had merely been fulfilling a back-up role in case he or Smith fell sick. Byrne would have none of it. "If anything happens to any lawyer," he said, "this case is going on. He is not going to be in one day and out another day without asking for relief." He wanted to know whether Benedict had in fact been briefed sufficiently well to take over at this stage of the trial if he had to.

Tucker doubted it. "I don't think that's a fair assumption, Your Honor," he said.

"It had better be," replied Byrne darkly, and he went on to make veiled threats about Benedict's chances of taking part in any other cases in California, if he did not treat the courts with proper respect.

On this, the fifty-seventh day of the trial, the judge had clearly decided it was time to show everyone who was boss. In the light of what had been, and what was to come, it was a curious episode.

TWENTY-THREE

OF ALL THE witnesses who came and went during those interminable months, none was more important than Captain Charles Bassett of Ridgefield, Connecticut. At the moment he appeared on the morning of Monday, April 24, there seemed a grave danger that the raison d'être of the trial—the conduct of Flight 806—was being lost amid the legal nonsense and abstruse technical detail.

The collective mind of the jury was a bemused miasma of wind shear and microamps, fly-downs and circuit breakers. It took the blunt certainty of Captain Bassett, focused on what happened during the last crucial minutes of flight, to bring the whole thing into perspective. Bassett was a catalyst, joining together the disparate strands of argument into a cohesive whole. To Dombroff and to Cathcart he was invaluable.

Bassett was sixty-three years old at the time of the trial. He had retired as a Pan Am captain some three years before, having flown for the airline since 1940 with a total of more than 31,500 flying hours. Twenty of his thirty-five years with Pan Am had been spent as a check pilot, training and qualifying other pilots, and he had spent ten years as captain of a Boeing 707. Nobody was going to suggest that Chuck Bassett did not know what he was talking about, and no one did.

Though he was appearing as a professional witness, having been paid $250 a day by the government for about thirty-five days of work on the case, Bassett had never before been in a courtroom. If this was a disadvantage, it did not show.

He was bluff, tough, and totally believable.

Dombroff began by taking him through his investigation: his study of the cockpit voice recorder and the thirty-two approaches he had made to Pago Pago. "Do you have an opinion as to whether or not the flight crew of Flight 806 acted in a manner consistent with Pan American's operating procedures?" he asked.

"No," Bassett replied firmly. "They did not."

Did he consider the approach to Pago Pago at night a black hole?

It was not a black hole to Captain Bassett, and he proceeded to blow the theory apart. It simply did not matter whether there were lights on the ground along the approach path or not, he said, because right down to the decision height of 280 feet the captain would be flying on his instruments, not looking outside. When he raised his eyes, he would have the runway lights in front of him. So much for the black hole.

Had the rate of descent of Flight 806 been established?

"Negative," Bassett replied, forgetting for a moment that he was in a witness box and not the cockpit. He went on to itemize the errors:

- The rate of descent had exceeded 1,000 feet per minute. There should have been a warning call at 800 feet per minute, and there was not.
- There should have been a callout at 100 feet above decision height. There was not. Nor was there a call at 500 feet above the ground.
- The speed of the aircraft, which should have been stabilized at 150 knots from a point some seven miles out, had gone up to 180 and perhaps 190 knots inbound from Logotala Hill.
- The flaps should have been put down at the intersection of the glide slope, and it had not been done. "I think it was just forgotten," Bassett said.

And so it went on; a dismal catalogue of all the things that Captain Petersen and his crew should have done but failed to do.

Dombroff read to Bassett an article published by Pan American in December of 1973. In view of what was to happen only a month later, and of what was to be discovered by the Hudson investigation, it had a sort of sick significance. Except, of course, that the jury knew nothing of Hudson and his report. The article read:

An evaluation of recent industry accidents and incidents again underscores the constant mandate of our business: safety. In a great number of cases, the accident or incident was due to improper execution of approved operating procedures. When this happens, it is an indication of deficiency in cockpit discipline, poor crew coordination and/or complacency. As a crew member, you have the responsibility to examine yourself and ensure that you are participating fully in the crew-concept mode of operation. Our entire operation is based on a team operation, not a solo performance. Total crew participation and alertness are absolutely essential to ensure safety and efficiency in all regimes of operation, but particularly during takeoff, approaches and landings. Share your operational intentions. Each crew members [sic] should know what is expected during an operation.

Be certain that you are observing proper cockpit discipline. The cockpit is your place of business, and a businesslike environment is a requirement at all times. Be certain you are not allowing complacency to enter into any part of your business. Double-check procedures. Challenge any part of the operation that could be wrong. Don't let paperwork interfere with the essentials of safe flight. Rule out complacency. Be certain you know, and are adhering to approved normal, abnormal and emergency procedures. Safety is our business. The pursuit of this has priority over all other duties.

The statement was admirable. Dombroff was intent on holding it up as an example of what the crew of Flight 806 should have been doing and conspicuously failed to do. He asked Bassett whether, based on instructions in the article, the crew concept had broken down on Flight 806.

"Yes, sir," the pilot said.

Byrne took exception to the first two sentences of the article and ordered them to be stricken as immaterial. But he could not strike them from the minds of the jury. They had been told in the clearest of terms that failure to conform to procedures was the cause of crashes. Pan Am said so.

Dombroff reinforced the point, drawing from Bassett his opinion that the crew had failed to be aware of their altitude, had failed to fly the glide path properly, and had failed to execute a missed approach when their rate of descent made it imperative.

The missed approach, Bassett said, should have been carried out not later than the decision height of 280 feet—at which point Flight 806 was descending at 1,500 feet per minute (25 feet per second). It should have been done irrespective of whether the crew had the runway in sight at that point, and failure to do so had endangered the aircraft. At 280 feet, descending at 1,500 feet per minute, they had 11.2 seconds before they hit the ground—fewer before they hit the trees.

Dombroff went through a damning list of twenty-three elements of the final approach. On each of them, one by one, Bassett gravely agreed that the crew had been at fault. The cumulative effect was great. At last the jury was getting a coherent picture of what had been done and what had not been done in the cockpit during the last moments of the flight, and this was reinforced a short while later when Dombroff broke off from his examination of Bassett to show a videotape.

Videotape had not been used before in aircraft litigation, and it proved to be remarkably effective. What Dombroff had done was to split the screen in two, using both the side elevation and a plan view of the final minutes of the flight. The glide path was a constant line, and the track of Flight 806 extended across the screen as the flight progressed. On the sound track, synchronized with the

WILLFUL MISCONDUCT   249

progress of the aircraft, were the voices of the crew, taken from the cockpit voice recorder. The jury watched and listened to the calm progress to final impact with horrified fascination. It was as though they were actually witnessing the deaths of ninety-seven people. As the demonstration ended there was a collective intake of breath, and then silence in the courtroom.

The picture had been worth a million words, but there were still a lot of words to come, many of them from Captain Bassett. It was during a short break in Bassett's testimony that the issue of the crew's training records raised its ugly head. Dombroff wanted to show them to the jury. He would be attempting to prove, he said, that the competence, or lack of it, shown by Captain Petersen and his crew on this approach was something that Pan Am should have expected.

Byrne grunted. He sometimes displayed an uncomfortable knack of getting to the nub of a question in a few words. "The only possible basis that these records could be used for," he said, "would be to show that they were lousy pilots, as demonstrated by their records, and they were lousy pilots on January 30, 1974, and that is what caused the crash."

Precisely so, but Dombroff seemed shocked at such directness. "I don't think you can attach a colloquialism to it," he said primly. "I think you can say that on January 30 the pilot did not properly fly a glide slope, and I think it's proper to say that not only did he not do so on that occasion but this is something he was unable to do throughout his career."

Byrne had put it better.

The judge retorted, "Now, not every time he's on the glide slope does he do the same thing, but there are occasions over a twenty-year period that he hasn't been able to stay on a glide slope when he's being checked. The only value that would have would be to show that he's not a good glide slope pilot."

"Well, isn't that the very issue in this case" challenged Dombroff, greatly daring.

But Byrne ruled against him. "You can't use his prior activities to show that he couldn't stay on a glide slope on some previous occasion, and therefore he couldn't stay on a glide slope here," he said. He refused to let the jury see the records.

Cathcart then came wading into the attack. The production of the training records was just as important to him, especially if he was to be denied the use of the Hudson report in his case against Pan American. He would try to introduce them, he said, in a bid to show that Pan American should not have allowed the crew to fly the aircraft.

"Denied," said Byrne.

Dombroff began to cry "foul." Part of the training records, he pointed out, had already been placed in evidence through Captain Baggott. There had been no objection from Byrne at that time, but then it had apparently been in order for Pan American to produce those records that were favorable to the crew.

It was an accusation of blatant bias by the judge. Surprisingly, Byrne ignored it. But it was not to be the last he heard of the issue. Not by a long shot.

Chuck Bassett was finally allowed to continue with his evidence, saying that he felt the crew of Flight 806 should have picked up the approaching storm on their weather radar and confirming that they appeared to have made no effort to make a missed approach. Cathcart began to cross-examine him, and suddenly the atmosphere in court became electric. With a flourish that would have done credit to Dombroff, Cathcart produced the Pan American operations manual that contained specific instructions regarding which routes aircraft could carry stored fuel along, and which they could not.

Tucker was on his feet immediately. "Irrelevant," he cried.

Byrne looked as surprised as everyone else. He called counsel to the bench to have the document explained to him, out of hearing of the jury.

It was his interpretation of the manual, Cathcart said, that Pan American procedures forbade the carrying of stored fuel from Auckland to Pago Pago.

Tom Smith protested. "That's certainly not what it means, Your Honor," he said. But Byrne was intrigued. He asked Cathcart if that was what Bassett was going to testify to.

Cathcart didn't know. He hadn't talked to the witness privately.

"Well, if that is going to be the testimony, it may well be relevant," Byrne said. Did Dombroff have any objection to Cathcart talking to his witness? That was the last thing Dombroff was going to object to. His only regret was that he had not turned up this piece of evidence himself. Byrne gave them an hour or two to talk it over.

The issue should not have been a surprise to anyone. The document had been in the hands of all the lawyers for many months, but it seemed that no one had bothered to read it, or at least to understand its significance. When they came back to the side bench again after the lunch break, Cathcart confirmed that Bassett would interpret the regulations in the way he had said. Tucker began to panic.

He claimed that Bassett did not have the qualifications to interpret the manual, having retired from flying 707s before the fuel policy was issued.

Byrne cut him short. "Does this manual restrict them from carrying stored fuel into Pago Pago?"

"Absolutely not," Tucker blustered. "From Auckland into Pago, absolutely not. I can bring in—"

But the judge interrupted him once more. By this time, he had read the document himself. "Well, what does this mean, then?" he asked, pointing at the relevant section.

Tucker had forgotten his reading glasses.

He went back to the well of the court to get them, then studied the manual intently. "Your Honor," he said, "you'll note that carrying stored fuel is done for two purposes. One, taking advantage of favorable fuel differential prices between stations, or two, reducing the likelihood of a diversion or en route fueling stop, enabling accelerated transits.

"Now, going over the page, item ten says: 'Do not load stored fuel on sectors without a code, unless necessary to ensure sufficient fuel for conditions that day.'" Tucker stopped his quotation abruptly. He had already gone too far, because his eye had raced ahead and caught the fatal flaw: against the sector labeled Auckland-Pago Pago, there was no code. He began to ramble meaninglessly, hoping to swamp the issue with a deluge of words.

He almost succeeded in confusing Byrne. Almost, but not quite. "I am not very pleased," the judge said, "with the possibility of the jury being badly misled as to what some of these regulations say." But he overruled Tucker's objection.

The Pan Am lawyer had one more try. He wanted to put Bassett through a voir dire examination to show that he was unqualified to interpret the regulations. "Okay," said Byrne.

"Can I do it outside the presence of the jury?" Tucker asked.

Byrne looked at him wryly. "No," he said. In that case, Tucker decided not to bother. The whole object of the exercise was to prevent the jury from knowing about those regulations.

And so Cathcart went ahead, leading Bassett calmly to the crunch point. First, he established that pilots were supposed to be familiar with the manuals, then that they were responsible for their fuel loads, then that they were not required to accept a load of fuel that might compromise the safety of the aircraft. Having laid his foundation, Cathcart introduced the vital section of the document.

"Does that chart indicate, sir, that it's possible to carry stored fuel into Pago Pago?"

Bassett said, "I would say, based on this page, it does not. It is not permitted."

It was simple, it was direct, and it proved to be the most important single piece of evidence in the whole trial: when Pan American sent Flight 806 into Pago Pago loaded with excess fuel, to crash and burn and to take the lives of ninety-seven people, the company was flaunting its own regulations.

Michael Brent, who was to become foreman of the jury, said after the trial, "That was the main point which we felt was flagrant and negligent. In their own records they said that you are only allowed enough fuel to go from one point to your destination, and then enough to take you to an alternate. They loaded up with all kinds of fuel in Auckland because it was cheaper. We felt that the weight of the fuel—to save a few bucks—it was flagrant. That was the company. Some guy down there loading gas, or even the supervisor, would not have had the authority to do that. It would have had to be the policy that they had to load up fuel on the planes when they left Auckland.

"We could say it was pilot error. We could say it was almost anything. But it was the company's fault."

TWENTY-FOUR

CATHCART'S CROSS-EXAMINATION of Bassett was not really cross-examination at all. The former Pan Am pilot had become a witness for the plaintiffs, and Cathcart was intent on milking him of every drop of evidence against the company.

Bassett testified to cockpit instruments that must have told the crew that they were going to crash unless they did something about it. Provided, that is, they were properly trained and qualified.

Against a background of mounting objections by Tucker, all of them overruled, Cathcart asked whether in his opinion, on the evidence, the crew of Flight 806 had been qualified to fly an ILS approach into Pago Pago that night.

"I would say, based on all the facts that you've mentioned, that they were not," Bassett replied.

At that point, Cathcart tried once again to get the training records of the crew before the jury. Byrne refused to give a ruling. It must wait, he said, until after Tucker's cross-examination.

Tucker began, and began badly, spending much time in any elaborate review of the instruments in the cockpit. The point he was trying to make was that Phillips might in fact have switched his own instruments to match those in front of Petersen, as required by Pan Am regulations, in spite of previous evidence that he had not. The problem was, as Dombroff was quick to point out, that the post-crash investigation had found Phillips's switches in the "off" position for the ILS. It had always been an agreed fact in the trial.

Tucker was promptly rapped over the knuckles by the judge for raising yet another false issue, but he stuck to it nonetheless, making confusion fearfully confounded. By the time Tucker had explored fifty-nine versions of which switch was which, a fog of incomprehension had begun to fill the courtroom. The Pan Am lawyer may have hoped that it would obscure what had gone before. He was a man so skilled in his trade that he could have made a complex issue out of a white line running down the middle of a straight road.

Tucker's contention, insofar as he had one, seemed to be that it was in order for the co-pilot to leave his instruments switched to the navigation beacon instead of the ILS system, because in the event of a missed approach the former information would be needed in the cockpit. Bassett's view was that Phillips's instruments should have been switched to the ILS so that the co-pilot could monitor Petersen's performance.

They could easily have been switched back if the captain had decided to go around again. All this took most of the day. Legal arguments over whether the jury should be asked to bring in a verdict at the end of the first part of the trial, before passing on to Boeing and the crashworthy issue, took the rest. That got nowhere either.

———

ON APRIL 27, Tucker resumed his attack on Bassett. This time he appeared to be doing a little better.

Bassett stuck to his view that Petersen should have attempted a missed approach and had not done so, but Tucker took him through the transcript of the cockpit voice recorder and got him to agree that there had been examples of crew coordination. Twenty of them, in fact.

Then Cathcart came back to the training records. He wanted them, he said, to prove through Bassett that the crew of Flight 806 had not only been unqualified on that night but were unqualified to act as professional pilots at all and should never have been entrusted with an aircraft by Pan American.

Tucker complained that the summaries of the crew's records, which had been prepared by Dombroff, were full of inaccuracies and misleading. Dombroff was cut to the quick. He had made no effort, he said, to emphasize either the detrimental things in the records or the good things. This was a touch misleading: in Dombroff's summary there *were* no good things.

Bassett, Cathcart said, had reviewed the records and had referred to one or more of them as being "atrocious." "I believe," he went on, "that he is prepared to state that these records buttress his opinion that this crew was not only unqualified on the approach but was also unqualified to serve as crew members in a cockpit for a flag carrier on a 707 aircraft. That this crew should not have been entrusted to fly a Boeing 707 airplane on a South Pacific route into Pago Pago with their records. Records that showed serious problems as far as their proficiency was concerned, as far as their ability to handle ILS approaches was concerned, as far as their ability to scan instruments was concerned, and as far as their ability to think and react as quickly as circumstances demanded was concerned. And you can go through these records—" Cathcart was getting quite carried away. Judge Byrne interjected: "What are you offering them for?"

In response to Cathcart's reply, which was to say it all again in different words, Byrne said, "Let me ask you this. Are Bassett's records admissible against him?"

Bassett's records? Cathcart did a swift double take. What did Bassett's records have to do with the case? Bassett had not been piloting Flight 806.

Byrne went on to say that although he was sure what Bassett would testify about the crew, he was not sure how he would support that conclusion. In any case, he said, he had decided not to allow the records right back to 1951 to be produced. If he allowed any of them, it would only be for the past five years. Dombroff struggled for more, and so did Cathcart, quoting at length from the contentious records, but well out of hearing of the jury.

Tucker protested bitterly that production of the records would have a horrendous prejudicial effect on his case, which was certainly true, and he seized on the hint thrown him by Byrne. If Captain Petersen's records were going to be admissible, then why not Captain Bassett's? What if they could show that he, too, had had problems in the past?

Byrne, having set him up, then cut Tucker down again. Did he want to show that Pan Am had been just as sloppy in letting Captain Bassett fly their airplanes?

Well, that was not exactly what Tucker had in mind (though there was no serious suggestion that Bassett had any skeletons in his closet). "Oh, I planted a seed here this afternoon," said Byrne wickedly. "Now I mention Captain Bassett, and I haven't heard any mention of his records in this whole trial, it seems very tempting for you. And when you get Captain Bassett's records, let me see them, and we'll see if you are going to offer them into evidence or not. It will be an interesting decision on your part." Tucker did not seem to be sharing the joke.

Byrne said that to him the one fair issue, and it did not seem to be an issue that interested any of the parties, was whether Pan Am was negligent in allowing the crew to fly. "If, for instance, there was evidence available to Pan American—recent, material, relevant evidence—that these pilots were just no good. And knowing that, Pan American let them fly and they crashed a 707 and killed a hundred people. Now there is corporate negligence on the part of Pan American, if those are the facts."

The records, Byrne added, could be used for that purpose, but not to the issue of whether Byrne considered the crew to be qualified.

It seemed a fine shade of difference, and it was certainly not enough to satisfy Tucker, who continued his efforts to keep the records out altogether.

Byrne said he would give a ruling first thing in the morning, but in the morning the issue had disappeared. Cathcart and Dombroff withdrew their application for the records because, they said, Bassett had told them that five years was not sufficient time on which to base a conclusion.

It was an anticlimactic end to such a spirited fight. Had that really been the reason, or had Bassett objected to the prospect of his own professional life coming under close scrutiny if the records were admitted? At all events, Tucker was happy. Now the jury would never know what manner of men it was who guided Flight 806 on its fatal journey.

No sooner had one contentious question been suppressed than another surfaced. This time it was the issue of Jack Hudson. Cathcart had been defeated before the trial began in his efforts to get Hudson's notorious report on Pan Am released from the judge's seal and placed before the jury, but he was not about to give up. There was still the deposition Hudson had sworn two years before, and it contained confirmation of most of the damaging allegations in the report. Cathcart had been trying intermittently for some weeks to have the deposition, or at least a summary of it, admitted. But Byrne had thus far refused to make a ruling, claiming that it was not in a form on which he could rule. There was a growing suspicion in the attorney's mind that the judge did not want to go on the record as rejecting the deposition, in case it was held against him in a court of appeal.

Now Cathcart tried a new tack. With Dombroff's assistance he wanted to put Hudson on the stand as a live witness.

"Is he controllable?" Byrne asked suspiciously.

Cathcart admitted that he could not control Hudson; he thought Dombroff could. Not so, said Dombroff.

Then Cathcart, who was willing to make almost any concession to get this star witness on the stand, suggested that Hudson might be examined in private before being turned loose on the jury. Byrne found the idea vaguely attractive, but a decision was put off until another day.

———

CHUCK BASSETT, who had been waiting patiently while all this was going on, was now examined once again by Cathcart. And once more the veteran pilot began reducing complex issues to basics the jury could understand. He was able to say quite simply that if Flight 806 had not been carrying stored fuel that night, its approach speed would have been reduced from 150 knots to 139 knots, and it would have been able to descend the glide slope at less than 800 feet per minute. It did not require a great feat of imagination to see what sort of difference that might have made, and Cathcart, wisely, did not belabor the point.

Tucker tried hard to shake Bassett but failed utterly, and Judge Byrne for once stepped in to make sure that the jury thoroughly understood before the Pan Am lawyer drew his usual blanket of obfuscation over the issue. Tucker withdrew, aggrieved. It was the conclusion of Dombroff's case, and the young government lawyer had every reason to feel contented. He had done what he had said he would do in his opening statement: he had made it all seem simple.

Cathcart, his work done by way of cross-examination and by Dombroff's witnesses, called no evidence of his own against Pan American beyond one brief deposition from a pilot. He had no need. Tucker, on the other hand, had considerable need to repair the fences that had been trampled down by Dombroff's small but thundering herd of experts. He chose as his tool the somewhat unlikely figure of David Alexander Hodges.

———

THE SECOND COMING of David Hodges to the witness box was akin to Samuel Johnson's account of a woman preaching: it was like a dog walking on its hind legs. The wonder was not that the thing was not done well but that it was done at all.

Hodges had been doing some much-needed homework since his first appearance, doubtless inspired by Benedict and Tucker. Now he had not only examined the Wilcox Mk IC glide slope transmitter, but he had brought its main working component, the mechanical modulator motor, into court with him.

Dombroff immediately asked him if this was the same type of motor as had been used on Pago Pago in 1974. Hodges, to no one's great surprise, did not know, but on Tucker's insistence that the part numbers were the same he was allowed to carry on.

It transpired that the purpose of Hodges's demonstration was to show that the glide slope motor, which was supposed to operate at a constant speed of 1,800 rpm in order to produce the correct fly-up and fly-down signals, could be made to run more slowly if the voltage was reduced. He had it rigged to a pulley so that the speed could be observed and did manage to make it run at 720 rpm when he cut down the voltage from 115 to 90. However, after confessing that he had pressed the wrong button, which made the whole thing meaningless, he packed in the demonstration and resolved to try again next day.

The following day was May 1. April 1 would have been more appropriate. Dombroff, showing unnecessary concern, tried to have the demonstration thrown out of court because, he said, it was a jury-rigged operation (an unfortunate turn of phrase) that bore no relation to the real thing. Furthermore, he claimed, it was not the same motor. Byrne rejected his motion. Dombroff then wanted an instruction from the judge to the jury on the purpose of the demonstration. Byrne denied that, too.

"Thank you, Your Honor," Dombroff said.

"You're welcome," Byrne replied blandly. Sarcasm ran off him like rain from the rocks of Connemara.

Hodges had removed the pulley from his motor and substituted a fan. Tucker asked him a few questions about it but seemed to lack confidence that the thing would work. He declined Hodges's offer to demonstrate it once more and handed him over for cross-examination by Dombroff. This was unavoidable, but unwise. Dombroff had once again been briefed by his good friend Dr. McFarland, who knew rather more about the Wilcox Mk IC glide slope than was good for any man—particularly Hodges.

The cross-examination began mildly enough, with Dombroff establishing what sort of motor they had in front of them.

"Now," Dombroff said, "on Friday you showed this motor operating on 90 volts at 720 rpm. Is that right?"

"Yes, yes," Hodges replied with enthusiasm.

At Dombroff's request he started the motor. It ran at 1,800 rpm. He reduced the current to 90 volts. It still ran at 1,800 rpm. Dombroff concentrated on the fact that this was not the identical motor to that at Pago Pago, having been made by a different manufacturer. However, it just so happened that he had brought along Dr. McFarland's motor, which was the right one. Perhaps Hodges would demonstrate with that? The scientist agreed readily.

And so another motor was brought into court, looking remarkably like the first one. This motor, however, was rather special. It had been unbolted from the FAA's operational facility at Miami airport the previous night, in response to an urgent plea from Dombroff, and flown more than 3,000 miles just to aid his cross-examination. The government attorney could not complain about lack of support.

Once again, the wires were coupled up. This time there was a piece of colored tape on the shaft with a stroboscopic light shining on it to register the speed. With the light set at 1,800 rpm, the tape would appear stationary when the motor was running at the same revolutions.

Like an alchemist performing some ancient ritual, Hodges reduced the voltage to 90, and then to 60, and then to 50 volts. The motor continued to spin merrily at 1,800 rpm. At 20 volts it was still doing so, and it began to look as though the Wilcox Mk IC glide slope transmitter could have run on fresh air if necessary. At 15 volts the motor finally stopped. It did not slow down, it stopped.

"Doesn't this indicate," asked Dombroff, "that this synchronous motor operates at 1,800 rpm, as it's designed to operate, or it does not operate at all?"

"No," Hodges said, "because we applied no drag whatsoever to the motor."

Strangely, Dombroff seemed to lose interest at this point. He established that the demonstration motor had the same load on that it would have had in actual operation, and then handed Hodges back to Tucker.

Tucker had picked up the suggestion that a little drag on the motor might do the trick. He first of all got Hodges to put his finger on the drive shaft, and sure enough the motor began to slow down. Unfortunately, however, Hodges's finger got too hot for comfort before they could take any measurements, so Tucker came up with another idea. Why not put on the fan from Hodges's own motor? That would surely provide some drag. Hodges agreed, and the jury watched with idle fascination as the fan was solemnly transferred.

The motor turned, the fan spun, the voltage was reduced, and sure enough, the motor slowed down. Tucker, in triumph, handed Hodges back to Dombroff once again.

Dombroff had him take off the fan once more. He brandished it theatrically, poking it into various parts of the machine as he talked. "Mr. Hodges," he asked, "where in the actual Wilcox Mk IC modulator does the fan go?"

Hodges was glad that he had asked that question. Well, actually, it didn't go anywhere. There was no fan attached to the real glide slope motor.

"The purple fan was to represent the drag that could develop in the unit when operating in American Samoa, where corrosion, fungus, or rust could form over a period of time," he said. Yes, that was it, the fan represented corrosion, fungus, or rust.

There was a feeling in the court that this splendid explanation had only just occurred to Hodges. If not, it was strange that Tucker had not brought out the theory in his own examination.

Dombroff, still poking at the intestines of the glide slope motor, found it an unlikely story.

"Assume," he said, "that there was no corrosion, rust, or fungus in this unit. Isn't it true, sir, that your purple fan doesn't represent anything to do with the actual operation of this system?"

"Well, with that assumption, you're correct," Hodges admitted.

"Did you see any record that said there was fungus, rust, or corrosion in the glide slope modulator at Pago Pago?"

"Well . . . no," said Hodges.

"Did you run any tests, switching the power back and forth, without this fan being hooked on?"

"Yes."

"What happened in terms of rpm?"

"Well, at 60 volts there was no change."

"And at 90 volts it still runs at 1,800 rpm?"

"Yes."

"So," Dombroff said, "if there was no corrosion, no rust, and no fungus on the glide slope modulator at Pago Pago, whether it was operating at 60 volts or 90 volts, it would still operate at 1,800 rpm. Is that correct?"

"That's correct," said Hodges. His credibility had hung by a single thread after the wet palm tree episode. Dombroff had cut that thread.

The episode was important in that it showed the remarkable lengths to which Pan Am was prepared to go to dredge up an excuse, any excuse, to get the airline off the hook. The resultant overkill effect was not lost on the jury. "They were clutching at straws," Michael Brent said later. "If they had concentrated on one reason why that plane crashed, I guess we might have believed them. But they tried for everything in sight, and all those reasons just couldn't have caused it."

TWENTY-FIVE

TUCKER'S second rebuttal witness was Captain John A. Walker, who flew Boeing 747s out of San Francisco for Pan American. Walker's evidence was mainly notable for being in direct contradiction to that of almost every other Pan Am pilot who had testified. Where they had claimed that Captain Petersen could have flown most of the approach automatically, with the autopilot engaged, he asserted that it had to have been flown manually. Where they thought that Phillips had been in error in not selecting the ILS on his instruments, Walker said that this had been the proper thing to do because the Pago Pago approach was quite unique: there would have been no time to reset the instruments (it involved moving one switch) in the event of an overshoot.

He also claimed that Petersen's route check to Alaska had been quite representative of the sectors he would fly from San Francisco because of its severe conditions, and that Petersen would have been unable to spot the storm approaching Pago Pago on his weather radar because of ground clutter.

As for the problems of handling a heavy aircraft on the landing approach, Walker laughed them to scorn. Heavy airplanes, he said, were more stable on the approach because they were less affected by atmospheric conditions. He could find no evidence on the cockpit voice recorder tape of a breakdown in crew coordination or altitude awareness, and as for allegations that the approach had not been stabilized, that was commonplace. Pan American pilots, Walker said, were lucky if they could conduct half their approaches in a stabilized condition, due to atmospheric variations. It did not stop them from making safe landings.

Captain Walker's loyalty to Pan American in the witness box was beyond reproach, and perhaps a little surprising in view of the way in which the company had treated him. Cathcart, who took first turn at cross-examination, established that at the time of the accident Walker had been vice president of Flight Training, Executive Division, and only two or three steps removed from Pan American's top job, president. He had been responsible for all the company's flight training programs, including equipment and financing, and had held this position since 1972. At the time of the trial, however, he was back flying an aircraft on the line and acting as a check pilot, having been transferred in 1975. It did not sound like a promotion.

Cathcart, of course, was unable to follow up any possible connection between the change in Captain Walker's circumstances and the strictures in the Hudson report. Judge Byrne had seen to that. But there was nothing to prevent him from making the pilot look slightly foolish, and this he did with some relish.

Was it not the ultimate test in crew coordination and altitude awareness, Cathcart asked, that the crew should make the aircraft do what it was supposed to do?

"Not necessarily, no," replied Walker blandly.

Well then, Cathcart said, was it a manifestation of altitude awareness when the airplane hit the ground 3,000 feet short of the runway?

"I don't understand your question," Walker said. Cathcart reworded it.

Walker replied, "It's entirely possible that the crew was well aware they were going into the ground 3,000 feet short, so I certainly could not question their altitude awareness. If the aircraft was out of control, they were aware that they were going down."

Cathcart nudged him further. "Is it the duty and responsibility of somebody, if they notice they are about to crash, to point that out to other crew members?"

"If it's abundantly clear to everyone in the cockpit that they are in trouble," Walker responded, "I'd find it unnecessary to call this trouble to the attention of other individuals."

Airline pilots are noted for their ice-cool behavior, but the jury may have felt this was carrying that legendary sangfroid to an unlikely extreme. To know that they were about to crash, probably to die, and to say nothing? As Cathcart once again established from Walker, the crew of Flight 806 had said nothing to indicate that they were in trouble. No emotion, no fear, no fright, no panic, no nervousness had disturbed their calm conversation on the way down. From a height of 400 feet to the point of impact, Cathcart said, the aircraft had dropped at 1,913 feet per minute. Did that not indicate it was out of control? Walker disagreed. It was, he said, an acceptable rate of descent, though he did admit that if it were done deliberately it would be against Pan American rules.

Walker was getting himself in an awful tangle. The essence of his testimony seemed to be that although regulations existed for flying Pan American airplanes, pilots were at liberty to disregard them in the light of their own experience. Potential passengers in the courtroom were taking careful note.

Cathcart stuck to his task, going through a long recital of the speed of Flight 806 on the approach compared to what it should have been and reminding Walker of the callouts that should have been made but were not. "Having reviewed all that material, sir," he said, "is it still your opinion that there is no evidence of lack of crew coordination on this approach?"

"Yes," said Walker.

"Is it still your opinion that there was no lack of altitude awareness on the part of this crew?"

"Yes, very certainly," Walker said.

Dombroff appeared content to let Cathcart handle this witness, since he was doing rather well. He asked only a few mild questions. Cathcart then turned to the question of whether or not Captain Petersen should have made a missed approach. He asked Walker whether good operating practice in 1974 required a pilot to go around again if, when he was less than 300 feet above the airport, his glide slope indicator showed he was substantially too high or too low.

"Absolutely not," Walker replied firmly. This was in direct contradiction to the evidence given by the other Pan Am pilots.

"Are you speaking now, sir, as the head of a training department," Cathcart asked smoothly, "or the former head of a training department?"

"No," replied Walker, "I am speaking for myself."

Cathcart persisted, "Was the policy or procedure of not executing a missed approach under the conditions just outlined the philosophy of the training department while you were its chief executive in 1974?

Tucker objected on the grounds that the question was unintelligible. He must have been the only person in court who did not understand it. Byrne overruled him.

There was a long pause. Walker was in a bind. He wanted to defend Captain Petersen and Pan American, but if he said "yes" it might imply that he had been running a sloppy training department. The fact that he had subsequently lost the job did not help either. Cathcart was waiting to pounce.

Finally Walker said, "The 'philosophy' or 'procedure'— I believe those were the words you used—was to execute a missed approach at any time it became necessary. It was never spelled out by a set of deviations from the glide slope, or was it set out in a set maximum descent rate. It depends entirely on the conditions that exist on the approach at the time."

"Are there any circumstances," Cathcart pressed, "in the way of rates of descent and glide slope needle deviations below an altitude of 300 feet, where the Pan American management would say: it is time to execute an immediate missed approach?"

"We have never specified such circumstances," Walker replied.

"Does good operating practice require that your crews be given some guidelines or criteria or limits as to when they can continue an approach and when it should be abandoned?"

Walker said, "Those guidelines have not been established, no."

Wearily, Cathcart asked Byrne to make Walker answer the question. Byrne repeated it. "Would it have been good operating procedure to have given them such guidelines?"

"Unnecessary," Walker said curtly.

Cathcart did not press the point further. He closed his cross-examination then and there, having left an indelible impression of the quality of Pan American training procedures under Captain John Walker.

If William Tucker had had his way, his next rebuttal witness would have been a certain Captain Clegg. But since Clegg was not on the list at that point, he had to ask the court's permission to bring him in.

Clegg was an Air New Zealand pilot, flying the DC 8. It appeared that on two occasions, in August 1974 and again in November of that year, he had experienced a hard fly-down indication on his glide slope instrument while making an approach to Pago Pago. It had happened inbound of Logotala Hill and before the flight path reached the crash site of Flight 806. He had not reported the first incident, thinking it was a fault in his own instrumentation, but he had reported the second to the CAP/IS operator. The latter had told him that as far as he could see the glide slope was functioning normally.

All this Tucker explained to Byrne outside the hearing of the jury.

There was an instant furor, and no wonder. It seemed to Dombroff a little late in the day to bring forward such evidence, especially since its existence had been known at the time Tucker presented his main case.

Byrne seemed to agree with Dombroff. Why had Clegg not been put on the stand earlier? By doing it now, said Byrne, Tucker was depriving the government of the opportunity to bring forward evidence to rebut it in turn or to produce the CAP/IS operator to tell what he actually said.

Dombroff backed this up and added a couple of extra points, but Tucker was insistent that he was bringing on Clegg only to rebut McFarland's testimony that there had been no changes in the glide slope installation.

"Let me ask you this," said Byrne. "Of all the speculation and insinuation that you have put on so far as evidence . . . here is a man who actually experienced a problem. He actually experienced a problem on the glide slope. And when do you bring him in? You bring him in when the case is all over, when the government has no chance to rebut this testimony at all, and when there is available evidence that, if it doesn't rebut it, at least will weaken it."

"There are a lot of terms for that, but I guess the one I want to use is that it's not fair."

"I don't think Your Honor is right, and I think Your Honor has put your finger on it," replied Tucker in a classic piece of doublethink. He lapsed into gibberish before Byrne intervened:

"Was this fellow on your witness list?"

"Yes, sir," Tucker admitted.

Well, said Byrne, if that was the case and he had not been called, the government was justified in assuming that he was not being used. He refused to allow Clegg to appear or, at least, to give any evidence about his alleged mishap with the glide slope. Tucker had to make do with Edgar A. Post as his next witness.

Post was an independent consultant specializing in weather radar. Tucker wanted to use him to show that the crew of Flight 806 could not have seen the coming storm as they made their final approach, and Post went most of the way with him. At least, he said, it would have been difficult to pick it out under those conditions, and almost impossible to take in the picture at a glance. Petersen would have had to study his radar screen for three or five minutes before being sure.

Cross-examined by Cathcart, however, Post confirmed that the storm cell would have been visible for up to seven minutes before the accident, and that it would have been foolhardy to fly an aircraft into such weather. Cathcart was able to suggest that if Captain Petersen had known the storm was there but had lost sight of it, he had been just as foolish to continue as if he had been able to see it all the way.

And so, part one of the trial ended on May 4, 1978. There were still a few unconsidered trifles lying around, such as the decision on whether or not Jack Hudson could give evidence, but Byrne evidently considered that since the jury would be there for a while yet, he could afford to wait. He had earlier, with some hesitation, rejected a plea from Cathcart that the jury be allowed to pronounce its verdict on the case against Pan American at this stage. They would simply have to hold it all in their heads while the second part of the trial, the case against Boeing, pursued its tortuous path.

After four months of learning how and why Flight 806 hit the ground, the jury was now going to hear what happened to those on board. It was going to be a harrowing experience.

TWENTY-SIX

THE SECOND PART of the trial would present Cathcart with enormous problems. Though it was indisputable that the passengers on Flight 806 had died in a particularly nasty way, that was a different matter from proving exactly what had caused their deaths and who was responsible. It was Cathcart's contention that they had died because the interior materials on the aircraft, when exposed to intense heat, gave off poisonous gases. He would also seek to prove that it was because of the inherent design of the aircraft that the main doors had not opened to allow the victims to escape.

But how was all this to be done? The separate items that go to equip the interior of a Boeing 707 are myriad, and Judge Byrne was pedantically insisting that he should identify the specific pieces that allegedly gave off the fatal gas. As a further complication, during the course of its seven-year life, the Boeing 707 that was Flight 806 had undergone many changes in its interior fittings. Before Cathcart could prove liability against Boeing on this count he had to establish that the manufacturer, and not Pan American, had been responsible for putting the dangerous fitments on board. It was a gargantuan task, made no easier by the fact that Robert Benedict had buried the wreckage before Cathcart's experts could get to look at it.

There was one strong factor running in his favor, however, and it was one that worried the chief Boeing counsel, Boyd Hight. "This case has a high level of emotional content," Hight said, "which could cause a trier of fact to make a decision which was not entirely justified by the cold hard facts."

Cathcart seized on the point, though since the jury had not yet been called in he was largely wasting his dramatic talents. "There is indeed some emotional element," he said. "I'm sure it was emotional to the people who had to undergo this event, who thought they had successfully survived a minor crash landing, only to find that they could not get off the airplane.

"The question of what materials were on the airplane, I know, is a question that has concerned the court. It has concerned us. Time and again, we have sent out interrogatories to Pan American and to Boeing to find out what was on the airplane. The airplane itself was buried, and the materials were burned before we could ever look at it, and we never got back any satisfactory answers, other than to check some microfilm records. I had somebody spend approximately two months going through 140,000 pages of microfilm to try and find out what had gone on and what had come off."

Cathcart went on to protest that it was impossible for anyone to identify the source of an atom of hydrogen cyanide found in a dead body and trace it back to a specific item that either Pan Am or Boeing had supplied. Nor should the law require him to do so. But it began to appear that this was exactly what the law would require. Once more he complained about the burial of the aircraft, and this time Tucker rose to the bait.

"We were ordered to bury it by the FAA," he claimed.

Byrne stepped in to separate them. "We've gone through this for nine months," he said. "Every time he wants to get under your skin, he talks about burying the aircraft. And every time, you get upset by it." Buried or not, he pointed out, they still had to determine what materials were on Flight 806, and they seemed to be some way away from that objective.

With his insistence that each tiny piece of the aircraft should be identified and examined to see whether it caused a death, Byrne was creating difficulties for Cathcart. He blamed the lawyer for failing to come up with the list. Cathcart retorted that it filled a book six to eight inches thick, and they still did not know exactly what was on board at the time of the accident.

"If you don't know, you're going to have a difficult time telling the jury," Byrne said. "And if the jury isn't given some specifics in the evidence, I am going to take the issue from the jury."

That was the last thing Cathcart wanted. The emotional reaction of the jury was his chief hope; if the case was to be decided by Judge Byrne his chances would he sharply diminished.

"I don't think, Judge," he said, "that is a burden imposed on the plaintiffs, who neither owned the airplane burned up while they were on board nor had the airplane buried."

Byrne was totally unmoved. That was exactly the burden he was placing on the plaintiffs. They could produce the evidence to prove their case, or he would take it away from the jury.

Finally, late on the morning of Tuesday, May 9, the opening speeches began and the second part of the trial was underway.

Cathcart, who went first, made considerable play of the burial of the aircraft, goading Tucker to fresh outbursts of fury. When all the darts had been placed, Tucker approached the bench like a bleeding bull to complain to Judge Byrne.

"There's nothing in the pre-trial conference order that has anything to do with the burial of that wreckage. It's a completely phony issue," he protested.

"It may not be an issue," said Byrne mildly, "but don't you think it's a fact in the case, as to why certain tests were not done? Isn't it fair to tell the jury that the wreckage isn't there anymore?"

Not to Tucker, it wasn't. "The way Mr. Cathcart put it —" he began.

Byrne cut him short. "The way he said it does not mean that it is not material to the case. He indicated, or insinuated, as you knew he was going to, that you did it in such a way before the plaintiffs' representatives could get there."

"That brings up the question as to what representative was on that island before this thing was buried," Tucker said. "I think that's a totally extraneous issue. But if we are going to go into extraneous issues, I think it is a two-way street."

Byrne was not to be bullied. He said, "I don't think that the fact that the aircraft was buried is extraneous. As to the motivation for burying it, who was on the island, or who was not on the island, I have no knowledge at all about that."

LEON MARTIN BOUNCED into the witness box on May 10. Stocky and balding, a sprightly sixty-one, he was to be the only survivor from Flight 806 to give direct evidence. The jury listened to his account with rapt attention. It would be unfair to say that Martin had enjoyed his experience on Pago Pago, but for such an extrovert the story lost nothing in the telling.

As a veteran air traveler, he told Cathcart, he had asked for and had gotten a seat next to an emergency exit; more for the increased leg room than for any suspicion that he might have to jump out of it. He was next to the forward exit on the starboard side, with most of the other passengers behind him. Cathcart asked him when he had first noticed something wrong.

"Well," Martin said, "I felt a little turbulence, and then a sort of fish-tailing action in the rear of the plane. This didn't disturb me any great amount, because I'd felt it before coming in on landings. Then there was a real rapid dropping of the airplane, and then I felt the aircraft strike an object. At that moment I knew we were crashing.

"I tightened my belt as hard as I could, and then I looked out of my window. I couldn't see anything. Then I braced myself by placing my elbows on my knees and grasping the seat in front and prepared for a crash, because I knew we were coming down.

"And then you could hear the scraping and the noise of the aircraft, and you could tell it was cutting through trees. As it came on down, the ride got a little rougher. There was a severe jolt, which I guess proved to be where the nose and the two engines struck the ground, then another jolt, and a harder jolt.

"By this time the airplane was on fire, because I brought my head up and saw that it was burning right where I was sitting. And I could see the flames, and it was a really profuse fire. It was a hard fire, and of course, I put my head back down and hung on harder until the aircraft came to a complete stop. It stopped with quite a sudden jar."

"Did you hear any screams," asked Cathcart, "or cries that you associated with pain?"

"No," Martin said. "I heard noises. I heard people yelling. I sat there for a brief moment, and I was aware of people making noise and people moving. There were people in the aisle. I believe they were moving forwards and backwards.

"I stood up, and for some reason decided to get out of there and get out fast. So I took hold of the exit window and opened it. That's when I got burned on the face and hands. I had the presence of mind to close that window quickly. I pulled that window shut. I felt that I had one way out, but that wasn't the real way, so I walked across to the middle of the aisle and looked out of that window.

"I could see I had a better way out there, because on my side the fire was really burning. On the left side of the aircraft, the window I was now looking out of, there just seemed to be a blooping of fire. Every now and again, there would be just a shot of fire coming up, and I figured that now I had two ways out and that was the better one.

"Then, I still don't know why, but for some reason I went towards the front of the aircraft. I don't know how far I went forward, maybe two or three seats, but I do know I was hit with a big black cloud, like black molasses. It hit me in the face, and it either knocked me down to the floor or I dropped to the floor instinctively, knowing that if there was any air that was where it would be. I very distinctly remember hearing someone up in the front forward cabin calling out a command for the people to quiet down, and then the man stopped right in the middle of his sentence. That was the instant when I was down, knocked down on to the floor."

Martin said the cloud of smoke seemed to come from the upper part of the cabin. He went on. "At that particular instant I really felt a bit of panic myself for the first time. Up until then I'd been, I think, rather cool and collected, but then I did feel really excited. I knew that all I had to do was to take a breath, and I would die. It frightens me still. That would have been the easy thing to do.

"But then I decided, I said to myself, 'No, Martin, not now, you, this way,' and I turned and made up my mind how to get out of the aircraft, and returned back to the window on the opposite side."

He found the forward emergency exit on the port side still closed. He opened it and no flames came through. "I dived or jumped through that door. I landed on the wing on all fours.

"The moment I landed I was on my feet and I was headed down that wing, that aluminum ribbon. Then, as I started out down the wing, I noticed a man on my left. It seemed that just as I got even with that man, or just as I passed him, I saw him slip and fall off the back edge of the wing. I went on down and jumped off the back part of the wing, somewhere past where the outboard engine probably should have been if it had still been there, and I remember hitting the ground very hard, again on all fours, because I didn't want to land on my feet and slip and fall."

Cathcart asked, "Was the top of the wing intact?"

"That wing was intact," Martin said. "That was like an aluminum highway to freedom for me. My only thought was to thank God that I had made it, and then to get out of there before that thing blew up. I'd seen airplanes blow up before, and I wanted to get away. So, I got back into the jungle, about forty or fifty feet. I turned around and looked at the aircraft, and I watched it. On the far side of that airplane the flames were just going all the way up to the heavens, and it was really burning, burning hard. There did not seem to be a great deal of flame or fire on my side of the aircraft at all."

Had there been any flames around the forward main entry door?" Cathcart asked.

"No," Martin said.

"Could you tell, from where you were, whether the door was open, closed, or somewhere in between?"

"When I saw it," Martin replied, "the door was closed. Both the forward and the back door were closed."

"Did you see any flame that would be in the way of people who wanted to come out through either of the emergency exits and use the wing as you used it?"

"No, sir," said Martin, and he added, "I'm sure people could have gotten out."

His last remark was stricken from the record by Judge Byrne.

After standing in the jungle for a short time, Martin said he remembered the man who had fallen from the wing and decided to go back to help him.

"Then I changed my mind, and then I changed my mind again. I went back towards the aircraft, towards the trailing edge of the wing, and got to Mr. Hinton just as he was getting to his feet. I helped him up, and then he said something about his wife. I reached down and helped her to her feet."

Martin went on to recount his meeting with Susan and Michael Rogers and their hair-raising ride to the hospital. He had seen no fire-fighting equipment on the scene, though four or five days later, he had gone back to the site of the crash and noticed that there was an access road running from the end of runway 5 to where the Boeing lay. He did not mention that he had stood on top of the wreckage and had his photograph taken.

The jury was absorbed by this first-hand account of the crash, though Brent was to say later, "Mr. Martin talked and talked about what he did, but by the time Michael Rogers came back to find his wife, Martin was already there helping her. He must have been out in ten seconds flat, but all these things were going on in his mind. There is no way he could have done all those things."

Cross-examined by Boyd Hight for Boeing, Martin said time and again that he saw no fire around the rear door of the aircraft at the time he escaped. Hight could make no real impression on his testimony, and neither could Tucker.

The rest of the survivors, Susan and Michael Rogers and David Pontiff, all testified by way of deposition. There were to be a lot of depositions in Cathcart's case, mainly because it was cheaper than bringing witnesses from far away, and much of the human impact was lost in consequence. One man who might have repaid closer examination in the box was Robert E. Burgin of the NTSB. Burgin had been in charge of a nine-man human factors and witness group, which had gone to Pago Pago to investigate the crash. In his deposition he said he "believed" the forward main passenger door on the port side had been jammed in a partially open position, but he had not tried to open the door himself and had no idea what caused the jamming. The question "Why not?" screamed to be asked, but there was no one in the witness box.

The autopsy reports, presented by Dr. Dean Wiseley, the Los Angeles coroner, were unpleasant. They would have been even more unpleasant if Judge Byrne had not stepped in to prevent the jury from hearing some of the details—and thereby being swayed in favor of the victims— but they could not be completely shut out. Ninety-seven people had died, and that was an inescapable fact. The bodies had been badly charred, many with their extremities burned away completely, and identification had taken six weeks. There had been sufficient evidence, however, to show that all had died from carbon monoxide or other forms of poisoning and, in the case of the crew, that they had not suffered heart attacks or been drunk at the time.

TWENTY-SEVEN

AS THE DEPOSITIONS ROLLED IN, several of them from NTSB investigators who confessed to giving scant attention to the question of why the doors did not open, the issue of who buried the wreckage and why began to assume greater proportions. From the beginning of this phase of the trial, Cathcart had fought a running battle with Tucker over the admission of evidence to prove the point. Though the evidence in question came from one of his own attorneys, Dennis P. Venuti, and by this time only existed in "summary" form, Tucker was firmly opposed to the subject being mentioned at all. When he finally submitted, having realized that after Cathcart's opening statement the subject could not be pushed under the rug, it was easy to see why.

Venuti exploded Tucker's claim that "the FAA made us bury it." In one section of his deposition that the jury was allowed to hear—quite a lot of it was cut out—he said there was no insistence by anyone that Pan Am should bury the wreckage. The FAA and the local authorities had merely given permission, but that was all. Neither Robert Benedict nor anyone else had discussed with him the possibility that the wreck of Flight 806 might be preserved for further investigation.

The importance of that decision became clear when the expert who would have been hired by Cathcart to look at the wreckage came to give evidence. Nelson Shapter, who had served with the airframe branch of the FAA in Washington for thirty-five years, was asked if an inspection would have helped him find out why the doors had failed to open.

Shapter replied, "If I could have seen it and actually been able to make measurements and literally to study the deformation that might have been associated with it, yes." Having been able to do none of these things, he had had to rely on photographs, and these seemed to show that the forward door had not suffered direct damage. It was not the same thing, and Cathcart rammed the point home time and again.

Shapter produced a number of FAA regulations, which were destined to bring the trial to a grinding halt. The first read: "Reasonable provision shall be made to prevent the jamming of external doors as a result of the fuselage deformation in a minor crash."

The second: "Crew and passenger areas shall be provided with emergency evacuation means to permit rapid egress in the event of crash landings, whether with the landing gear extended or retracted, taking into account the possibility of the aircraft being on fire."

And the third: "The structure shall be designed to give every reasonable probability that all the occupants, if they make proper use of the seats, belts, and other provisions made in the design, will escape serious injury in the event of a minor crash landing (with the wheels up if the airplane is equipped with retractable landing gear) in which the occupants experience the following ultimate forces relative to the surrounding structure: 2G upwards, 4.5G downwards, 9G forwards, and 1.5G sideways."

According to Shapter, the forward G-force on the passengers aboard Flight 806 had only been 2.5G. As the aircraft scythed through the trees, each separate impact had absorbed some of the tremendous energy, and the Boeing 707 had done a good job in soaking up the crash forces and keeping its passengers alive.

But the fact was that in the end the passengers had not survived, and the issue concerning the court was whether this should be considered a "minor crash"—in which case Boeing would have been in breach of FAA regulations—or whether it was something more. Byrne's problem was that the FAA had not bothered to define what was meant by the term "minor crash," and that he had to rely on what the alleged experts told him.

This had its own hazards. As he remarked plaintively to the counsel gathered around him, "There appears to be no difficulty in getting either an FAA employee or an ex-FAA employee to give you two totally diverse interpretations of their own regulation."

Hight contended that when the FAA referred to the structure of the aircraft, it really meant only the seats and seat belts. When Byrne doubted him, he suggested that the judge call the FAA.

"From my experience thus far in trying this case," Byrne retorted, "it would depend who answered the phone." He decided to send the jury away and question Shapter himself.

Did the load factor of 9G apply to the doors?

Shapter said it did.

Could there be such a thing as a minor crash landing away from an airport?

Yes, Shapter replied. The definition of whether it was minor or not depended on the G factors involved in the crash, not on its location.

Byrne asked him if he had looked at the affidavits of any of his colleagues on this subject, and Shapter said he had seen one by a George Bogert.

"He's totally incorrect, I assume," said Byrne ironically.

"He's incorrect in my estimation," Shapter replied.

Byrne had not got very far and decided to let Hight take over the questioning. "Are we going to have any other problems like this come up?" he asked. No one dared to answer. It was all too likely.

Hight, for his part, was pushing the line that if the FAA had certified the aircraft, including the doors, then it must have conformed with the regulations.

"They might have goofed," Byrne interrupted. "The plaintiffs have been saying that all along. They just goofed up. The FAA made a mistake, so what does that have to do with the interpretation of this regulation? Certainly, they certified it. But perhaps the FAA missed it, and so did Boeing."

Hight decided that if interpretation of the regulations was what Byrne wanted, interpretation he should have. He brought up his own FAA witness, George D. Bogert. Bogert had retired from the airframe section of the agency's western region in 1972. He, too, had worked for the FAA for thirty-five years.

As far as Bogert was concerned, a minor crash was one in which an aircraft was under control and came down on a level surface without obstructions.

Byrne took over the questioning once again. Was there anything in writing from the FAA to back that up? Bogert, to the judge's despair, knew of nothing. And having confirmed that the regulations applied to the doors and the structure surrounding them, he then remembered why he was there and said they were aimed primarily at the attachments of the seats and the safety belt.

Byrne persisted: "When you were certifying aircraft, did you believe that the aircraft frame and doors should be designed to give every reasonable probability that all the occupants would escape serious injury in the event of a minor crash landing with the G-forces laid down?"

"Yes," said Bogert.

"And if the doors and structures were not designed to give reasonable probability of all the occupants escaping serious injury in the event of a minor crash under those forces, the doors and the frame were not designed in compliance with the regulations. Is that correct?"

Bogert needed the question repeated before he replied, "Yes, sir, they would not have met this requirement."

That must have lifted Cathcart's spirits, but a moment later Bogert was telling Hight that the value of G-forces in the regulations only applied to the occupants, not to the structure of the aircraft. They were all getting nowhere rather slowly.

It was the following day, with the jury still absent and the legal argument raging, that Byrne remembered that they had never asked Shapter for his definition of a minor crash. Byrne was a man to leave no stone unturned. He got Shapter back into the witness box and asked the question.

This was unfortunate. Shapter was a man whose use of the English language had been dulled by a lifetime's exposure to bureaucratic gobbledygook. He said, "From the regulatory point of view that I have indicated, which includes all those sections of Civil Aviation Regulation 48 to which we refer, there isn't a clear definition, in so many words. The concept, if I can put it in that frame, embraces both the load factors that are developed at a minimum level, not necessarily that you can't develop higher levels, but that is the order of magnitude that would be expected not to be exceeded insofar as a minor crash landing is concerned from a design point of view. It is not a value that necessarily occurs in every landing or things of this sort, but if they do exceed them then it becomes, in terms of the structural aspect, something greater than a crash landing."

Quite so.

Byrne emerged from this fog of verbiage with a decision to make. Confused or not, the issue was important, for if he ruled that the Pago Pago disaster rated as a minor crash, then regulations had been broken. Boeing, and very possibly the FAA, would suffer as a result.

He said, "My determination, if I had to decide right away, would be that I wouldn't pay any attention to what either witness said. That is no criticism of the witnesses, but I might as well take a dictionary definition of a minor crash landing. Here are two witnesses, both from the FAA, both with substantial responsibility, and both interpreting the term entirely differently."

But after a lot more argument from Cathcart and Hight, Byrne did make a ruling: "I find that this section is not applicable to the question now being presented, and do not believe that the section applies to doors and fuselage structure, and does not apply to the type of landing that is here involved."

It was a strike against Dan Cathcart, and an important one.

Shapter's testimony went on, but it was now more limited. He was able to say, in effect, that it was good design philosophy to design airplane doors so that people could get out of them in an emergency. In the case of Flight 806, since the fuselage had survived the impact and there appeared to have been no undue forces in the cabin, the doors should have opened. They had not done so. It still left a lot of questions unanswered, but it was becoming plain that with the wreckage buried beyond recall they never would be answered.

———

ON WEDNESDAY, May 24, the trial slipped gently from confusion into chaos. The issue was that of the materials used to furnish the interior of Flight 806—not so much from the point of view of whether they were dangerous, but what items were there and who had installed them.

To Dan Cathcart it must have seemed so simple at the outset. He had a living survivor, Leon Martin, to testify to the presence of dense and poisonous smoke in the cabin. He had the undeniable presence of fire, and he had medical evidence to prove that those on board had toxins in their blood of the kind released by burning plastics. From there, it was surely a short and simple step to proving that those who put the plastic material on board should be indicted for causing the death of the passengers and crew. There were, after all, only two possible culprits: Pan American or Boeing. With luck, he might get a verdict against both.

Alas, the step was neither short nor simple. From the moment he produced his first witness on the subject, it became clear that this was to be a microcosm of the whole trial, an exercise in legal gamesmanship in which truth and justice were of little importance when set beside the personal feuds of the attorneys.

The witness in question was Dennis Craig Jones, a young second-year law student who had been employed by Cathcart to go through the vast quantity of records. It quickly became apparent that Jones had suffered from two severe handicaps: he had been brought into the case suddenly and late, and furthermore, the documents were, in any case, incomplete.

The story, as it unraveled over tortuous hours and days of argument, went something like this: Boeing, in its own defense, had requested Pan American to produce documents to show what changes had been made on the aircraft since its delivery. Pan American had complied, and one of the Boeing attorneys, Sally Treweek, had gone to New Jersey where the documents were stored. There she found about half a million pages of information, of which she had 140,000 pages microfilmed.

Cathcart had taken a shortcut. Instead of going to the original source, he had had Jones review the Boeing microfilm, which was no small task in itself. For more than six weeks, he had skimmed through the material, stopping every twenty or thirty pages to see if there was anything relevant. What Cathcart had to put in evidence, therefore, was a précis of a summary of what was on the airplane and who put it there. For Byrne, it was simply not enough. "I want a list of every specific item that you contend was a basis of fault in this action," he said.

Cathcart tried to bluff his way out: "We contend that everything that was in that cabin, Your Honor, which was non-metallic, was a basis of fault."

Byrne raised his eyebrows. "If that's what you are contending," he said, "I have never heard that contention before. In other words, they should have been sitting on metal seats?"

It was the reduction of Cathcart's argument to absurdity. "No, no, no, no, no," he replied.

"They should have had a metal carpet?"

"Not at all," Cathcart said.

Byrne: "Maybe I misunderstood."

"It's our position," said Cathcart in some desperation, "that those materials were all inconsistent with passenger evacuation in a post-crash environment, because they would produce an environment in there that was hostile and lethal to the passengers."

But the judge was not to be swayed.

He said, "I want a specific list of each item that you contend was in that aircraft, be it the toilet seats, be it the handle on the water dispenser, that you are contending that Boeing was either negligent in putting on the aircraft, or was a defect in their design of the aircraft, or that Pan American was negligent in putting on the aircraft. Then you can summarize your records and show me and the jury whether, for instance, the curtain or the toilet seat, or whatever it might be, was put on by Boeing, put on by Pan American, or put on by Boeing and changed by Pan American."

That was exactly what Cathcart could not do, and he knew it. Byrne blamed him for failing to do his job properly; he blamed Byrne for making rulings that rendered his task impossible, and both Boeing and Pan Am for indulging in gamesmanship. Byrne himself suspected there had been "a little hanky-panky" going on, but he was not going to budge from his stand: he wanted the complete list and, if necessary, Pan American would have to produce the documents and sort them out—all half million pages.

Tom Smith was aghast. "That," he said, "is going to take an awful long time."

"It might," agreed Byrne.

———

BY TUESDAY, May 30, nothing much had happened and Judge Byrne was getting angry. When Cathcart suggested he had put forward sufficient evidence already and it was up to the other side to prove him wrong, Byrne snapped back: "To me it's totally incredible that the plaintiffs and defendants have never made a study to determine what was on their airplane and who put it there. Now one side is contending that the other side is liable because of the things they put on the aircraft. The other side says, we are not liable for anything we put on the aircraft. And nobody seems to have analyzed, in all the years of discovery in this case—all the untold hundreds of thousands, if not millions of dollars that have been spent in the preparation of this case—no one has apparently made an analysis of what was on the airplane."

Sally Treweek got up to explain how overwhelming her task had been, and how with three assistants it had still been impossible to copy all the documents. Byrne faced the problem that if the plaintiffs had been lulled into believing that they had all the necessary material, as they claimed, he ought to intervene to help them. On the other hand, if they had merely been inefficient that was their own responsibility. But which was true? One by one the attorneys swore their innocence.

Finally, he reached a decision. He would allow Cathcart to go ahead and use the material he had but insisted that a foundation would have to be laid for each and every item. It was not much help. Jones came back to the witness box for an unhappy session during which he was forced to admit that he had read less than a quarter of the documents. Cathcart tried to boost his testimony by producing one of his employees, a man named James Gibbons, who had reviewed Jones's work. But that was not a signal success, either.

Boyd Hight, in a breathless sentence fully three hundred words long, moved to strike the testimony of both from the record. Jones and Gibbons, he said, had not reviewed all the documents available, were not competent to assess them, and had made numerous mistakes.

Cathcart fought hard, for without this evidence his case against Boeing was in tatters, and if he was going to do any better for his clients than the strict limit on damages laid down by the Warsaw Convention, he would be left with proving willful misconduct against Pan American. Denied the use of the Hudson report and the crew training records, and with no precedents in his favor, the chances of this were not rosy.

Byrne's ruling faced both ways. He found that Jones's and Gibbons's testimony was insufficient to lay a foundation for the evidence, but he denied the motion to strike it. He would wait to see what happened. No wonder Cathcart asked for a pause in the proceedings to see exactly where that left him.

———

THE DAYS TICKED by into June and still the legal arguments continued. Byrne began to complain of the unfortunate effect on the jury. Finally, with the whole issue still unresolved, Cathcart tried to break the logjam by calling Matthew Radnofsky.

Radnofsky was an independent consultant on fire-resisting materials, whose curriculum vitae filled seventeen pages of the court transcript. He had been called to help with the aftermath of the Apollo spacecraft fire in 1967, in which three astronauts were killed, and had subsequently been involved in the design of space suits. The jury began to wonder whether Cathcart was about to contend that Pan American should have issued space suits to the passengers on Flight 806, but it turned out otherwise. The core of Radnofsky's testimony was that at the time the Boeing 707 was built, less flammable materials were available than those actually installed.

This sounded fine, until Radnofsky was forced to admit under cross-examination by Hight that he had recommended wool for use in aircraft upholstery, and that burning wool produced hydrogen cyanide. He had probably made a mistake, he said, in not carrying out sufficient tests.

A week later, on June 13, Radnofsky was still in the witness box, most of the intervening time having been taken up with interminable legal tussles on the issue of the aircraft's contents. Byrne's ruling had solved nothing, and he was making increasingly testy comments about gamesmanship among the attorneys. Cathcart's case was proceeding like a one-legged man trying to climb a mountain, and he gave up the unequal struggle the following day.

TWENTY-EIGHT

SEEN IN RETROSPECT, Cathcart's case against Boeing was not a howling success. Had he drawn a bead on one example of plastic on board Flight 806, proving its presence and toxicity, he might have fared better. But he chose to fire both barrels indiscriminately at the whole interior and became so confused by the legal ricochets that his aim was lost. He committed the same error that afflicted William Tucker in the first half of the trial: he overstuffed the jury. In Tucker's case this may have been deliberate tactics. If he made the case too complicated for the jury to understand, there was always the chance that Judge Byrne would take it away from them and decide the issue himself. In all the circumstances, this would have given Pan Am a better chance. The same reasoning could not apply to Cathcart; he needed the human sympathy that only a jury could give him, and he muffed it.

By contrast, the Boeing case, which opened on June 15, was a model of simplicity. Boyd Hight, who was later to achieve prominence in the Carter administration, began by calling one of the designers of the 707, Howard Warren Smith. Smith could hold his head quite high. After all, the fuselage of Flight 806 had withstood the crash and kept its passengers and crew alive until after the impact. Though Cathcart tried hard to shake him on the design of the doors, Smith's theory was that there must have been local damage by a tree or some part of the aircraft, possibly the nose wheel, and his reasoning retained a certain logic.

The man who had actually designed the doors was Allan William Opsahl, who had worked as an engineer for Boeing for the past thirty years. He had worked out the design, which was revolutionary at the time, in 1955. It had remained basically unchanged ever since and had even been sold to the Russians.

The unique feature of the door, Opsahl explained, was that it achieved two objects: it functioned as a plug for safety during pressurized flight but opened outward for easy evacuation. It did this by moving inward a few inches when the handle was rotated, at the same time folding its upper and lower edges inward to clear the frame. The door could then be pushed straight out. The design, Opsahl said, had specifically allowed for some distortion of the doorframe in a crash.

Still, it was beyond question that the doors had failed to open on this occasion, though he believed that the rear one, at least, had been operable after the crash.

Cathcart had only one line of attack open to him, and he played it for all it was worth. He suggested that it might have been impossible for a stewardess to open the door those vital inches inward if there had been a crush of panic-stricken passengers trying to get out. The position of the bodies, of course, did little to support this theory, but it was worth a try.

Opsahl admitted that the door had not been tested under such conditions, though he had conducted an experiment himself with five men crowding behind him and found no particular difficulty. However, they had never used a woman in the same circumstances.

Until Dr. Edward Parish Radford appeared on the stand for Boeing, there had not been much challenge to the theory that the victims of Flight 806 had died from inhaling poisonous gases, whatever may have caused them. But Radford, who boasted the somewhat gruesome distinction of being an expert on death by fire, had a different idea. He claimed that neither carbon monoxide nor hydrogen cyanide had played a significant part in stopping the evacuation. There had not been time for such gases to build up, especially from the interior furnishings.

What had killed those on board Flight 806, according to Radford, had been nothing more complex than extreme heat and the accompanying lack of oxygen caused by the fuel fire. They had, in effect, been caught in an immense oven, which was bound to kill them if they did not get out within twenty seconds.

It was simple, it was believable, and none of Cathcart's efforts could shake Radford from this view. He was a strong witness.

IRVING PINKLE WAS a man who loved to crash airplanes. In his time, he had crashed forty or fifty, all for the cause of science, and he came to the witness box to reconstruct the last fatal moments of Flight 806.

Pinkle described how the nose wheel must have folded up on impact, becoming trapped against the belly of the aircraft as it made its wild slide across the rocky ground. Stones and other debris would have joined it in a jumbled mass beneath the fuselage, striking massive hammer blows to rip open and break up the structure.

At first impact, the fuel from the ruptured tanks would have spurted forward, enveloping the aircraft in a fine spray that would explode in a ball of flame. Huge quantities of fuel would have spilled out when the aircraft came to rest, unable to soak into the ground because it was already saturated with rain. It had poured into the gully, where the wind whipped the fire into greater fury, concentrating the flames on the torn belly of Flight 806 like a gigantic blacksmith's forge.

Pinkle's evidence was graphic and delivered with an almost ghoulish relish. It certainly held the attention of the jury.

Amid mounting objections from Cathcart, who could see his case melting away like the snows of yesteryear under all this talk of unbearable heat, Pinkle said he felt the smoke experienced by Martin came directly from the fuel fire. He went on to say, "It's my opinion that the rate of heating of the fuselage, through the floor and sides, raised the interior temperature to intolerable levels within the first minute, to temperature levels which people cannot support for more than about ten seconds."

The floor, Pinkle said, would have reached a temperature of about 600°F in less than a minute, which was beyond the limit of tolerance for the most rugged person. Smoke and gas would have been rising through the ventilation vents at floor level.

THEY WERE NEARING THE END.

It was time to clear up some of the legal detritus that had been left lying around unresolved for weeks and months. Cathcart began by returning to his favorite theme: the burial of the aircraft. "It's our belief," he said, "that the running over of the airplane with a caterpillar tractor, burying it in a hole, is a willful suppression of evidence. It denied us the opportunity to have it examined and to analyze it."

"Your Honor," Tucker retorted indignantly, "that is one of the most ridiculous arguments I have ever heard in this trial. With due respect to my friend Mr. Cathcart, that machine is sitting out there in the middle of a navigational aid, in the middle of an airway facility. What is Pan American going to do? Hold it until the plaintiffs get around to looking at it?"

The judge thought for a moment, then came down on the side of Pan American. "I don't believe there is sufficient evidence," he said, "to allow the jury to be instructed that there was a willful suppression of evidence in this case." And that was that.

But there was another, more serious issue still lurking. The question of Jack Hudson—his report and his deposition—had since the outset been haunting the trial like Banquo's ghost. Though the proper moment for this evidence was long past, Cathcart was not about to give up trying to get it in, nor Tucker abandon the fight to keep it out.

Hudson, Tucker said, had not conducted a specific investigation into the crash of Flight 806 but only into the affairs of Pan American. And anything he might have to say on that subject would be hearsay, speculation, and conjecture.

Byrne had now seen the summary of the deposition—something he had been demanding for weeks—and felt that though some of it was inadmissible, some was not. Cathcart, nurturing the reasonable suspicion that Byrne wanted to cut out all the interesting bits, felt it should all go in. Hudson's opinions, he said, related to Pan American's operation and the adequacy of crew training and pilot checking.

"It's been our effort in this case," he said, "although unfortunately we have not been completely successful, to show that this accident, or the causes of this accident, began with Pan American management in New York. They set the policies which Pan American management in San Francisco carried out, and which resulted in a crew that was criticized by several people in this case as being less than adequate."

Byrne began to go through the deposition line by line. Some of the material, he said, if properly obtained and put in evidence, would have been admissible. In its present form it was hearsay. "If there's somebody in the FAA up in San Francisco that evaluated Petersen and had an opinion that he was a lousy pilot, that might be admissible," he said. "It might be, but this isn't admissible."

Finally, Cathcart surrendered. It was as though he could not bear to see his cherished evidence, on which he had founded so many hopes, subjected to the death of a thousand cuts. "In view of the court's rulings," he said, "we will not be reading any portion of Mr. Hudson's deposition summary. There is nothing left in it of value to our proceedings." He was dignified in defeat, but it must have hurt.

They passed on to a couple of depositions from minor witnesses, duly trimmed, and then the evidential phase was over. It was June 28, and they all went away for two weeks to prepare their final speeches and the instructions to the jury.

———

ON JULY 12, when the court reassembled, there was a fresh and unexpected problem. Richard Fitzgerald, one of the six principal jurors, turned out to be a motor racing enthusiast. He had overturned his car during a race and had broken a few assorted bones with the result that he was heavily encased in plaster. After all this time, it seemed that he would not be able to participate in the final decision. They would have to find someone from the reserve panel to put in his place.

Who should it be? Here was a fresh opportunity for wrangling. As Byrne began to run through the names, there were suggestions that one or two had not been as wide awake during the proceedings as they might have been. Though, as Tucker said, "If we are going to exclude everybody who has closed their eyes during this trial, there are a couple of candidates a little more sophisticated than Mr. Callaghan [the juror under discussion at the time].

Byrne took the remark personally. "We don't have peremptory challenges of judges in federal courts," he said. Tucker virtuously denied any such suggestion.

In the end, the choice came down to a woman, Mrs. Anita Ford, leaving Michael Brent as the only male member of the jury. The selection was at the root of some strange things that happened later, and for an odd reason: Mrs. Ford had formed an intense personal admiration for William Tucker.

———

SUCH CONSIDERATIONS WERE NOT EXACTLY what Judge Byrne had in mind when he instructed the jury on the legal aspects of the case. "Our system of law," he said, "does not permit jurors to be governed by sympathy, prejudice, or public opinion. This case should be considered and decided by you as an action between persons of equal standing in the community, of equal worth, and holding the same, or similar, stations in life. A corporation or a government is entitled to the same fair trial at your hands as a private individual. The law is no respecter of persons. All persons, including corporations or governmental agencies, stand before the law and are to be dealt with as equals in a court of justice."

Having thus disposed of the Orwellian concept that some persons are more equal than others, Judge Byrne settled down to review the issues in detail. It was a rational and fair sum-up, as simple as could be expected in view of the self-generating complexity of the trial.

As for counsel, they prepared to spend the remainder of the week on their closing submissions. This was the last chance. Few adjectives would remain unused, few withers left unwrung.

———

CATHCART WENT FIRST, belaboring Pan American for violating their own fuel procedures and for flying an aircraft at maximum weight into a hazardous airport with an unqualified crew. He had a lot of things to say about Pan American, all uncomplimentary, and then he turned to dead Captain Petersen and dead co-pilot Phillips, ghostly on either hand.

"It is difficult for me to stand before you," Cathcart said, "and criticize the human performance and human failure of men I cannot look in the eye, and who cannot answer me back. It is a very awkward and uncomfortable position to be in, because those men are defenseless to my criticisms. But I have to say it, and what I have to say perhaps will be regarded by many as ugly. It certainly won't be complimentary, but it has to be said.

"This crew unfortunately did not make one mistake, they did not make two mistakes, they made almost all the mistakes you can make in flying an approach to land at an airport. The crew itself left an indelible record, so in a sense it is speaking as to what it did.

"If the actions of this crew could be explained—or tolerated or justified— 'The World's Most Experienced Airline' should have plenty of pilots who could review what this crew did and explain it or justify it.

"So as I criticize these men I criticize them not as defenseless men and not as completely silent men, and I hope when I do criticize them that you people will understand that the passengers in this case, through denial of any responsibility whatsoever by Pan American for the injuries and deaths here, are given no choice but to speak to you of the conduct of the Pan Am crew."

And Cathcart went on to describe the last minutes of the approach in fine detail, taking the evidence of the cockpit voice recorder.

"There is not an ounce of concern," he said, "expressed by anybody in the cockpit. There is someone humming throughout the approach. Totally complacent, totally oblivious as to what is about to happen. There is no 'Hey man, look out, you are too low' or 'Look out, you are off the glide slope' or 'What the heck are you doing?' or 'Pull up' or 'Go around' or anything. There was nothing. No warning, no indication of any kind. The crew was totally oblivious of where they were, what they were doing, how they were doing it, or how the other fellow was doing it. An approach that was made with every procedure called for in the manual violated."

He itemized each and every alleged misdeed. "It isn't one mistake; it isn't two mistakes; it isn't little mistakes. They are enormous mistakes, and when you look at them all, there is only once conclusion: that tragically Pan Am's management and Pan Am's crew set the circumstances at Pago Pago for a tragic accident that was the consequence of both negligence and willful misconduct."

With the case against Boeing, Cathcart was less sure-footed. He made maximum play of the burial of the wreckage, blaming it, in effect, for his failure to put on better evidence. He wound up in mid-afternoon with a whimper rather than a bang.

It was Tucker's turn next. Expanding before the jury like a pouter pigeon, he boomed at them boldly: "It is our position today, it was our position over one hundred trial days ago, and it has been our position since the action started that Pan Am was not guilty of negligence, Pan Am was not guilty of wanton misconduct, and the sole cause of this tragedy was the acts of the FAA, coupled with the acts of the National Weather Service, and enhanced by the acts of individuals running the airport."

Tucker paused briefly to consider if there was anyone he had missed. The baggage loaders at Auckland, perhaps? The odd itinerant seagull? God, in his capacity as rainmaker? But no, he left it there. It was simply anyone at all except the crew, to whom he gave glowing references.

Had he made the technical issues too complicated for Mr. Cathcart to understand? Tut tut, he was sorry about that. But his obligation was not to make glide slopes and the like comprehensible to Mr. Cathcart but to the jury. And that he was sure he had done.

The jury stared at him blankly.

Had the aircraft been overweight? Well, it had taken off from Auckland without any trouble, and it had had a heck of a lot more fuel on it then. So that had to be all right. As for the issue of stored fuel, it was perfectly permissible to carry it from Honolulu to Pago Pago, Tucker said grandly—presumably hoping that the jury would forget that Flight 806 was traveling from Auckland and that on that sector it was forbidden.

Tucker wound up with a flourish: "The basic problem resolves itself on what drove this aircraft into the ground. Was it Captain Petersen, Mr. Phillips, Mr. Green, or Mr. Gaines? Were they oblivious to what was going on on that flight deck? There was well over 30,000 hours [of experience] on that flight deck. Those people had a lot to live for. How can you say that the evidence in this case shows that they were oblivious?

"How can Mr. Cathcart say the evidence shows they were oblivious in the light of the environmental conditions that existed on the night in question? In the light of the down-drafts that were occurring? In the light of the visibility problems? In the light of the showers and the rain cells? How can you say, in the light of Mr. Saunders's testimony, that the environmental conditions were such in those last five seconds that it was possible to pull that aircraft out?

"Mr. Cathcart is going to say, why didn't they do it before? What notice did they have before that last seven seconds or nine seconds or five seconds that they were about to encounter that type of extreme down-draft and wind shear? What notice did they have that at that critical point when they were approaching these areas of down-draft and wind shear that the glide slope was going to malfunction? That there was going to be a power interruption? That the mechanical modulator was going to slow down? That they were going to get a false fly-down indication? What indication did they have? When Mr. Cathcart addresses you again, test each of his final arguments with your common sense."

It was quite remarkable. Tucker had taken all his many theories, ignored the fact that cross-examination had blown them to pieces, and presented them as immutable truth.

Mark Dombroff, who was next in line to address the jury, was not impressed.

———

WHEN MARK DOMBROFF was in law school he learned an important dictum: "When the facts are against you, you pound the law; when the law is against you, you pound the facts; when both facts and law are against you, pound the table."

He glanced at Tucker as he repeated it. There had, said Dombroff, been a good deal of table-pounding in the courtroom during the course of this trial. He went on: "It's a simple case. I told you it was a simple case when I addressed you back in March, and it is a simple case today. What has made it complex is the manner in which Pan Am, and to a much lesser degree the plaintiffs, have attempted to present it to you. They have presented a complex case in an attempt to cover the issues with some sort of smoke, to create issues which don't exist. We have seen the birth of many factual issues in this case. We have seen lawyers father these issues. They just don't exist."

Not having been involved in the second part of the trial, Dombroff had had time to sharpen his final argument to a fine edge. He was to speak for several hours, but the nub of his argument was encapsulated in those first few sentences.

"What caused the crash?" he asked. "The four men at the front end of the aircraft. It is a tragic thing to say, and a terrible thing to say, but that is what did it. And no amount of squirming and wriggling and putting up smokescreens will detract from that.

"Frankly, after listening to Pan Am's evidence in this case, I don't know what caused the crash. Did the hand of God cause the crash? Was it wind shear? Was the angle of the ILS too great? Was there reverse sensing? Was there fly-down?

"Boy, that was one heck of a night when all these things happened at once. That was one heck of a seven seconds. That would really rank up there with the creation of the earth, because I can't think of any other time when so many things happened at once."

Cathcart, he said, had acknowledged that there was nothing wrong with the ILS system at Pago Pago that night, or with the National Weather Service or with the CAP/IS. "I wish he had acknowledged that a long time ago; I would have felt better for the past six months. That has to tell you something: that people who don't have this self-interest in terms of protecting their clients, who represent those who were sitting in the back of the aircraft, drinking coffee, reading magazines, and looking forward to getting home, say that none of these things had anything to do with it."

Dombroff ran through the evidence with devastating effect, demolishing one Pan Am witness after another. Even James Leet, he said, the general manager of the airline, had admitted that he had never heard of any problems with the navigation aids at Pago Pago prior to the crash of Flight 806. "Well, there weren't any comments, there weren't any negative reports, there weren't any inadequacies until lawyers got hold of it. You have seen the birth of a child of this litigation. It is a natural wonder of the world. You have seen this litigation give birth to issues, to facts, to contentions that nobody could have imagined before this crash occurred. It is a sham. All of it is a sham."

He stoutly defended Bateman, the CAP/IS operator, who had been accused by Tucker of contributing to the accident by not passing on the latest weather report. "He didn't have it in time," Dombroff said. "Mr. Bateman didn't sit on the thing. He wasn't saving it for a sunny day. He wasn't going to deprive anyone of any information. He told them there was a bad rain shower, he told them he couldn't see the lights, he told them he thought he had a power failure; but the aircraft talked him out of it. The crew said, 'Well everything is fine here, still bright to us; we are getting everything.' They talked him out of it. What was the man supposed to do?

"Let's talk about stored fuel," Dombroff continued. "No matter how you argue, no matter how you squirm, no matter how you read it, Pan Am's manual says: 'Don't carry stored fuel from Auckland, New Zealand, to Pago Pago.' It says do not load stored fuel to sectors without a code unless necessary to ensure sufficient fuel for conditions on that day. There is no evidence that it was necessary to load stored fuel for conditions on that day. It does not matter whether you are allowed to load stored fuel from some other direction into Pago Pago. It doesn't matter whether you were allowed to put all sorts of extra passengers and cargo on the aircraft. Maybe they were permissible. The manual says: Don't load stored fuel. Don't do it. You can't squirm out of that."

And so on. With heavy use of sarcasm, Dombroff was steadily cutting William Tucker into tiny pieces and tossing them to the jury like scraps to a dog. When he finally sat down, Tucker was given two hours to make his riposte. The Pan Am lawyer rose heavily, oozing indignation.

Tucker said, "I have been accused in this case of fathering issues, fathering palm tree theories, giving birth to the idea that the glide slope was erroneous. If I were to step from behind this podium and turn sideways, you could tell I haven't given birth to anything for a long time. It will be a while before I do."

Tucker treated the jury to a view of his ample profile. It was his one attempt at humor, but he was too angry to be funny. Dombroff had not only attacked him, he had attacked his witnesses. Worst of all, he had attacked the crew of Flight 806. He recounted the accusations.

"Those are the charges I resent," he said. "I don't resent him attacking me personally or accusing me of making up facts or accusing me of making up theories. But I do resent that he has attacked the crew."

Dombroff's assault had shaken Tucker to the core. He had no real answer to the charges, and his whole demeanor showed it. Never a man to use a single word when ten would serve the purpose, he now piled phrase on phrase in a jumble almost totally devoid of meaning. When they reached the end of the day, with Tucker still in full flood, he asked Judge Byrne for a half-day adjournment.

Byrne refused the request. "You just had a week or ten days," he said.

"All right. All right," said Tucker with ill grace. He continued the following morning, but nothing got any better.

———

BOYD HIGHT DID a competent job to round off the case for Boeing and then, finally, Cathcart came back for the last words. He reserved his strongest attack for Pan American.

"Pan Am's position is this," he said. "'We didn't fail to exercise the highest degree of care. We were not to blame. We were not negligent. We don't owe these people anything.' Throughout this case and throughout this argument, these people who were paying good money to ride on their airplane, and did not get delivered safely, did not even get one word of concern or sorrow from this air carrier. They continue to say: 'We are not to blame.'"

It was true. The Rogerses, the Hemsleys, the Carters, the van Heerdens, the Simpsons, and all the rest could testify to that. No one had said they were sorry. In an odd way, certainly not a way that had any place in the sterile environment of a court of law, it had become the most important thing of all.

Cathcart went on: "In almost five years of traveling back and forth across the States and the Pacific in order to gather evidence, we have heard and continue to hear, 'We are not to blame. It was the glide slope that failed.' We have lost, and our people have lost, almost five years of wasted time. And you, members of the jury, have lost almost seven months of trying an issue which never had any substance.

"As much as I would love to prevail against the government on the faulty glide slope, I cannot do it. I cannot become a party to it. If there was ever the slightest doubt, that doubt was erased by Mr. Dombroff's argument."

It was good psychology. Cathcart was presenting himself as an honest man, above the barnyard scramble of the courtroom floor, who was prepared to sacrifice advantage for the sake of truth. He felt, and he was probably right, that the jury would draw a contrast between his attitude and that of Pan American. But it was also genuinely felt. Cathcart did, and does, have real concern for the victims of Flight 806, but he wanted the recompense to come from the proper quarter.

He wound up by quoting Tucker, who had said that nobody in their right mind would have allowed an aircraft to crash. "But they did it, they did it, they did it," cried Cathcart, shaking his fist for emphasis. "And there is no one that has come here and said they did not do it. So, if doing this is an example of somebody not in their right mind, then I submit to you that we have met each and every element of willful misconduct in this case.

"All the rules that were broken, all the compromises of safety by the crew and by management, guaranteed not that an accident might happen, or could possibly happen, but indeed that an accident would happen."

The argument was over. On the morning of Tuesday, July 25, 1978, the jury in the Pago Pago case retired to consider their verdict.

TWENTY-NINE

THE FIVE WOMEN on the jury had picked Michael Brent to be their foreman. They made the decision long before the end of the trial, and they were not to know how much trouble it would subsequently cause.

At first the discussion in the jury room went quickly. Cathcart's case against Boeing, which had given him such immense problems, was disposed of within fifteen minutes and dismissed out of hand. "We felt," Brent said later, "that with all the garbage that plane went through, and yet it still came to rest with everybody living, it was held together pretty good. They were trying to prove the doors didn't open. Well, when you consider how the structure of the plane was torn out, I don't care what kind of structure it was, it was going to impair the operation of the doors." The question of the interior materials apparently never got a second thought. So much for poor Mr. Jones and his exhausting trek through 140,000 pages of microfilm.

But the first part of the trial, in which Pan American and the government were doing battle to escape liability for the accident itself, was less easily settled. Though five members of the jury, including Brent, reached a fairly quick decision that Pan American was to blame, they could not convince Mrs. Anita Ford.

"The reason was," Brent said, "that she liked Mr. Tucker. It was just personal feelings. That was why she couldn't say Pan American was at fault: she didn't want to hurt him."

The five had been convinced by two main factors: the carriage of stored fuel and the training of the pilots. Though they had only been given the briefest adverse snippet from Petersen's past record and had no knowledge whatever of the Hudson report, it had apparently been enough. "The guy had failed and failed on his first try," Brent said, "and they were always giving him a second try. He didn't get a second try this time. This is why we felt the company should have had different training programs."

It was extraordinary. With so much information kept from them by deliberate design, the Pago Pago jury had still come to exactly the same basic conclusion as Jack Hudson.

But still the five could not convince Anita Ford. Brent began to grow irritated. "We didn't have any big argument or fight," he said, "it was just that she was basing her ideas on a personal thing, not on evidence. I kept saying, 'Give me the evidence that makes you feel this way,' and she would say, 'Well, I don't have any evidence, but I just don't feel like it's all Pan Am's fault.' We would go on like this all day long."

Another juror stepped in constantly to calm things down. Then finally, on the afternoon of Thursday, July 27, Mrs. Ford finally capitulated. "Okay," she said wearily, "I'll agree with you guys." Brent took the form on which they had to place their verdicts and marked it as fast as he could before she changed her mind. The envelope was sealed until the next morning.

The atmosphere in the courtroom was electric. Brent was given the sealed envelope, opened it, checked the contents, and handed the verdict to Judge Byrne. The jury, because of the number of cross-petitions in the case, had had a lot of questions to answer. Byrne went through them one by one.

"Was the United States negligent?"

"Yes," came the answer.

"Was such negligence of the United States a proximate cause of the accident?"

"Yes."

Mark Dombroff's heart sank. He lowered his head between his hands. He had given three years of his life; he had brought his marriage close to the breaking point; he had spent $250,000 of the taxpayers' money; and all for what? He had given a good performance and he had a good case. He knew he had had a good case. And now the jury had rejected him. True, the jury's verdict against the government was only advisory, though they did not know that, but he doubted if it would be reversed by Judge Byrne. At that moment, his whole career seemed to dissolve into fragments. The government would have to pay for the loss of the aircraft as well as an untold sum in compensation for the death of the occupants. Mark Dombroff was a broken man. He did not even hear the questions and answers as they rolled on.

"Was Captain Leroy Petersen negligent in failing to exercise ordinary care in the operation of Flight 806?"

"Yes."

"Was the negligence of Captain Petersen a proximate cause of the accident?"

"Yes."

The same questions and answers were given for Phillips and Green. Only Gaines was acquitted of responsibility.

The smile that had formed on Tucker's lips as he heard the verdict against the government was beginning to fade. It vanished altogether as the verdicts on Pan American were read out.

"Was Pan American World Airways, through the acts or omissions of its employees, negligent in failing to exercise ordinary care in its operation of Flight 806?"

"Yes," came the answer.

"Was this a proximate cause of the accident?"

"Yes."

And then came the most important question of all, the question that had never been answered in the affirmative in all aviation history and on which depended the victims' chance of overturning the Warsaw Convention and recovering realistic damages: "Was Pan American World Airways guilty of willful misconduct in the operation of Flight 806?"

The jury's answer was "Yes." Cathcart had made it. He had lost the case against Boeing, but he had succeeded in doing what even he, an eternal optimist, had thought hardly possible. He had broken the Warsaw Convention.

It had been done with a little help from his friends, and the chief of those, Mark Dombroff, was in no state to offer congratulations. Yet it was still not over. The fat lady had yet to sing.

Suddenly Michael Brent stood up in the jury box.

"Yes, Mr. Brent?" said Byrne, sounding surprised.

"Your Honor, did you read the question pertaining to the United States?"

"Yes, I did."

Brent hesitated. "I believe I've got it marked wrong," he said.

And he had. In his haste to get the form marked up after Anita Ford had changed her mind, Brent had put a cross in the wrong box. He said ruefully later, "As soon as Judge Byrne read it back, I said to myself, 'Whoops, that isn't what we meant to do. All the jurors looked down at me as if to say, 'What did you do?' I felt terrible. I had to put it right straight away."

The attorneys conferred briefly at Judge Byrne's side. "He said he marked them wrong," said Dombroff, suddenly returned to life.

"He said he *may* have marked them wrong," Tucker corrected.

Byrne decided to give the form back to Brent. "Just take a look at the answer that's there and see if there is any problem. We'll see what we can do from there."

Brent took a quick glance, though he hardly needed to. "Yes, sir, there is a problem," he said.

They took a little while to sort it out. Had Brent marked the form wrongly, or had the jury changed their minds overnight? Byrne sent them back to the jury room once again.

This time when they emerged, all was clear: the government was acquitted of each and every accusation; the verdicts against Pan American still stood.

Mark Dombroff could live again, this time in triumph, and Dan Cathcart was jubilant. Neither of them could have had any way of knowing that this was not the end. It was little more than the beginning.

BOOK THREE

No Surrender

THIRTY

THE TRIAL SETTLED NOTHING. When their first
elation had subsided, the victims of Flight 806 began to
realize that they were almost as far away from getting
recompense as they had ever been.

Failing settlement, there would now have to be a
separate trial for damages on each of the outstanding cases
against Pan American—57 at this time—and the claimants
would have to come from the four corners of the earth to
give evidence in Los Angeles. More time would be wasted
and more expense incurred.

It was also abundantly clear that the airline intended to
fight every inch of the way. Pan American and its insurers
had taken the willful misconduct verdict very hard and felt
they had been ill-used by both judge and jury. They
intended to launch an appeal just as soon as Judge Byrne
had gone through the formality of signing the judgment, and
when the verdicts in the damage trials came up it seemed
likely that they would appeal against those, too. Cathcart,
for his part, had every intention of appealing against the

verdict in favor of Boeing, and he had a few other assorted legal tricks up his sleeve. The lawyers were going to be working for their contingency fees for a long time to come.

However, one thing had changed. The United States Aviation Insurance Group now knew that unless the trial verdict was reversed on appeal, they could no longer rely on the protection of the Warsaw Convention. Within a matter of days, Robert Benedict was back on the scene in Los Angeles, armed with his own private calculations of what juries might award in the individual cases and prepared, once again, to talk about settlement.

Cathcart, Demanes, and Jefferson, the triumvirate of the plaintiffs' discovery committee, met Benedict during the first week in August. Though they were duty bound to pass on the new offers to their clients, their initial response was for immediate rejection. In truth, the figures now being put forward by Benedict were very little different from those offered during the abortive settlement discussions in January.

There was an extra $10,000 for Michael Rogers, bringing his offer to $25,000, but Susan's compensation remained at $125,000. The Hemsleys were offered an extra $25,000 at $325,000 and Leon Martin would get $25,000—an increase of $10,000. But many of the new offers were exactly the same as those made previously.

With a verdict of willful misconduct in their pockets, the attorneys saw no reason to advise settlements at this stage on those terms. They were confident that the juries in the coming damage trials would award far higher figures, and there was another aspect to be considered: the possibility of punitive (as opposed to compensatory) damages against Pan American.

This particular mirage had been hanging over the horizon for a long time, but nothing could be done about it until the liability verdict was in hand. Now there was an understanding that if matters between the parties were not settled by August 22, they would go back to court and have the question of punitive damages decided by the same jury. In these circumstances it was little wonder that Benedict got a frosty reception.

Alas for the claimants, it never happened. Judge Byrne, acting on his own, ruled that the finding of willful misconduct against Pan American was not sufficient to justify punitive damages under Californian law. He would not let the issue go in front of the jury. And that was that, at least until the appeal stage. It began to look as though Cathcart had been justified when he wrote to his clients a month before the end of the trial:

Our change of judges from Judge Hall to Judge Byrne has proved to be a change for the worse. Judge Hall was at all times sympathetic to the plight of the passengers and their families, and did his best to lighten the burden imposed on them as to the quantum of proof required. This unfortunately has not been the case with Judge Byrne.

Judge Byrne has made it as difficult as possible upon the plaintiffs in the measure of proof required before our evidence has been deemed admissible. Whenever judicial discretion could be exercised, as to the admission or exclusion of proffered evidence, his discretion has always been exercised so as to favor the defendants. He has demonstrated an attitude which at times has been antagonistic towards the plaintiffs, and extremely solicitous to the defendants, particularly Boeing.

At the time he wrote this, Cathcart was going through the toils of trying to present his evidence on the interior materials in the aircraft. Had he known what troubles Judge Byrne was to cause him over the ensuing months, he would not have been so restrained.

———

ROBERT BENEDICT, meanwhile, was a busy man. The possibility that Pan American had received the verdict they deserved never crossed his mind for one moment. Benedict's view was that there had been a serious miscarriage of justice, since it was demonstrably out of the question for the "World's Most Experienced Airline" to be guilty of willful misconduct. Aside from the behavior of the judge, about whom he felt almost as resentful as did Cathcart, there seemed to Benedict to be only one explanation: Pan American had been the victim of foul play.

It was an ironical obsession. While Cathcart and his clients were convinced that they were being cheated, delayed, and held to ransom by an insurance organization intent on avoiding its liabilities, Benedict was no less sure that his company was being taken for a ride. As he saw it, he was being prevented from paying reasonable compensation—and getting rid of the Pago Pago case—by a bunch of greedy lawyers.

Now he had to contend with a willful misconduct verdict as well. He set off to find a culprit, and his eye lit on Michael Brent.

Brent lived in a neat single-story home in Fountain Valley, just outside Los Angeles, with his wife and two teenage sons. He was still recovering from his seven-month ordeal in the jury box and trying to settle down once more to his job with the telephone company, when the burly stranger arrived at his door one evening.

He did not recognize Benedict from his days in court—Benedict had not been there very often—and expressed no surprise when the insurance chief introduced himself as "a private investigator employed by William Tucker."

The object of his visit, Benedict said, was to question Brent about what had gone on in the jury room so that the Pan American lawyer could see where he had gone wrong and avoid making the same mistakes in future.

It was a plausible story, if totally false, and Brent did not mind talking. He was an amiable man, and his conscience was clear. He invited Benedict in and entertained him with large quantities of soft drinks. The big lawyer was on a diet at the time.

Not being an attorney, Brent saw nothing especially unusual in being questioned about what had happened in the jury room. He was not too sure what Benedict wanted, but he was quite willing to cooperate. As they talked, a stenographer who had accompanied Benedict took it all down. The "private investigator" asked him whether he felt that anyone had acted wrongly in the jury room by talking about the trial while it was in progress. Brent told him of one woman who had remarked that the claim against Boeing should not even be in court, though he had thought nothing of it at the time. Benedict wanted to know her name.

"He was trying to get me to say stuff like that," Brent recalled later. "He was asking me a lot of questions about this lady that lived in Alhambra [Mrs. Anita Ford]. He was trying to get me to say that she and I had a big argument, a fight. We didn't. It was just the fact that she was basing her ideas on a personal thing, not on evidence."

What Benedict was trying to do was to get proof that the jury foreman had perjured himself when being questioned by Judge Byrne before the jury was chosen—that he had deliberately concealed his knowledge of aircraft navigation systems and had subsequently influenced three or four members of the panel, who had wanted to find against the government, into changing their minds.

Benedict got, or thought he got, what he needed from his interview with Brent. He re-donned his proper identity and went to Judge Byrne to apply for a mistrial in a bid to start the case all over again.

But Byrne would have none of it. As Benedict was to confess in an interview later, Byrne was angry with him for approaching Brent and forbade him to question any of the other jurors. He also refused to have Brent brought to court for full examination.

Nevertheless, the insurance man refused to give up. His attack on Brent was to form the linchpin of the Pan American appeals court brief when it was finally filed some three years later. This brief was a remarkable document. It said:

> The foreman of the jury, Michael Brent, has admitted under oath that he intentionally withheld from the court and from the parties information concerning his experience with aircraft navigational equipment, and that he did so because he was afraid that the parties would not allow him to sit on the jury if they knew of his experience. . . .

Mr. Brent's sworn statement makes it clear that he appreciated the importance of the court's enquiry about aircraft navigational instruments and that he intentionally withheld material information about his experience. During voir dire, the court asked Mr. Brent, "Did you have any instruction at all on the navigational apparatus on the aircraft?" Mr. Brent's answer was, "No, sir."

The brief made repeated references to Brent's alleged "sworn statement" to Benedict, who was not named but merely described as "an investigator." This was passing strange, because Brent had taken no oath, made no affidavit, and signed nothing. In fact, he had no communication with Benedict or anyone else connected with the trial after that evening. The "sworn statement," which was quoted at length in the brief and did not in any case add up to very much, was apparently no more than a transcription of the stenographer's notes. Yet it was presented to the Ninth Circuit judges as the equivalent of holy writ.

There was another misleading thing about the brief. Aside from the fact that Michael Brent would have been delighted to have been excused from jury service and was shown on the court record to have taken every opportunity to get up and confess something about himself that might get him off the hook, he did actually say the things that Benedict accused him of concealing. The question and answer selected were the last in a series of exchanges between Brent and Judge Byrne. The full sequence read:

Brent: "While I was in the navy three years I worked on aircraft."

Byrne: "What type of work did you do on them?"
Brent: "On the radar."
Byrne: "You were in the cockpits then?"
Brent: "Every time I worked on them, right."
Byrne: "Did you have any instruction at all on the navigational apparatus on the aircraft?"
Brent: "No."

The full version conveys a somewhat different impression than the selected quotation used in the brief. He had given them a description of his job as a fire control technician; he had told them that he worked on radar sets in aircraft cockpits. What more did they need? Brent himself said later that he had been rather surprised not to be excused from the jury at this point, though in practice he had found his previous experience of very little relevance during the trial. But at the time he had felt that the judge and the attorneys were the arbiters of whether he should be disqualified from service. Was it his fault that no one took any notice of what he was saying? Was he really guilty of "concealment or mendacious conduct," as the brief alleged?

But in August 1987, the appeal stage was very far away, and, in the meantime, Robert Benedict had other fish to fry.

THIRTY-ONE

THE SETTLEMENT OFFERS MADE at the beginning of the month had been left on the table with an expiration date of September 1. Two of them, at least, were getting a positive response. In the cases of John Carter and Johannes van Heerden, where the offers of $150,000 and $250,000 were the same as they had been back in January, Cathcart now felt it was right to advise acceptance. The plain fact of the matter was that both families were desperate for money. Each had asked Cathcart, through Pilkington, to settle.

But the offers were conditional. In all, eight strictures were laid down by Benedict, all of which had to be satisfied before Pan American's insurers would pay up.

All these conditions except one—that the settlement offers must remain confidential—were aimed at ensuring that once the money had been paid, Pan American would be free of any further liability. This did not seem unreasonable, but Cathcart was having trouble with the terms of one paragraph. It read: "A complete release of all defendants including, but not limited to, Pan American, the estates of the deceased crew members, the Boeing Company, the United States of America, and their agents, servants and employees."

Cathcart worried about the wording of this condition, for he feared that Boeing and the government, having won their case in court, might descend on his clients with a bill for costs. In any case, since as far as he knew neither of these parties had authorized Benedict to negotiate on their behalf, what right did he have to request a release for them?

He therefore wrote to Tucker on August 31, the day before the expiration date, accepting the offers on behalf of Carter and van Heerden but asking for an added assurance. He wanted Benedict to guarantee that Boeing and the government would relinquish any claim for costs against his clients. If this was done, he was quite willing to agree to the condition and release all three defendants.

Though it seemed odd that Benedict should be asking for a release from liability for clients he did not represent, there was nothing sinister in his motive. He was ensuring that if Pan American won their eventual appeal against the government, they would be able to reclaim from the United States most if not all of the money they had paid out to Cathcart's clients. Cathcart, understanding this perfectly well, thought that the caveat entered in his letter was a mere formality. He was wrong. His letter to Tucker of August 31 was to spark off one of the most bizarre episodes in the whole case.

The reply that came on September 7 was not from Tucker but from Benedict, and it was not what Cathcart expected. After restating the eight conditions, Benedict said:

Prior to the commencement of any settlement discussions before Judge Francis [the man appointed by the court to oversee any settlement negotiations at this point], you appeared to agree in substance to these conditions. I advised you at that time that these conditions were non-negotiable, and intended to protect the interests of Pan American with respect to any settlement in view of the ambiguous information which we have received to date concerning appropriate facts in many cases involving foreign decedents or foreign heirs.

Prior to September 1, 1978, I received no acceptances of any of the outstanding offers of settlement based on the conditions as outlined previously to you and set forth above. Accordingly, as of September 1, 1978, all of the outstanding offers of settlement made to you in any case arising out of the accident have been withdrawn.

The letter went on to reject Cathcart's acceptance of a week previous, on the grounds that it was not unequivocal, and to make fresh offers, again conditional on the eight points. This time the figure in the Carter and van Heerden cases was drastically reduced: $100,000 each.

Dan Cathcart was furious. To his mind he had accepted the Pan Am offer in good faith, raising no more than a minor legal query, and the company was now refusing to honor the bargain. He had a simple explanation for what had happened: Benedict had discovered that the Carters and van Heerdens were in desperate straits and had withdrawn the offers in the confident expectation that they could be persuaded to settle for less.

Cathcart gathered his anger around him like a cloak and prepared to do battle.

———

THE MATTER WAS MORE complex than Cathcart supposed, and, in his heart, he must have known it. The clue to Benedict's apparent volte-face had been contained in his reference to "ambiguous information," and these alleged ambiguities were at the root of his determination not to pay up.

Benedict had been sleuthing again.

On August 13, two days before the settlement conference with Judge Francis, and a date Benedict remembered because his room at the Century Plaza Hotel in Los Angeles was broken into, he had acquired some information. Exactly where he got it from is unknown. His informant told him something he had not known before: that John Carter had filed a divorce petition just before he died, in which he stated that he had never supported his paraplegic son and had never made any medical payments.

To comprehend the significance of this, it is necessary to understand what constitutes a legitimate claim for compensation after death in an aviation accident, as far as the law is concerned. Sentiment plays very little part in the assessment of the value of a life. What matters is what a man has been earning, how long he would have lived in the normal course of events, what his expectations were, and how much he was contributing to the support of his family. The heirs of those who died on Pago Pago, with the assistance of their attorneys, had had to compile these somber statistics at a much earlier stage of the case. They were known as "damage brochures," and they were the raw material from which claims were constructed and offers made. In the case of John Carter, the damage brochure prepared by Cathcart had contained no mention of a divorce petition.

Cathcart's brochure, dated July 10, 1975, had given details of his wife and five children, and of his earnings during the five years before he died. These had varied from $4,000 to $6,400 a year. From this, by some magic of arithmetic involving the rate of inflation, Cathcart had calculated Carter's maximum future earnings at $81,598 per year, and had computed a claim for damages of $642,171—of which $50,000 was for conscious pain and suffering. He never expected to get this amount, of course.

The brochure contained details of Richard Carter's paralyzed condition, adding that he had had a nervous breakdown and might be suffering from epilepsy, and put the potential contribution of his father to the family income at $3,150 a month. Of this, $1,100 was reckoned as the dollar value of his "care, comfort, society, and protection."

When Benedict got his information, his antennae began to twitch. Was someone trying to take his insurance company for a ride? He dispatched another Los Angeles attorney, George Manfredi, to New Zealand, to take sworn depositions from the entire Carter family. For good measure, he also instructed him to interview Grace van Heerden and her son. He had his suspicions about that case as well. Cathcart was informed, and both he and Pilkington were present when the affidavits were taken. It was an expensive exercise.

The Carters were interviewed at the Royal International Hotel in Rotorua—which is not quite as grand as it sounds—on September 16, 1978. It was not a happy occasion for the family or for Cathcart. Lucy Carter's testimony disclosed that she had learned of the divorce petition some six months after her husband's death, although she had never actually seen it until Manfredi showed it to her. It was also revealed that John Carter had done nothing for financial support of his family after the separation, beyond the minimal payments he had to make under the formal separation agreement. Suggestions in the brochure that the couple were trying for a reconciliation were also found to be baseless.

But had Lucy Carter deliberately lied in order to increase the value of her claim against Pan American? Anyone who met this blunt, feisty little lady would find such a thing hard to believe. The answer may lie elsewhere. Virtually all the overturned claims were made in answer to an inordinately long and detailed list of questions submitted by the Pan American attorneys in early 1975. They ran to thirty-nine pages of legal foolscap, and many of the queries were inapplicable or difficult to understand. Pilkington and Morrison went through the questionnaire with Mrs. Carter and took her answers away to be prepared. When the resultant document was completed in June 1975, it was signed not by Mrs. Carter but by a female employee from Cathcart's office.

Rightly or wrongly, it was Mrs. Carter who had to suffer. The situation was made even worse by her daughter Julie's assertion that her brother Richard had never had a nervous breakdown and had suffered only one short seizure, which was prior to his father's death. It was, Manfredi recorded on his return, "a very different situation" to that which Pan Am had been led to believe existed.

———

THE PROBLEM with Johannes van Heerden was that no one could be sure just how much he did earn before his death on board Flight 806. There always seemed to be plenty of money—enough for trips to Europe every year and generous gifts to his children. And he ran his own shoemaking factory. Yet van Heerden told no one, not even his wife, how much he was making. He did not even leave a will.

All this posed a great problem when the attorneys came to draw up Mrs. van Heerden's claim for damages. In retrospect, it might have been better to have been totally frank about van Heerden's somewhat nebulous financial affairs, and to work something out on that basis. But the legal profession, like nature, abhors a vacuum, and somehow or other, neat and convincing rows of figures had to be found to fill the void in van Heerden's fiscal record.

Thus, it was that when the damage brochure in the case was filed, the figures were there in confident abundance. On page three his earnings at the time of his death were given as $50,000 a year gross, $30,000 net. It was estimated that after 1975 his income would have risen to $100,000 a year.

Exactly who computed these figures was unclear. Whoever it was, he was certainly not guilty of the sin of consistency. By page five of the brochure, van Heerden's income when he died had risen to $75,000, which was not bad going for two pages of typescript.

By the time the inflationary factor was built in, van Heerden's earnings were forecast to rise to an annual $325,000 had he lived to retirement age, and what with one thing and another the total damage claim came out at $1,069,847.67. The odd sixty-seven cents were a nice touch, giving an air of verisimilitude to the whole operation.

It would have taken a more innocent character than Robert Benedict to fail to note some slight problems with this brochure. In fact, his offer of $250,000 spoke of more generosity than his enemies gave him credit for.

However, now that the trial was over and Benedict had his dander up, generosity was a thing of the past. The van Heerden claim was going to come under close scrutiny.

The deposition of Grace van Heerden was taken by Manfredi in Auckland on September 13. It had to be continued the following day, because Mrs. van Heerden was not strong enough to complete her answers in one session. Her diabetes and her heart trouble had left her in a very weakened state. Common sympathy might have dictated a brief session and a recommendation for an early settlement, but sympathy was in short supply that day, and settlement was not the name of the game. Manfredi questioned her at length, seeking to find inconsistencies between her sworn answers and those she had made on the questionnaire three years previously, which formed the basis of her claim.

Unhappily, there were many. Mrs. van Heerden had been asked previously about her state of health and had said that she was diabetic but otherwise well. But her deposition revealed that her condition had worsened dramatically since her husband's death; she had spent three months in a Sydney hospital in 1974 and had twice been hospitalized with angina. None of this had been disclosed.

She was asked about any periods of separation during her marriage to Mr. van Heerden, to which she had replied "not applicable." This may have been a misunderstanding about the form of words, but the fact remained that with the exception of brief visits they had lived apart almost continuously between 1968 and the time of the accident. For nearly four years, she had been living in New Caledonia while he worked in New Zealand, and shortly after she returned to New Zealand, he went to Samoa to open his new shoe factory. This made it difficult to believe the contention in the damage brochure that the van Heerden family was "emotionally very close" and "enjoyed being together." There was also a good deal of doubt cast on the extent to which van Heerden was supporting his family during this period. His widow now admitted, which she had not done before, that during her time in New Caledonia she had supported herself and her youngest son by running a boutique. The brochure had stated that they were wholly dependent on van Heerden and that he had paid for everything. It was unfortunate, to say the least.

As for van Heerden's income, the figures proved to be totally unverifiable. Mrs. van Heerden testified that she had no idea what his earnings were at any time and had found no records. Yet they had lived well, at one time owning three houses, cars, and a caravan. Van Heerden was a mystery, wrapped in an enigma, and his widow's deposition had done nothing except add fuel to the fire of Robert Benedict's determination not to pay up.

———

IN SPITE OF ALL THIS, Dan Cathcart was not about to surrender. On December 18, 1978, he launched an action in the district court in Los Angeles to enforce the settlements and to recover his expenses for the trip to New

Zealand. The case was heard before Judge Manuel Real, not Judge Byrne, and Cathcart won the day. When Pan American still refused to pay the Carters and van Heerdens, he pounced.

Cathcart now had the force of law behind him, or so he thought. He acted swiftly to place a writ of attachment on Pan Am's bank account in San Francisco, which meant that his bailiffs could go in and seize whatever money was there to pay the settlements.

It should have worked, but luck was not on Cathcart's side. Whether it was pure chance or whether someone leaked his intent was never clear, but when the bailiffs descended on the vaults, they found the Pan American account almost empty. There was only $3,672.72 left, and with that they had to be content. One story had it that the previous day had been a bank holiday in New York, where the bulk of Pan American funds were kept, and that an anticipated transfer of money had not been made. It was possible. Whatever the reason, the result was a fiasco. Cathcart took the $3,672.72, split it equally in two and sent it off to Mrs. Carter and Mrs. van Heerden. Then he considered his next move.

From his office window on the edge of Beverley Hills, Cathcart could see the big jets coming and going from Los Angeles International Airport. The spectacle gave him an idea. There was an old tradition of nailing a writ to a ship's mast; why not stick one onto a Pan American jumbo? The plan had more than one attraction. It would not only make the airline pay up to get the release of their valuable aircraft, but it would bring immediate publicity to his whole cause. Dan Cathcart was not averse to a little publicity. He calculated that Pan American would feel very differently.

Alas, the best laid plans . . . Careful inquiry showed that many of the blue-and-silver giants were not owned by Pan American at all. They had been sold by the company to financial interests and leased back. It seemed impossible to discover which aircraft were still in Pan Am's ownership and which were not.

Cathcart was uneasily aware that if he slapped a writ on the wrong one, the consequences could be very expensive. With reluctance, he abandoned the idea.

Benedict, meanwhile, had decided to appeal against Judge Real's verdict. Benedict would appeal against the last trump.

He was greatly aggrieved that the case had gone against him, especially after Manfredi's efforts in New Zealand, and he took it to California's second appellate district court. This occupied more time, but that was not about to worry the insurance company. Cathcart had exhausted his efforts to attach Pan American property in California, and they could afford to wait.

Even if they lost, the money would have garnered more interest in the meantime.

As it happened, however, they did not lose. On January 26, 1981, the appeal court handed down a ruling that overturned Judge Real's verdict in favor of Cathcart. California law, stated three judges unanimously, laid down that the acceptance of a settlement offer must be absolute and unqualified.

By asking that his clients be relieved of cost claims from the United States and Boeing, Cathcart had made a qualified acceptance. Therefore, it was not valid.

Strictly speaking, Pan American would have been justified in asking for the return of their $3,672.72 at this point. Fortunately for Mrs. Carter and Mrs. van Heerden they did not do so, but the cases were put back in limbo. Cathcart refused an invitation from Benedict to take them to immediate trial and decided instead to await the outcome of the other damage cases.

Nothing was going to happen until those were disposed of anyway.

THIRTY-TWO

AT LONG LAST, in the late summer of 1978 came the moment for which so many families had been waiting. Their individual cases were about to be tried, the damages they would get being decided by separate juries. There was no question that they would get something. The sole issue was how much. From New Zealand, from Australia, from Samoa, and from various parts of the United States they came, dressed in their Sunday best and heading for the courthouse on Spring Street, Los Angeles.

Michael and Susan Rogers had to travel a long way. In the middle of 1978, they were at last fulfilling their ambition, shattered by the crash of Flight 806, and were traveling around the world on an overdraft. By the time they reached America they had run out of money completely, and Cathcart had to put them up at a cheap hotel in the city. Although the Rogerses had set up regular mail drops in Europe, the attorney had had some difficulty locating them. He had sprayed Europe with telegrams asking them to contact him and eventually had tracked them down in southern Greece.

Friends and acquaintances in New Zealand were convinced that the Rogerses had already made a fortune from their damage claim. Michael, thanks to some overblown stories in the local press, had been nicknamed "the six-million-dollar man," and no amount of explanation would convince anyone that they were not rich at all.

From the outset, Susan and Michael were unhappy with the way the trial was conducted. They disagreed with Cathcart over the choice of jurors. He wanted to exclude any attractive women; Susan felt that only another attractive woman could truly appreciate what her scars meant to her. Michael wanted older men because he felt they would know the value of money; Cathcart said such men would have fought in the war and be unsympathetic toward injuries. In the end, they got the jury the attorney wanted.

But the real shock came when they discovered just how little of their suffering the court was to be allowed to hear. And how little of the circumstances of the case. Judge Byrne, before whom all the damage trials save one were heard, refused at any point to allow the fact that Pan American had been found guilty of willful misconduct to be mentioned in front of the jury. Nor would he permit any reference to others killed or injured in the accident.

"At one point," Michael said, "I started to talk about how it was when I was in the hospital, and how horrible it was with all the other people injured. Straightaway the judge cleared the court of all the jurors and gave me a lecture that I must not refer to anyone else. If I made another reference to it at all he would disband the jury and we would have to start all over again.

"As a lawyer myself, I didn't think he was acting correctly. I submitted to him in a very respectful manner that the jury could not possibly appreciate our position unless they knew the full enormity of the accident and the fact that other people were killed and injured. He would not accept that position."

Cathcart was also disturbed. "The cases have been tried in a somewhat sterile environment," he wrote to his clients. "Judge Byrne will not permit us to tell the jury anything about the accident, or the liability jury's finding as to fault on the part of Pan American. In this environment, it is impossible to get anyone mad at Pan Am. It is difficult to get them truly to understand what Pan Am has put the victims of this accident through. Unless the settlement picture changes, and I see no reason for it to change, it will be necessary to try each and every one of the remaining cases to a verdict."

———

THERE IS no doubt that Pan American was fortunate that Judge Byrne ruled as he did. Juries in full possession of the facts, especially the willful misconduct verdict, would almost certainly have given far higher awards.

"It was a joke," Michael Rogers said later. "The proof lies in the fact that we met all the jurors bar one immediately after the trial and told them everything. They were absolutely scandalized. They just could not believe the truth when we told them. They were shocked. They didn't say they would have doubled the award, but from the way they were speaking it would not have surprised me."

Yet the Rogerses were not unduly disappointed with the awards they did get. The jury gave $353,000 to Susan, who in spite of plastic surgery still showed scars on her face, hands, and arms; they gave $75,000 to Michael. The figures were well in excess of what Benedict had been offering by way of settlement, apparently justifying Cathcart's decision to go to trial. They went back to their hotel for an early night, thinking that judgment would be signed the following day and that within three months it would all be over. Little did they know.

———

WHEN THE CALL came to the four Hemsley brothers—Desmond, William, Roy, and Edward—they were spread out between India, Mexico, and New Zealand. They paid their own fares to Los Angeles. "Thank God we had the money," William said later. "Otherwise don't ask me how we would have got to the trial. Nobody ever suggested they would pay the cost. We were simply told to get there, and we had to be there."

The brothers had been having a turbulent time in the intervening years, largely through the emotional strain of having lost their parents and sister on Flight 806. Edward's marriage had ended in divorce, and he found that the trauma of Mary's death had destroyed his wish to have children of his own. "It would be too much to handle," he said simply. "I could not have a child myself and suffer again the agony of losing that child."

Roy had given up his medical studies at Otago, had spent a year doing nothing, and had then taken up archaeology. William had traveled, unable to settle down after his plans of going into business with his father had been dashed. Desmond had become a hippie. They were all worried about the impression Desmond would make on the court and bought him a new suit when he reached Los Angeles.

On the night before the trial, Dan Cathcart invited them all to dinner at his home in Beverley Glen. He was not at his most tactful. William recalled later, "He said it was probably better that we didn't get the money anyway, that we didn't need it. That just blew me away. We went away that night and Edward and I got so drunk we could not even sit up in bed. We just could not believe that we had been taken right down the chute."

There were many things about the trial of their case that disturbed the Hemsley brothers, not least the final verdict. But what really stuck in their collective craw was the discovery that Judge Byrne had eliminated the death of their sister from the action altogether. He apparently held that because as a child she was making no financial contribution to the family, her death merited no compensation whatever from Pan American. He went further: he would not allow the fact of her death, or even her name, to be mentioned in the courtroom, lest the jury feel sympathy and increase the amount of the award.

Cathcart commented afterward, "Byrne maintained as sterile and unemotional an environment as you possibly could in a courtroom. You almost felt you should wear a mask and gloves and never let any emotion creep in as to what had really happened to these families. He did his best to keep the verdicts down. We had a nice time with him."

William Hemsley was bewildered by it all. "I just could not believe what went on in that trial. Everything was suppressed to a point where I felt like walking out of court. My sister, just as much as my parents, was a part of the family. The trial had a different tone altogether if we were not allowed to mention her. She was very special to the family. I just could not believe that this was happening. It frustrated me so badly that I just didn't care. I lost a lot of interest in the trial after that.

"There was no point in us being there, anyway. After this incredibly long, drawn-out case, which had left us in the air for so long, Pan American had been found guilty of willful misconduct. And now, during our trial, they changed the terminology for the jury and just said that Pan Am was 'legally responsible'. I had to sit there and listen to this, and I just could not believe it. I felt my presence in the court was an absolute waste of time.

"All I could keep thinking at the time was that the trial was a fix. I just wanted to get up and say at some stage, 'I had a sister called Mary,' and throw the whole thing out. Edward was so frustrated that at one point he just let go. He used the word 'Mary' and it had to be explained who Mary was. The judge stopped everything and said to the jury that the case could be stopped and retried, but since Edward was as young as he was, he would allow him to mention the fact that he had a sister.

"He didn't even say she was killed in the accident," added William bitterly.

At the end of the day, the Hemsleys found that their parents' lives had been valued at $190,000 each—a total of $380,000, out of which would have to come the lawyers' contingency fees and expenses. It was more than Benedict's settlement offer, but not all that much more, and there was no telling when they would actually get it. Inflation, the word of the day, had already taken care of the difference. There would still be the appeal to come. The Hemsleys were disgusted. They felt they had been ill-used by the judge, less than well served by their counsel, and had received no sympathy from the jury, whom they suspected had kept the award low because the Hemsleys were foreigners.

Three years afterward, in 1981, Edward Hemsley said, "We have seen the value of money halved since the trial, and it can conceivably be ten years before we get anything. Inflation isn't taken into account at all. We will eventually get little more than enough to buy an ice cream."

———

A YEAR WENT BY, and by the late summer of 1979 all the damage trials had been completed except one. Judge Byrne's tactics, deliberate or not, had proved remarkably successful in keeping the damages down. The total compensation figure now stood at less than eight million dollars, which was not much greater than the settlement figure on offer at the beginning of 1978. By the time inflation was taken into account, it was probably less, and because Pan Am intended to appeal each and every verdict the victims had still not gotten any money.

The one outstanding trial was that of the Simpson case, involving the children of Herbert and Eunice Simpson who had fought so hard to save their parents' lives. It was delayed and delayed and delayed again, and it did not come before the court until July 23, 1980.

The Simpson case was a little different from the rest. They were not only suing Pan American for the death of their parents but also for the airline's failure to evacuate them.

Judge Byrne, however, knew a trick worth two of that. He told the jury at the outset that the damages to be assessed would be identical under either claim. "So," he said, "regardless of whether you find Pan Am liable or not liable for the failure to evacuate, you will be called upon to assess the same damages, the identical damages, and those damages will not be increased or decreased by any finding you make on the evacuation issue."

He went on to place a further barrier in the path of the Simpsons. They could refer to any conversations that they had had with Pam American employees, he conceded, "but not for the purpose of indicating any grief, sorrow, or anxiety on the part of the heirs because that element of damages commenced only after the death of the deceased."

The grief, sorrow, and anxiety caused by the conduct of Pan American were, of course, the whole point as far as the Simpsons were concerned. But not in the eyes of Judge Byrne. At least they were able to tell their story in open court, and that was some consolation.

After a week of trial and a day of deliberation, the jury came back to find that Pan American had been negligent in not evacuating Herbert and Eunice Simpson but that this had not been a proximate cause of their deaths. In other words, the jury felt that they would have died anyway. They awarded damages of $225,000 in each case—a total of $450,000.

Robert Benedict had valued the lives of the Simpsons at $50,000 each.

THIRTY-THREE

AS IT HAPPENED, the delay in the hearing of the Simpson case was of little consequence to Herbert Simpson Jr. and his sisters. Nobody else had been paid yet, and the appeal process had not even begun. The Pago Pago cases hung in uneasy limbo, and none of Dan Cathcart's efforts could shake them loose.

The reason for the long delay was encapsulated in two words: Judge Byrne. Under California law, the verdict of a jury cannot have any effect until the judgment is officially signed by the judge in the case. The procedure is a formality, usually assigned to the clerk of the court, but until it is carried out the appeal process cannot begin. Once the judgment is signed, the parties have thirty days in which to appeal against the verdict, but if they do so, they must post with the appeals court a bond of one and a half times the amount of the damages.

The court rules lay down that the judgments must be signed "forthwith." But Judge Byrne did not sign. He did not sign the jury verdict in the liability case that found Pan American guilty of willful misconduct, and he did not sign the verdicts in any of the damage trials.

Dan Cathcart became increasingly concerned. He went to Byrne and made a motion urging him to enter judgment, protesting that his clients needed the money and that every week the value of the money was shrinking because of inflation. Byrne received the motion courteously, took it under submission, and did nothing. Cathcart presented another motion. Judge Byrne could not, or would not, sign his name.

The months went by. Even Pan American, who were being actively helped by Judge Byrne's prevarication because they could happily reap large amounts of interest on money that would otherwise be tied up in the appeals court, made a motion. That got nowhere either.

With some reluctance, though not much, Cathcart decided to take an extreme step. He applied to the Ninth Circuit Court of Appeals for a writ of mandamus, which would order Byrne to perform his duty as a judge. This was a considerable embarrassment for the appeal judges; they were being asked to censure one of their own judicial brethren, and they, too, stalled for some weeks. Finally, they ruled that because this was a complex matter, they would give Byrne a further six months to enter judgment.

Exactly what made it so complex was unclear. True, Byrne had one other issue to decide: whether or not the claimants were entitled to pre-judgment interest on their damages. By this time there was quite a lot of money involved in the decision, because if such interest was paid, as Cathcart claimed it should be, then it would be at the rate of 7 percent right back to the date of the accident. The interest would be simple, not compounded, but it would still raise the total amount payable in each case by about 35 percent.

"Judge Byrne has ducked this decision in every way possible," wrote the frustrated Cathcart to his clients in December 1978. And he continued to duck it for many, many months, eventually deciding, to Benedict's delight, that interest would only have to be paid on such actual financial losses as medical and burial expenses. Pan American would get away with paying peanuts in terms of interest.

Nineteen seventy-eight moved into 1979, and 1979 trundled forward. Still no judgments were signed, and Cathcart told everyone that Byrne's motive must be that he wanted to delay the appeals in the hope that the cases would be settled and somehow go away. There was no hope of that.

Cathcart was watching the calendar; the clock had long since ceased to have any significance in the Pago Pago case. Six months to the day after the first appeals court ruling, with Byrne still silent, he applied for another writ of mandamus. This brought some response from Byrne himself, who announced that he had now reached a decision on pre-judgment interest and would be entering judgment "shortly." He asked Cathcart to withdraw the writ.

"This I will not do," Cathcart wrote to his clients. "I do not trust Judge Byrne to follow through on any announced decision, or to enter judgment until he is forced to do so. I am convinced that the filing of the writ is the only thing which has caused him to begin to do that which he should have done over a year and a half ago." It was now February, 1980. Cathcart added:

Because so much time has elapsed from the date of the verdict to the present time, I intend to ask additionally that the amounts of the verdict in each case be adjusted for interim inflation, and that the increased amount be entered as the judgment in each case.

It is extremely difficult to be patient, particularly when the delay and hardship being inflicted on you are totally unnecessary, and a product of a judge whose concern on how he will look in the eyes of his brethren continues to work unnecessary delay.

Cathcart might just as well have saved himself the trouble. Not only was his inflation plea to be rejected, but the Ninth Circuit must have had undying faith in their judicial brother. After a long delay, they rejected the second application for a writ. Byrne had assured them that he would act—on his judge's honor, he would. It transpired, however, that Cathcart knew his man better than they did. More months went by, and nothing happened.

Even Benedict was astonished at this turn of events, later describing the appeals court's treatment of Judge Byrne as "extremely lenient."

There was only one thing left to do, and in the fall of 1980 Cathcart did it. If the formal legal process could not get action out of Judge Byrne, then he would try the court of public opinion. A Chicago newspaper had been showing interest in the case, and Cathcart decided to cooperate with them and tell all.

———

THE RESULTANT ARTICLE rehearsed the history of the affair and contained quotations critical of Judge Byrne from attorneys on both sides. Byrne himself refused to comment, but at last, he was needled into action. He began to sign the judgments.

There were more weeks of confusion to come. When the sighs of relief had moderated, and the lawyers began to look at what had actually happened, they found that Byrne had only signed the dockets in one place, and not in two as he was supposed to do. The date for the appeals process started slipping back again while the errant signatures were rounded up from November 1980 to January 1981. It was now seven years, almost to the day, since Flight 806 had plunged into the jungle. "Whether it was Machiavellian on his part or a clerical error, I don't know," Cathcart said later. "I have very strong suspicions that Machiavelli played a role."

And now there were new barriers. Every time a judgment was entered, Pan Am filed a motion for a new trial, based on their allegation of Michael Brent's deception. And every time a motion was made, Judge Byrne had to rule on it. The motions were all turned down, but the rulings did not come swiftly.

At this stage, motions and counter-motions were flying thicker than medflies in California, and Cathcart was encouraging his flock with the idea that Pan Am had somehow left it too late to launch their appeal. This proved not to be so. Finally, a date was set for the filing of the first appeal brief: September 28, 1981.

The due date arrived, but the brief did not. There was jubilation in the offices of Cathcart and Dombroff. "Holy shit!" cried Mark Dombroff's secretary, a lady of mature years and great respectability who had, like everyone else involved, developed an emotional attachment to the Pago Pago case over the years.

Cathcart and Dombroff, after a hurried telephone consultation between Washington and Los Angeles, decided to launch a joint motion to dismiss the Pan American appeal on the grounds that it was out of time. But the luck that carried Benedict along so happily on such occasions did not desert him now. Pan American, pleading that their printers had let them down, delivered the tardy brief and were duly excused by the court of appeal, which dismissed the Cathcart/Dombroff motion.

The appeal was set remorselessly in train, to drag on, perhaps for years. An optimistic Cathcart felt the whole thing could still be wound up early in 1982, but Benedict was forecasting 1984 at the earliest.

For the victims of Flight 806, waiting, ever waiting, there remained one small chance of final retribution. It would not bring payment of their claims any closer, but it might just get them extra payment from Pan American's insurers by way of punitive damages. Cathcart called it his "get even" case.

At some point back in the mists of time, Cathcart, Jefferson, and Demanes had realized that they might have an action against Benedict under the California Insurance Code. This laid down that it was unfair practice in the insurance business if a company did not attempt, in good faith, to make prompt, fair, and equitable settlement of claims in which liability had become reasonably clear.

Well, reasoned the attorneys, since there was no question that a liability of up to $75,000 per case was known to exist under the Warsaw Convention—and in spite of repeated requests USAIG had refused to pay that much on account—they must be liable for damages under this code. They took the case to court in August 1979. It was rejected. So, they appealed, which they were able to do, since their case (as distinct from all the other cases) had not been heard by Judge Byrne but by another judge, who had entered judgment immediately. The appeals court turned them down, but it did so in terms that gave cause for hope. What the appeals court said, in effect, was that the case had been launched too soon. Cathcart and company should wait until the main appeal in the Pago Pago case had been decided and should then come back with more ammunition.

Two paragraphs in the ruling gave special cause for hope:

> While appellants must await the conclusion of the federal action before bringing an action against the insurers wherein they seek a remedy under the Unfair Practices Act, we point out that the position of the insurers that because they have "no duty to pay $75,000, no duty has been breached, and they cannot be sued for inflicting emotional distress on this basis" is completely untenable.
>
> It is difficult to conceive under the allegations of the complaint that companies or groups engaged in the business of insurance, with experienced claims personnel, could not have long since made knowledgeable evaluations of the liability and damage features of the claimants' claims against Pan Am, especially since the accident occurred on January 30, 1974, and the jury in the federal action held that the willful misconduct of Pan Am was a proximate cause of that accident.

And it went on to give a stern reminder to USAIG of their duties under the insurance code.

The part could have been put more briefly and with greater clarity, although the meaning was plain: unless Mr. Benedict mended his ways and paid up, there would be a nasty reckoning at the end of the day.

THIRTY-FOUR

IT HAD BECOME A WAR—A long, grinding war of attrition, in which neither side was about to give up. The two generals, Benedict and Cathcart, schemed and plotted fresh maneuvers to outwit each other, while the poor bloody infantry—the victims of Flight 806—waited and suffered in the trenches. There was no end in sight.

All the niceties were gone now, swallowed up in a welter of mutual dislike and mistrust. Each side would blacken the character of the other without a second thought, and an outside observer needed to remember that the first casualty of war is truth. On one thing alone they stood united: their hearty disapproval of Judge Byrne and all his works. All of them, that is, except Mark Dombroff.

Dombroff, though he had suffered fairly severely at Byrne's hands during the trial, described him later as "the finest courtroom judge I have ever worked in front of, and the most charming man I have ever met." He sympathized mightily with Byrne's problem in taking over the Pago Pago case in midstream from Judge Hall. "That's a hell of a task to put on a judge."

But then, Dombroff was a winner, and one who had become firm friends with the judge after the trial was over. His description of Byrne would not even be recognized by Robert Benedict.

During an interview in his New York office, in the fall of 1981, Benedict said of the judge, "I have some very strong feelings about his failure to administrate this case properly. This particular case is a tragedy from the standpoint of the disposition of major air crashes in the United States in the last five or ten years. It is a tragedy to those people who were directly affected by it, primarily the survivors and relatives of the victims. It's a tragedy for those people who spent millions of dollars in litigating the case, and it is a tragedy for society in general because more money has been spent by the parties, both plaintiffs and defendants, and the court system, than the cases are worth from a fair damage standpoint. I think we have to agree that what happened in Judge Byrne's court was a tragedy, and it was a gross failure by Judge Byrne."

Benedict's attack moved from the professional to the personal. "Judge Byrne is a bachelor," he said. "He is a very popular bachelor in California. He is a very social man. According to conversations I have had with numerous lawyers in California, he takes a great deal of time to make any decision that requires homework. There are other cases where he has taken an inordinate amount of time to make a decision.

"In the courtroom he's a very bright, articulate, and attractive performer. He's bright and intelligent. There is no doubt that his failure to render these judgments for over two years was inexplicable in judicial, legal, or logical terms. Both we and the plaintiffs made requests that he should do so. The courthouse records are in a shambles. There are exhibits we know have been lost. There are orders which cannot be found. It makes it extremely difficult to put together the record on appeal.

"It is a glaring example of how civil litigation, particularly in air disasters, is incapable of being handled by our judicial system, if the wrong individual supervises the administration of that litigation. In this particular case, Judge Byrne turned out to be the wrong individual."

Cathcart, though he regarded Benedict and all his works as inventions of the devil, did not dissent from this judgment. "Judge Byrne," he said, "did everything he could to stonewall this litigation. We could not get him to enter judgment. The rules required him to do it forthwith; it is normally done in twenty-four hours or less. It is a ministerial act—the clerk does it. He would not let the clerk do it. He held these things up for over two years, hoping we would give up and the case would go away, hoping that Benedict would have a change of heart and conscience and would settle these cases, or something."

In a deft attempt to kill two birds with one stone, Cathcart accused Byrne of being intimidated by Benedict throughout.

But for all the shot and shell that flew from the entrenched positions, the central mystery remained: what was it that turned a relatively minor air crash into the longest, most costly, and most bitterly fought lawsuit in world aviation history? What motivated Judge Byrne, Robert Benedict, Dan Cathcart, William Tucker, and Mark Dombroff to act as they did? To put it down to a clash of strong personalities, as some would have it, is to state the truth—but not the whole truth.

Some of the central characters seem easily explained. Tucker was a lousy courtroom lawyer, being well paid to do the best he could with second-rate material. Dombroff was fired by personal ambition. For Cathcart, a routine search for profit became a crusade on behalf of his clients when all reasonable chance of making money had disappeared.

But what of Judge Byrne? He was known to have ambitions of his own—a seat on the Supreme Court was rumored. Was he merely, as Cathcart put it, "protecting his ass" against possible reversal by the court of appeals? There had to be something more.

All roads, in the end, lead to Benedict. Robert Benedict, vice president of the United States Aviation Insurance Group, a friendly, helpful man, but one with a steely purpose and an undefinable sense of menace beneath the bland exterior. Benedict, the unabashed enemy of the contingency fee lawyer. Benedict, éminence grise of the Pago Pago case and private investigator extraordinaire. When Robert Benedict speaks of his role in the Pago Pago affair there is an air of injured innocence that is almost convincing. Almost, but not quite. There are flaws in the argument.

At the root of Benedict's policy was always the belief, persisted in to this day, that Pan American was not and never could have been guilty of willful misconduct. Though he admitted during his interview that "if we could have verified much of what was in the Hudson and Thomas reports we would have taken a different perspective," there is no evidence to show that any attempt was made to verify them. There is much evidence that every attempt was made to suppress them, and successfully. Therefore, it followed, according to this belief, that Pan Am would be protected by the Warsaw Convention and that maximum damages would be limited to $75,000 for each passenger. That the jury found otherwise was quite irrelevant.

Benedict claimed that from the moment of the crash his company "had always offered $75,000 to each of the passengers with the exception of two of three, one of whom was Leon Martin, whose injuries we did not consider merited $75,000." This contrasts with Cathcart's insistence that he constantly demanded such an interim payment for his clients and was refused. Faced with this point, Benedict modified his position.

"We did not have information which would persuade us to tell our insurers that you should pay these people $75,000," he said. "We wrote to Cathcart and Jefferson in 1977 and asked them to give sufficient information to evaluate these cases. We said that we would make advance payments on the following conditions. Firstly, we needed to know whether the deceased had been financially supporting the individuals. Secondly, that the money would be used by the survivors and not in pursuance of litigation. Thirdly, that the money would go to the client and not to the lawyers, and fourthly, that we should have a complete release on the amount of the claim being paid.

"We never got those assurances. The sticking point appeared to be that the majority of the people on this airplane were of meager means. Most of them were not supporting anybody, and the plaintiffs' lawyers never did sufficient investigation of the families to be able to make an accurate assessment."

With such conditions, it was hardly surprising that Benedict did not get to pay out any cash. His insistence on prior disclosure of means (with the implication that the needy would have to be content with less) was not quite the same as the open-handed offer he had described previously. Also, his hatred of contingency fee lawyers was showing like a debutante's slip.

He said later in the interview, "Every person who has someone killed or injured in a major disaster has always gotten their money. The only question is when and how much. The third question is how much is it worth when they get it? Who are the people who make money out of litigation? The lawyers make the money, on both sides. If Cathcart, Demanes, and Jefferson had come to Pan American in February 1974 and said, 'Give us $75,000 times so many seats and we will agree to split this up,' they would have gotten it. But then they, the lawyers, would have gotten no money."

Close examination of the various settlement offers shows, in fact, how closely Benedict was sticking to the notional calculation of 91 passengers x $75,000, a total of $6,825,000. His offer of January 1978, which embraced the remaining fifty-seven cases, amounted in all to $6,875,000, of which $50,000 was a sort of bonus to be spread around the fifteen people who had already settled for low figures. It is also worth noting that in spite of his insistence that Pan Am was willing to settle for $75,000 in all but two or three cases, twenty-seven of the 1978 offers were for less than this amount, and so were all but two of the cases previously settled.

Benedict claimed that his offers came within a few percentage points of what the juries finally awarded and had been calculated on an estimate of what would happen in court. The figures hardly bear this out. Hans Richter, for example, was offered $35,000. The jury awarded him $304,000. John Handis was offered $100,000. The jury awarded $335,000. Susan Rogers was offered $125,000. The jury assessed her case at $353,000. Wane Tyler was offered $100,000. The jury award was $375,000. The Garth family, in which the parents and three children died in the crash, were offered $275,000, which included $75,000 for the lives of the children. Even though Judge Byrne excluded the deaths of children from the damage trials, the jury still gave the Garths $390,000.

Yet Benedict himself admitted that there was a sterile atmosphere in the courtroom for the damage trials and that the verdicts had been "conservative" in relation to what the plaintiffs' attorneys had expected. "Conservative" is one word for what his own offers had been. There are others.

During the course of the settlement negotiations, Benedict had urged Judge Byrne to order the claimants themselves into court to testify about their circumstances. "If you make that order, these cases will always settle," he said. "The plaintiffs' lawyers will always overestimate the value of the case." Byrne refused, something that Benedict considered to be a grave mistake. In his world there was no room for sentiment or finesse. If widows and orphans whose menfolk had been killed by Pan American wanted to lay their hands on his money, they would have to come and ask for it. And justify themselves.

But it could not be said that Robert Benedict had not learned a lesson from the Pago Pago fiasco. Others might have suffered hardship—"I know nothing about hardship in any of these cases," he said—but he had been put to a great deal of trouble by the infuriating persistence of Cathcart and company. And even though the long delay had probably reaped the insurers a profit in terms of accumulated interest, they had still had to pay out something like $2,500,000 in legal fees and expenses. "If any message comes out of this case," he said, "it is that there has to be a better way to deal with this kind of situation."

There were a few veterans of Pago Pago who would breathe "amen" to that.

Robert Benedict's "better way" was to be put into operation almost as soon as he realized that the Pago Pago case was heading for the Grimpen Mire into which it subsequently tumbled. It took the form of a three-page mimeographed letter, which was sent post haste to the relatives of those killed in subsequent airline disasters. The Tenerife collision and the crash of the American Airlines DC 10 at Chicago were the outstanding examples.

Even before the letter arrived, one of Benedict's representatives would have been on the doorstep to express condolences and offer help. The letter merely provided confirmation. This was certainly a far cry from the off-hand treatment accorded the Pago Pago claimants.

The letter expressed sympathy, forbore intruding at a time of personal grief, and provided helpful information about the identification and burial of the victims. The crunch, however, came on the last page:

> During this period of time, you may be in need of funds because unexpected expenses have been incurred, or as a result of losing the one to whom you normally look for financial support. In order to attempt to minimize any such current hardship, we are prepared to advance funds to you periodically as you need them if you will

call or write. Money damages can never compensate for the loss of a loved one, but this is the medium recognized by the law for compensating victims and the families of victims in air disasters. We will be writing to you again within the next two weeks to obtain certain information to assist us in evaluating the loss which you have incurred. Upon receipt of this information, we will extend an offer to settle your claim. It is our intention to see that you receive fair compensation for the loss which you have sustained. It is also our hope that you ultimately retain as much of the compensation as is properly due to you without unnecessary diversion of large amounts to legal expenses.

You may find yourselves under pressure to sign a contingent fee retainer with an attorney, whereby his fee is a percentage of the final award. The rationale for such a percentage fee is that the lawyer risks getting no fee if there is no recovery. There is no such contingency in this case. There is also nothing to be gained by a precipitous lawsuit. We do suggest that it would be in your best interest to evaluate the offers which will be made to you and obtain the help of your attorney based upon a fee for the work involved rather than a percentage of the settlement or award.

The letter was signed by Robert Benedict. It was, on the face of it, an eminently helpful document designed to protect the innocent from falling into the hands of legal entrepreneurs. It offered immediate money, with the promise of more, and it promised a speedy conclusion to the whole sorry affair.

No doubt if queries were raised, the awful example of Pago Pago could be trotted out to show what happened to those who entrusted their fate to the contingency fee lawyers.

It did not, of course, point out that widespread acceptance of this advice was going to save the insurance company an awful lot of money.

Mr. Benedict's offers were not noted for their insane generosity.

The contingency fee fraternity was madder than wet hens. They had been dealt a swift kick in the wallet, and it hurt. There was not much they could do about it except intensify the scramble to be first on the doorstep, but they resolved to get the whole thing out in the open. A debate was duly staged between the lawyers and their implacable foes from the insurance industry at New Orleans in August 1981.

The occasion generated more heat than light. Robert Benedict was supposed to be there to defend his new policy, but at the last moment, he found a pressing engagement somewhere else. This did not go unremarked by Lee Kreindler, a noted contingency fee lawyer who was leading the debate for his colleagues. "One thing Bob Benedict is not," Kreindler said, "and that is unintelligent. He decided it would be prudent to be elsewhere at this time."

Having set the tone, Kreindler took it from there. "What happens," he said, "and I have difficulty in restraining myself when I talk about this because I think it is so disgusting, is that almost immediately, with people in the depths of despair suffering unbelievable grief, they get a letter following up a personal visit. Someone from the insurers has knocked on the door. Before bodies are identified, certainly before they are buried, claims adjusters knock on the doors of poor widows all over the country and say, 'We want to help you.' They say, 'This is a terrible time, we offer you our condolences, and we recognize that you may have some financial difficulties. Don't worry about it. Here is a check for $10,000. If you need more you can get more.'

"Then, after the introductory stuff, the claims adjuster says, 'We hate to bring this up, but you have certain rights and you will be hearing about the rights you have. You may be solicited by people who want to handle your case. We caution you that there is no need to hire a lawyer.

"There is certainly no need to hire a lawyer and pay a contingency fee. We are not going to deny liability in this case; we are going to pay you what you are entitled to. Contingent fees are justified by contingencies, and the possibility of losing. There is nothing like that here. You are entitled to a lot of money—maybe $500,000.'

"I think it is absolutely disgusting; just unseemly. Of course," Kreindler went on, wrapping a mantle of virtue tightly about him, early settlements were highly desirable. "Lawyers have no vested interest in human misery. None of us have any interest in fees we might get for representing people in an accident. The only criterion is what is good for the accident victim.

"What the insurance company does is to assess the real value of the case. Then it deducts a substantial amount for the plaintiff's contingency fee. It deducts an additional amount for defense costs. So that in a million-dollar case you might get an offer of five or six hundred thousand dollars. Later it will go up. If you take out these other factors, it is not necessarily a bad offer under the circumstances.

"I say it is an effort to make a cheap settlement—a settlement that will cost the defendant insurance company less than the conventional method of handling the case. If it doesn't work and the plaintiff goes to a contingent fee lawyer, then the policy is one of resistance. They take great pride in not increasing the amount of money. They take a very tough position, to the point where they have been criticized quite harshly by the judges."

It was true, Kreindler admitted, that some lawyers did engage in ambulance chasing themselves. "It is unfortunate, and it is not the general rule, but it happens." He did not condone the practice for a moment.

But for all its anger, Kreindler's argument had a fatal flaw: if the offers were really reasonable; if they achieved quick settlements and gave the victims as much as they would get after paying their legal fees but sooner, where could the objection to Benedict's scheme lie? The answer was too obvious to be worth stating, though that did not stop Bob Kraft from stating it.

Kraft, a defense attorney frequently employed by Benedict, was standing in for the USAIG executive. He said, "With the underwriters now doing what the plaintiffs' attorneys have always said they should do, the contingency attorneys are hurting. This is why they are defending themselves by attacking the underwriters. They are trying to make it seem somehow improper. Worse, some have tried to overcome this by intensifying their attempts at solicitation and by taking significant contingency fees, even when there is no significant contingency.

"Many contingent attorneys also try to put roadblocks in the way of the underwriters by trying to keep them from getting the information necessary to make early offers. That is an awfully effective way to stop underwriters from settling your cases. They also delay litigation for as long as possible, by doing all the things they used to claim that underwriters did. These delays are important to the attorneys for one primary reason: they help them justify their fees. They disguise the error of rejecting the original offer. Their role is at best superfluous, and more likely detrimental, to their clients.

"Those who still look at plaintiffs' attorneys as the Robin Hoods of modern-day litigation are just out of date when it comes to aviation. The shoe is now on the other foot."

It was stirring stuff. If everyone meant what they said at New Orleans, the world of aviation litigation was now littered with knights on white chargers, all selflessly defending the interests of the innocent. The victims of Flight 806 would have been very glad to hear it; not that the new policy was about to be of any benefit to them. There would be no retrospection. They could continue to wait for their compensation as they had waited for the past eight years. Robert Benedict would happily sign checks for the victims of new disasters, but at the mention of Pago Pago he clenched his fists.

"We don't pay these people for one simple reason," he said. "We don't believe we were negligent."

For Richard Carter, angry and frustrated in his wheelchair, such words were small consolation. The money owed to his family would never mend his broken spine, but it could have made life more tolerable. It would have helped his mother, too. Lucy Carter, as mentioned earlier, had refused a widow's pension, having been told she would have to pay it all back when the award came through. She had continued in her low-paying job, turning down promotion, because she believed that if she earned more Benedict would pay them less. The years of poverty had been endured, and nothing had come of it.

Now Lucy Carter, in the Pacific winter of 1981, was reduced to writing urgent pleas to President Reagan, demanding that he take a close look at his country's legal system. All else seemed to have failed. "They are using us, the little people, to feather and line their own pockets," she said bitterly. It had not escaped her notice that when the lawyers came to take her deposition in 1978, they had adjourned the proceedings for "a damn good lunch." She and her children had stood outside on the pavement and shared a pie.

For Susan and Michael Rogers in their home at Waihi Beach, the problems were different but no less acute. Michael fretted over vanishing opportunities—wanting to use his compensation to invest in land, to grow trees—and seeing inflation eat away at the unpaid award like corrosive acid. Now the dream was almost unattainable.

Susan still worried about her appearance, wearing heavy makeup to cover the scars on her face and clothing to disguise the rest. Her dancing career, the most important thing in her life, was gone. "You can't dance cabaret with these scars," she said. "It's that simple. I was offered a chance of an audition in a nightclub in Auckland. But the chap who offered it did not know what was under my clothes. They expect you to look pretty good up there." She had finally returned to teaching modern ballet after years of being unable to face a class, but it was no substitute for the career she knew, she just knew, she could have had.

She was bitter about the way she had been treated by the lawyers throughout the case. "I won't be patronized," she said. "I am not a dumb blonde, and the fact that I'm a dancer does not mean that I don't have a brain. All the way through, the more polite I was, the more helpful I was, the more like an idiot they treated me. That is what I was really angry about. I was told that as a married woman I had no claim. I am totally against that. Because you are married and have found your man, it apparently doesn't matter if you are scarred. Had I been single, it would have been quite a different thing.

"It was put to me that I was a dancer, I was married, and therefore my career was not really a career and was going to be very short. What a load of garbage. The best dancers don't peak until they are twenty-eight to thirty, for a start. That was ten years away for me.

"I think it was because I was so polite. Had I been a little more forceful, perhaps they would have listened. I don't know."

"We have both become very cynical, very frustrated people," said Michael. It was patently true. Nor was it the crash that made them that way, but the unending legal struggle. Frustrated cynicism had become a Pago Pago disease, endemic among the victims, and even seen among the lawyers. Few were able to express it as well as Edward Hemsley, now eight years older than the callow young attorney who went to Hawaii and learned more than was good for him.

"This tragedy," Hemsley said, "is being deliberately prolonged. Nobody will recognize that or have the humanity to conclude the affair and learn from it. It is something they have allowed to fester, and with absolutely no regard to the human element. They have covered up. They have refused to recognize the facts, just as they have refused to conclude. It is those things which are the most damning to my eyes.

"If it is not Pan American, it is the insurers. Within the insurers it is probably a department, and within the department it is probably one man.

"What I find very difficult to understand at times is the warped economics of this whole process—the fact that Pan American and the insurers can spend such an enormous amount of money in prolonging this matter at the expense of those people who have been most damaged. It seems to me they do not, at the end of the day, win anything but damnation out of this. They will, instead of paying the claimants, pay their advisers, their insurers, their advertising people, all the hangers on, together with enormous court and associated costs.

"Somebody needs to be taught a resounding lesson. Somebody needs to be taught that the loss is not the airplane, the loss is not just those lives that go with it, but the enormity of the loss is the immense human tragedy of the aftermath.

"The people in the airplane lost their lives, and that is an end of it. But each of those people left others behind, and for them there has been no release, no ending. They are still living with it. They are still suffering. That is where the real loss is suffered, and though time heals it might take twenty, thirty, or forty years. Perhaps it will only end when those people die themselves, some of them under circumstances one would not like to think about, and perhaps as a direct result of the accident.

"I think that an airline involved in this sort of situation should be directly responsible to those people, to assist them in every way they can and to help them cope with the situation. I think it would do them a lot of good if they did. I think they would engender more public sympathy if they did that, rather than waiting a discreet month or two before splashing huge amounts of money about to counter the effects in advertising. If this thing had been dealt with humanely and efficiently right from the word go, then a thousand times less suffering would have resulted, at a cost of millions less to Pan American. Why it was not so dealt with, we shall never know."

Edward Hemsley, a small-town lawyer in New Zealand, had summed it up rather well.

POSTSCRIPT

On February 15, 1984, ten years and two weeks after
Flight 806 plowed into the jungle at Pago Pago, Pan
American World Airways finally relented and paid up.
They had little option. Two months previously, the Ninth
Circuit Court of Appeals had removed their last legal fig
leaf by granting Dan Cathcart et al. a petition for rehearing.
The result of this was to affirm on appeal all the judgments
for damages, plus the award of pre-judgment interest in
some of the cases.

The much-disputed claims of Lucy Carter and Grace
van Heerden were settled out of court and never came to
trial.

It was over.

And yet . . . and yet there was still some unfinished
business. The victims may have been compensated, the
lawyers may have drawn their fees and licked their wounds,
but for one man the story of Pago Pago could not end there.
For Dan Cathcart the affront to natural justice had been
too great for simple victory to bring satisfaction.

And so a new action was filed before the California court. Under California law, an insurance carrier must act in good faith, not only in its dealings with those it insures but also toward the claimants. It was on this legal foundation that Cathcart hoped to achieve justice for his clients.

Cathcart's complaint, laid before Judge Pamela Rymer, charged his opponents with "unfair and deceptive acts and practices." In an exhaustive catalogue of their alleged misdeeds, he accused them of burying the wreckage, failing to attempt fair and prompt settlements, prolonging the litigation to increase its costs, and economic coercion.

"The conduct of the defendants," his indictment thundered, "was intentional, willful, malicious, oppressive, outrageous, and done with a heedless and reckless disregard of the rights of the plaintiffs, all for the purpose of inflicting severe economic, physical, and emotional hardship and deprivation on the plaintiffs."

For each of his clients who chose to join in this new battle, Cathcart claimed three things: damages of $500,000 for "severe mental distress, mental suffering and anguish, and physical suffering"; punitive damages of $15 million each; and the interest earned by Pan American on compensation withheld for more than nine years.

He was nothing if not ambitious.

The group of plaintiffs was smaller now. Some of the victims were precluded by the terms of their settlements from suing for bad faith. Others, notably Susan Rogers, had simply had enough of litigation and declined to join in.

At the time this book was first published by W.W. Norton in 1984, Cathcart's "get even" action had yet to come to court. For me, however, there was to be a curious postscript.

Some two years later, when my wife and I had settled in Virginia's Shenandoah Valley, I received a strange telephone call. It was from an attorney representing the United States Aviation Insurance Group. Would I, he asked, be prepared to appear as an expert witness when the case against his clients came to trial in Los Angeles?

"Why me?" I asked.

"Because," he said, "you seem to know more about this case than anyone else."

Probably true, but I can only assume that he had not read the book. For the defendants, I would have been a greater disaster than any of the witnesses called by William Tucker.

Alas, it never happened. A few weeks later, I was informed that the case had been settled out of court, and my services would not be required. Pity.

The terms of the settlement, of course, were kept under seal. For a fleeting moment, I contemplated returning to room 64G to satisfy my curiosity. But no, enough was enough.

FOR FURTHER DISCUSSION

1. What made you decide to read this book?
2. Given how hard Pan Am and the insurance company worked to keep the accident out of the news and deny responsibility, how could Cathcart have approached this case differently to influence the ultimate outcome?
3. Would you describe this case as a David versus Goliath fight? Why (not)?
4. Has reading about this case changed your traveling behavior? How and why?
5. Imagine a member of your family was lost in Flight 806. How do you think your family would react to the legal mess that followed? Would your family pull together, like the Hemsleys? Would your family be torn apart, like the Carters?
6. What was the most frustrating thing you read about Flight 806 and its legal battle? What was the most uplifting?

7. In your opinion, how did Judge Byrne impact the outcome of this trial?

8. Was there a specific section of the book that left an impression on you, good or bad? Share the passage and its effect.

9. What do you think about the author's research? Was it easy to see where the author got his information? Is the author's overall account of the events credible?

10. Do you think more information about the pilot's and co-pilot's records should have been presented to the jury? Why (not)?

ABOUT THE AUTHOR

William (Bill) Norris has been a professional writer since the age of sixteen, when he joined his local newspaper as an apprentice reporter. After ten years of working for various newspapers in England and Africa, Norris was appointed as Parliamentary Correspondent to the prestigious *Times* (of London). He is one of the youngest people to hold this position. He remained in this role for seven years, revolutionizing the art of the "parliamentary sketch" before transferring to become Africa Correspondent for *The Times*, covering political events and wars in Biafra, Nigeria, Angola, the Congo, Mozambique, Botswana, Zambia, Tanzania, and Zimbabwe.

In 1968, he became ITN's Political Correspondent while also covering overseas stories, such as the Paris Riots happening that same year. He transitioned to freelance work in 1980 after moving to the United States. In 1997, Norris became the Associate Director of the PressWise Trust (a British media ethics charity) where he counseled young journalists to promote journalistic ethics.

Along with being an experienced writer and journalist, he has a strong public speaking background. He has spoken to students at the University of London and was the keynote speaker at both the World Health Organization conference in Moscow and a European Union conference on journalistic ethics in Cyprus.

He now resides in the South of France with his wife Betty, two cats, and two exhausting dogs.

EXCERPT FROM SNOWBIRD

Even before the pig flew over the windshield, Andrew Barnes knew he had made a mistake. This was not the runway he was looking for. It wasn't a runway at all. The brown strip rushing towards him in the landing lights of the twin-engine Rockwell Turbo-Commander was nothing more than a rutted country lane.

The flickering lights that he had taken as threshold markers were actually the headlamps of an ancient truck, jolting along and minding its own business.

"Oh, shit," said Andrew Barnes.

There was no going back. Flaps extended, nose high, the Turbo-Commander was committed to landing. The engines screamed in fine pitch as they swallowed the last few gallons of fuel in the tanks. The stall-warning horn blared in protest.

On the ground, an astonished Colombian farmer stood on his brakes and lurched into a ditch as the monstrous shape skimmed the roof of his truck and struck the road only yards ahead.

"Hang on tight," shouted Barnes. Paralyzed with fear, his two passengers hardly needed to be told. With a spine-jarring jolt, the main wheels touched and stayed down as the fully stalled aircraft fell out of the sky. The nose dropped, and they watched with horrified fascination through the windshield as the Turbo-Commander began a wild charge down the track. Barnes fought for control, stabbing at brakes and rudder pedals, miraculously dodging the trees and bushes that flashed past the wingtips. And then the road turned. There was nowhere to go.

The aircraft left the path, crossed a ditch, smashed through a hedge, and hurled itself into a farmyard. Startled chicken scattered in all directions.

And a pig flew over the windshield.

With a final expensive crunch, the Turbo-Commander plunged its nose into a wooden fence. And stopped.

———

Andrew Barnes told me that story on the first day we met. It was not a chance encounter. Some three weeks before I had had a telephone call from Michael Knipe, then foreign news editor of The Times. Michael, an old friend from my own days with that once-distinguished newspaper, was calling to do me a favor. At least, he hoped it was going to be a favor. He sounded a trifle nervous.

The Times man in New York, said Michael, had just been interviewing an odd character who was one of the witnesses in the cocaine-smuggling trial of Carlos Lehder, down in Miami. The witness was an Englishman, now living in Pennsylvania, who had an extraordinary tale to tell about the cocaine-smuggling business. Furthermore, he seemed to want it converted into a book and had asked the

New York correspondent if he knew any good authors who might be interested. The message had been passed on to the Foreign Desk, and Michael had thought of me. Nice of him.

"What do you know about this guy?" I asked. Not a lot, it turned out. Just that his name was Barnes, that he had smuggled large quantities of cocaine for the Medellin cartel, and he was probably heading for a lengthy spell in prison. From the sound of it, he deserved no less.

At this point I knew no more about the Medellin cartel than the next man, merely what I had read in the press and seen on television. But it was enough to induce revulsion. By all accounts, these were unscrupulous crooks who had poisoned a continent and amassed a king's ransom in the process. On the way, they had murdered scores of men who attempted to expose their conspiracy. And some of those men, I now remembered with an odd churning in the pit of my stomach, had been journalists. From the tone of Michael's voice, clear across four thousand miles, I could tell he was thinking the same thing.

"Just thought you might be interested," he said rather lamely. "I've got his telephone number if you want it."

Why not? There was no harm in having the option. I scribbled down the number and sat looking at it pensively long after our conversation ended. I wondered about the personality of the man who lay behind that number, and I wondered even more about his associates. I had never met a drug smuggler, at least, not knowingly. Curiosity did battle with prudence, and for the moment, prudence won. I pushed the slip of paper to one side and got on with the rest of my life.

It was not a good time for authoring in the Norris household. In spite of splendid reviews for my last book and the sale of the film rights to Hollywood, there was no prospect of a commission for the next one. I was caught in the usual dilemma of the nonfiction writer: No publisher will sign a contract and pay an advance without a fully researched outline of the project. But research involves time and travel, and time and travel cost money. That money ought to come from the publisher's advance—it is what advances are supposed to be for—but in practice you cannot get one without laying out large amounts of your own cash long before you see the check. Which is fine if you have it. It was not the first time I had been in this catch-22 situation, but try as I might I could find no way out of it. I ought, I thought, to give up the nonfiction trade and write novels instead. The trouble was, I was not very good at fiction.

My passion of the moment was the Lindbergh kidnapping case. Others, notably Ludovic Kennedy in his excellent book *The Airman and the Carpenter*, had proved conclusively that Bruno Richard Hauptmann was innocent of the crime, but no one had yet been able to identify the true guilty party. I believed I had a clue to his identity through newly discovered evidence, but believing it and proving it were two very different things.

For months, I had been chasing phantoms and spending money I could ill afford in pursuit of the final truth. I had even flown to Scotland to interview Betty Gow, the Lindbergh baby's still-surviving nursemaid, only to have the door literally slammed in my face. In the United States, too, hostility and evasion were greeting every inquiry. I knew I was on the right trail, and that given sufficient time and money, persistence would pay off in the end. Time, I had. Money was a different matter. As the days passed and the crock of gold at the end of my investigatory rainbow grew no closer, I found my eyes drawn more and more to the scrap of paper lying on my desk and the telephone number of Andrew Richard Barnes. Perhaps, after all, it was time to face reality, to put the Lindbergh project on the back burner, and to tackle something that, on the face of it, looked straightforward. Something, moreover, that ought not to cost an arm and a leg to research.

My long-suffering agent in New York was mildly encouraging. My wife, faced with the prospect of her middle-aged husband associating with ruthless criminals, was appalled. Four years of exposure to American television violence did not help. "These people are worse than the Mafia," she said. "You could get yourself killed."

With some asperity, I pointed out that I had survived more dangerous assignments in the past. I had been under fire in Biafra, Zimbabwe, Angola, and Mozambique. I had been in the thick of the Paris riots in May 1968. By comparison, the prospect of rubbing shoulders with a drug smuggler was pretty small beer.

"You were younger and sillier then," she said.

That did it. I rooted out the scrap of paper and made the call.

Barnes seemed agreeable enough on the telephone, and more than willing to meet with me. The time and place could be of my choosing. I pondered the question. Aside from the fact that his house in Pennsylvania was a three-hour drive from my home in Virginia's Shenandoah Valley, did I really want to stick my head in the lion's mouth at this first meeting? At least my own place boasted three large and faithful dogs of fearful mien, plus, as a last resort, the family firearm. There was the small problem of persuading my wife to accept a drug-smuggler as a houseguest, but I hoped, correctly as it turned out, that curiosity might win the day.

"Come for the weekend," I said.

During the intervening days, Betty and I speculated on what our guest would look like. Suave and sinister was the consensus of opinion. Probably slim and dark-suited, with a palpable air of menace. We were certainly unprepared for the shy giant of a man who unfolded himself from an ancient Ford Mustang in our driveway on that Saturday in late April.

Andrew Barnes was big. Very big. He looked down at us from a height of six-foot-three, and his chest strained at the buttons of his jacket. There was some surplus fat there to be sure, but a hell of a lot of muscle underneath it. The face was bucolic. It was the sort of face that belonged on an English farm laborer, not on a drug smuggler. The eyes were blue and, God damnit, they had a sort of innocence about them.

Barnes came towards us, a battered leather case in one hand, brushing the hair from his eyes with the other. He wore it long with a pronounced fringe, as though in memory of the Beatles, and I became aware that the dogs had stopped barking. They were crowding round him, sniffing his legs and showing every sign of pleasure as he bent down to pat them. Great, I thought. The one time I invite a criminal to my home, and you silly bastards fawn all over him. But they were right. For all that he had done, and it was plenty, there was no harm, no violence in Andrew Barnes. A dog's judgment is not often wrong.

We shook hands, and I made a mental note that his grip was firm and dry. The hands themselves, though, were surprisingly small. Smaller than my own. It was as though they had stopped growing in his early teens, while the rest of his physique burgeoned into manhood. It was not the only thing about Andrew Barnes, I was to discover, that betokened arrested development.

His voice, too, was a surprise. I had expected an English accent, perhaps similar to my own. But what came out was a sort of mid-Atlantic twang, neither one thing nor the other, but more American than not. His speech, like his whole manner, was diffident. Courteous and gentlemanly— an odd word to use in this context, but totally appropriate— but with a sheepish air about him. As we stumbled through the formalities and finally sat down in my study to begin the first of many interviews, I came to realize that he was more nervous than I. Every few seconds he would take a comb and pass it through his perfectly ordered hair, like an errant schoolboy facing his headmaster and wondering what to do with his hands.

But he could talk. Oh my, how he could talk. At first, as names and dates and places poured out in an unrelenting stream, I began to wonder if he was not too articulate. Was it possible that this was a well-rehearsed tale being recounted for my benefit, a fictional farrago concocted with the object of making big bucks out of the book? If so, I thought wryly, this guy is singularly ignorant about the rewards of authorship, let alone the Son of Sam laws.

Slowly, I came to realize two things. First, his astonishing power of recall was largely due to the fact that he had just spent weeks and months being grilled by agents from the FBI and the U.S. Drug Enforcement Administration, not to mention sundry lawyers while he stood on the witness stand in Miami.

Second, and more important, Andrew Barnes was using me as a confessor. In terms of his atonement, going to jail and paying the price was not enough. He was inwardly driven to tell the story of his misdeeds in the utmost detail to the widest possible audience. There was no altruism in it. He was not out to educate the young and prevent them falling into the same trap.

At root, he neither knew nor cared whether his revelations would have any effect on the long-term future of the drug trade. All that mattered to Andrew Barnes at this point in time was to get the whole thing off his chest so that he might, one day, make a fresh start. In short, he needed to cleanse his soul.

I am no psychologist, still less a priest, and the reader must judge as the story unfolds whether such a public *mea culpa* is justified. When it comes to evil intent, having got to know Andrew Barnes rather well, I will vouch for the fact that he is not in the same league as the man he met on a Florida airfield on December 26, 1977.

FICTION TITLES BY WILLIAM NORRIS

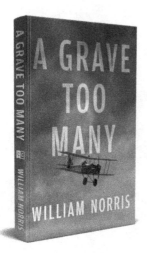

Available now, wherever books are sold.

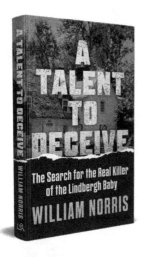

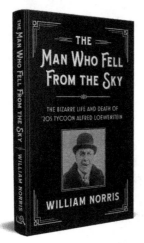
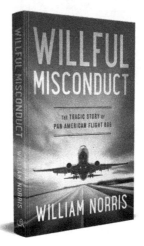

CamCat
Perspectives

VISIT US ONLINE FOR
MORE BOOKS TO LIVE IN:
CAMCATBOOKS.COM

FOLLOW US

CamCatBooks @CamCatBooks @CamCat_Books

Printed in the USA
CPSIA information can be obtained
at www.ICGtesting.com
LVHW040318180224
771680LV00009B/36/J